HOW TO MASTER THE ART OF LISTING REAL ESTATE

BY
TOM HOPKINS
THE NATION'S #1 SALES TRAINER

ISBN 0-938636-06-5

CONTENTS

PART THREE: CONTROLLING YOUR EMOTIONS AND ORGANIZING YOUR SKILLS

INDEX

PART ONE
A FAST OVERVIEW

1
WHY YOU SHOULD BECOME A LISTING CHAMPION

The prime reason is money. All listing champions make more than the average doctor or attorney does. Listing champions enjoy higher incomes than those earned by college professors, middle management executives, and airline pilots. Many listing champions are paid between two and ten times as much as the average person in these other professions, and a few listing champions regularly collect even more.

But they don't do it without effort, or without first learning their business.

Please understand that I'm talking about champion listers, not average salespeople. The truth is shocking: the average salesperson doesn't make enough to stay in the business. Worse yet, thousands of new licensees quit real estate before they've made their first dollar at it. Then all their time goes for nothing, and all their costs gurgle down the drain.

It's so unnecessary.

Everyone who has enough intelligence and discipline to acquire a license can be successful in real estate. All it takes is the proper training and a reasonable amount of effort. The training I can give you; the effort you must give yourself. Now, while you're resolving to put forth mighty efforts to succeed, also resolve to make an effective effort to learn how to earn.

What do I mean by being "successful" after putting out "a reasonable amount of effort?"

I can answer that question for myself but I can't answer it for you. Plug in your own definitions; they're the only ones that really matter to your future hopes and present realities. However, for better understanding between us, let's agree that real estate success begins when you're taking home twice as much money as the average factory worker does.

That's not much money. But it is a start—and we all have to start at the bottom rung of real estate success, don't we?

Where's the top rung, you might ask.

It keeps going up too fast to put in a book. But here's one sure thing about real estate's top rung of success: there's room on it for you. And here's another: the top rungs can't be seen from where people are when they're struggling to stay in the business.

I know about that struggle. I lived it every day through the longest and hardest six months of my life—the start of my real estate career. I know now that I could easily have avoided my 180 days of agony; all I had to do was learn how to list and sell in the beginning. If you've been in real estate less than six months, you're ahead of where I was at the same stage of life. You already know that you need training. That knowledge is precious. I didn't stumble onto it until I was at the bitter end of my resources.

My case illustrates the main trouble with new recruits in the real estate industry. All too often we make our beginners practice on qualified people. No other prestigious profession allows this. In the other well-paid callings (law and medicine are familiar examples), the license comes only after years of expensive training. In real estate, we get our license first. Lots of us are confused when it comes in the mail. It confused me. I thought that little piece of paper meant I had qualified to earn a professional's income. As I soon found out, it meant no such thing.

Real estate was a wonderful opportunity then. It is a wonderful opportunity now. It will continue to be a wonderful opportunity in the future—for those willing to do its work. But we can't go straight to the pay window; we have to acquire expertise first. All licensed professionals from accountants to zoologists learn their trade before they cash in, so why shouldn't we? But there is an exciting difference about real estate—our training period is measured in weeks, not years.

Unfortunately, many new people in real estate waste their early weeks in the business because they don't react creatively to being—probably for the first time in their lives—within striking distance of professional status. They don't take themselves or their opportunity seriously enough. They stick to their old get-by attitudes. Instead of giving their opportunity all they've got for half a year, they vacillate. They wonder if they'll like it and, by wondering, rob themselves of drive. They waste their energy finding excuses for not doing what they know they must do in order to succeed.

If you regard real estate as just another job, you'll certainly fail to achieve much, and you're not likely to be in business next year at this time. When you hang your new real estate license on a broker's back wall, you go into business for yourself. You plunge into a battle to survive that's far keener than most people experience while working for wages or a salary. Real estate is not a position in which you build up seniority, accrue company benefits, and go on strike for more money. When you want more money in real estate, you just go out and make it.

"But they don't train me," many new people in real estate keep saying. "How am I supposed to know what to do if my company won't train me?"

I had that misconception too. I thought my company would train me. Every company I'd ever worked for ran me through an on-the-job training program first. When I went to work as a bridgedeck specialist, they trained me. It went like this: "See those steel bars over there? Carry them up that ramp." That's on-the-job training. And you know what? Nobody pays much for jobs you can learn in four seconds. But they will train you while they pay you.

Another reason why you should become a listing champion is power. Champion listers and strong listers control the business. Sellers come to them because of their reputation for getting houses sold; buyers come to them because of their reputation for having desirable properties. Wise brokers treasure agents who get their share of saleable listings over those who don't.

Why? Because one of the unique features of the resale housing brokerage business is that we have to create our own stock in trade. That's where about half the income* lies, in the inventory-creating activity known as listing. And it's the more secure half. Without

---

*This is true of most, but not all, areas.

listings, a brokerage office has nothing to sell of its own. Buyers tend to work with the offices that have signs on interesting properties. The office without a good inventory of listings soon feels its sales drying up. Unless you're a strong lister, you'll always be hanging by your fingernails in real estate.

Another reason why you should become a listing champion is that listings can make you money when you're out of town. I think you'll agree that it's almost impossible to work with buyers unless you're right there with them. If you've arranged with another agent to cover for you while you're away, that's not true of listings. There's nothing sweeter than having your vacation paid for by a listing that sold when you were skiing down a mountain or wiggling your toes in the sand thousands of miles from home. Nice things like this frequently happen to listing champions. When they start happening to you, your morale will get a terrific boost.

Maybe at this point you're wondering exactly what I mean by the term *listing champion*. To explain that, we first need to talk about *listing banks*.

If you've just started to think about a career in real estate, this concept may be new to you. Perhaps you're not positive exactly what a *listing* is. (Skip the next two paragraphs if you are familiar with these terms.)

The agreement between a broker and an owner wanting to sell property is called a listing. It must be in writing and conform to many laws and regulations. The most commonly used kind of listing agreement states that the seller will pay a fee if the property is sold within a limited time for the specified price and under the specified terms. The listing also shows (a) how the fee is to be calculated and (b) how it is to be divided between the listing office representing the seller and the selling office representing the buyer. (Brokers have separate written agreements with their agents spelling out how the fee will be divided between the office and the agent.)

A *listing bank*—it's often called a farm—is a group of up to 500 houses assigned to one agent as his or her special territory.

A *listing champion* is a real estate agent who earns more in listing fees from his or her listing bank than any other agent does.

A *listing superchampion* earns more than all other agents combined do in his or her listing bank.

And, when it's spelled with a capital "C" in this book, Champion refers to an agent who is trained in the Tom Hopkins Champions Unlimited method.

Can this really happen? Do listing superchampions actually exist? Certainly. I was one myself for several years at my listing bank in Simi Valley, California. After that, I managed a real estate office and developed a team of strong listers, champions, and superchampions of listing.

Then I began training people by the thousands to do the same thing. Now, in the two nations of North America, hundreds of superchampions of listing, thousands of listing Champions, and tens of thousands of strong listers use the Tom Hopkins method. All these people are highly competent, highly paid professionals. Yet we need still more of these fine people in this industry. We need you.

Did you notice that I didn't say your listing bank will be your exclusive territory? Companies that own the products they sell may give exclusive territories, but real estate brokers are in an entirely different position. Only rarely do they own what they sell. Since they lack a manufacturer's absolute control of inventory, they must adopt rules that are realistic for their own operations. In addition to the competition you'll face from other real estate firms, you'll probably find that, under certain circumstances, agents from your own office can take listings in your bank. Expect those circumstances to occur frequently. Then it won't be such a terrible shock when you discover that there's a new listing in your territory, and it was taken by an agent whose desk is just down the aisle from yours. But the rules that allow him to do that also allow you to take listings all over town under the same circumstances. So learn the rules. Get comfortable with them by understanding their logic. Think positively. Concentrate on what you can gain rather than what you can lose.

Another powerful reason why you should become a listing champion is to gain what I call "mobile security." This is one of the great benefits of professional status. What mobile security means is that you can take your specialized knowledge and skills wherever you like and earn a professional's income with them.

And here's yet another reason for attaining championship listing power. Real estate brokerage has to be performed by local people. No development overseas can drive your company out of business, and no one anywhere can invent a gadget that will make you obsolete. The practice of real estate gets more complicated every year, and this trend has to continue. Why am I so sure it will? Because our population is increasing but our land area is not. This means that the pressure of people on the available space will intensify, leading to more and more complex real estate arrangements. The need for ever more skilled and knowledgeable real estate professionals will continue to grow throughout your career. Everything positive that you learn about real estate not only contributes to your present prosperity, it also contributes to your future security as well.

The price of becoming a listing champion is high. Most people think that it takes too much effort and demands too great a sacrifice of free time. Maybe you're one of those who won't pay the price. That's all right. If money is your only concern, you'll always be poor in spirit no matter how much wealth you accumulate. So make the choice that's right for you. We all have to decide at what point making more money becomes less valuable to us than having more time for ourselves and our families.

But remember that you don't have to pay the high price of becoming a listing champion in order to earn a substantial income from listing fees. The thousands of strong listers I've trained are proof of this.

You may be thinking, "I'll bet none of those successful people had to overcome my handicaps and disadvantages, or fight my problems."

You're right.

None of them had your exact set of problems—many of them had far worse troubles of their own. I know strong listers who get around on crutches. Others are blind. Gary Wahlquist was a listing champion throughout his losing fight against leukemia.

Edie Roman didn't do well in school because of her heartrending childhood. So when her first marriage ended and left her with small children to support, Edie had no job skills to support them with. After a rough period of low paid menial work and welfare, this determined lady became a strong lister. Now Edie Roman is a broker who operates her own office in San Leandro, California.

Many of today's listing champions had to learn English first, and some came to real estate with no previous work experience except stoop labor in the fields. Other listing winners had to battle various kinds of prejudice along their road to achievement. Life gave every one of these people plenty of excuses for failure—but they chose success anyway. You too can find excuses in your life, or you can turn your back on excuses and opt for success.

What will it be?

It's your free choice.

Please realize one vital point: it truly is *entirely* your free choice whether you fail or succeed. Once you accept this fact, nothing can deny you every bit of success that you're willing to earn.

In the chapters that follow you'll find all the techniques you need to acquire listing power. Before you turn to them, take a moment to read part of the letter I received three years ago from Bob Baldwin of Alexandria, Virginia:

"I made $7,237 in October because I started doing the things you mention in your listing seminar. Had I not gone out and listed properties, I would have made only $1,830 that month . . . the best part is knowing that this is only the beginning."

Now let's move on from *why*. Let's take a look at *how*.

2

HOW TO ACQUIRE LISTING POWER

Referrals are the best source of new business. A referral is a fee that calls up or walks in and says, "Take me, I'm yours." But if you don't have the knowledge and skill that's required to earn a fee, the people who were willing to pay it (before they discovered your ignorance and ineptitude) will walk right out again and leave you empty handed.

Referrals will usually give you the benefit of the doubt for a little while. Other sellers won't. Your chances of listing them are gone the moment they decide you lack expertise. Put yourself behind their eyes. Would you trust a large transaction to a stranger you think is incompetent? Of course not. Then don't ask your prospects to make that unwise decision.

How do you avoid making this common mistake? By acting on my first method of acquiring listing power: gain knowledge. Here's what you must know:

● THE INVENTORY. A thorough understanding of the real estate that's available now in your service area is essential. This knowledge is your basic expertise. You can never have too much of it. The more formidable your fund of inventory knowledge is, the more formidable your listing power will be.

- **FINANCING.** A practiced discussion about *the financing options that you can guide prospective buyers to* is one of the most effective methods for demonstrating your expertise to sellers.

- **YOUR SERVICE AREA.** Being aware of and appreciating the benefits that your area offers prospective buyers is a mark of the professional that assures sellers they are in good hands.

- **THE FORMALITIES.** A full understanding of the legal requirements, forms, and business procedures involved in the transfer of real estate ownership is vital.

The second way to acquire listing power is to learn the skills of working with people, of getting them to like and trust you, of leading them to decisions that benefit them and earn you a fee. We'll cover this thoroughly in later pages.

The third requirement for acquiring listing power is to go out on the street and put your skills and knowledge to work. But what about referrals? Can't you wait for people to come through the door on a referral?

Sure you can. Thousands of new licensees do; it's one of the most popular ways to fail in this business. Don't confuse the referrals and walk-in traffic that your company generates with the true referral that comes specifically to you because you've earned it.

There's a pitfall here that's easy to fall into. If you depend on your company's leads, call-ins, and walk-ins for your basic income, you're not lift to that firm, you're drag. When they start losing altitude, they'll have to get rid of the drags.

Look on company-provided business as a bit of sauce that makes your meat and potatoes taste better, but never think of it as the main course. With this attitude, and with a determination to develop several dollars in fees on your own for every dollar you make from company-generated activity, you'll truly be in business for yourself. Only by believing in and acting on the premise that you're a business of your own can you develop the professional skills that will give you high income and mobile security.

The fourth and most important way of acquiring listing power is to deserve referrals. You do that by using superior knowledge and superior skill to render superior service. The referrals will come when you've earned the right to ask for them and not before. However, many new salespeople do such a good job on their first transactions that they start getting referrals very early in their real estate careers. Make that your goal. Without a steady flow of referrals, high earnings are difficult to achieve.

Now let's touch briefly on specific systems for gaining high-performance listing power. Later chapters will explain each of these systems in detail.

TURNING DOORBELLS INTO DOLLARS

The money in real estate is behind the doors that line your town's streets. To get whatever share of that money you want, you have to ring doorbells. If you're saying to yourself right now, "I'm not going to do that—no way," then I challenge you to explore exactly why you have these feelings. Most people simply say, "Well, I hate to ring strange doorbells."

Do you really think that's unusual?

I'll tell you a secret. Everybody feels exactly the same way. That is, everybody who doesn't know how, and everybody who hasn't made a whole lot of money doing it, hates to ring strange doorbells. But when you're prepared, when you know how, when you've had a lot of success doing it, you won't hate ringing doorbells anymore. Maybe you won't love it—but you'll get out there and do it regularly without feeling any distress.

After making money at it for a few months, there'll come a time when you'll go out and knock on doors to cheer yourself up when you're feeling down. Do you find that hard to believe?

Trust me. It'll happen. If you'll put the principles in this book to work for you, you'll discover that you not only "get lucky" when you ring doorbells, you also get your enthusiasm recharged. You'll find that you make new contacts and unearth new opportunities while you're raising your spirits by ringing doorbells and talking to people.

What a precious skill to acquire. Do you really want to deny yourself this wonderful fountain of earning power?

Three things make doorbell ringing easy. First, have a reason for doing it. Second, rehearse plenty of things to say. Third, have the right attitude. We're going to talk a lot about attitude in Chapter 12 because attitude is where most real estate people—and salespeople of all kinds for that matter—destroy themselves. For the time being, accept the fact that this book will give you many ways to enhance your attitude so that you can turn doorbells into dollars.

But I'm not going to stop there. I'm also going to give you specific, proven techniques—the exact words—that you can use to break down the barriers that are in the minds of the people behind those doors. You're going to get a complete system that works. So get your manager to mark off about 500 houses on a map and assign them to you. Get started as soon as you can on creating the listing bank that will be the foundation of your real estate fortune.

But remember one thing: you won't have much impact in your listing bank until you get out there and start ringing doorbells.

CANVASSING THAT COUNTS

What makes canvassing count?

Getting appointments to see people. When you sit down at your telephone to canvass for listings, your aim must be to arrange to meet sellers. We're concentrating together on listing real estate in this book, and in my companion volume we'll concentrate on selling real estate. But the two functions often mix in actual practice—when you're canvassing, you're not only looking for people who want to sell their home, you're also looking for people who want to buy real estate. Champion listers also sell a large volume of real estate, which is the fifth source of listing power: the ability to sell what you list.

In Chapter 8 we're going to explore the techniques of moneymaking canvassing in detail. I'm going to show you how to act and what to say so that you'll get the appointment to work face-to-face with qualified people. Then—and only then—do you have the opportunity to earn a fee. In other chapters I'll detail exactly how you turn that appointment into a listing. Acquiring listing power is a process of learning a variety of skills and facts and then putting them all together in a series of smooth performances. That is, you learn a method that works, and then you keep using it over and over. You'll find it all in these pages.

GETTING PEOPLE TO LIKE AND TRUST YOU

Champion listers have an aura of integrity. People feel comfortable with them. People believe they can rely on the champion or strong lister's word. They respect the lister's knowledge of real estate.

All through Part Two (Chapters 5 through 11) we're going to be studying this basic skill of getting people to like and trust you. You'll find many hints and insights and specific techniques for making this happen. For years, I've been telling my audiences that being able to get people to like and trust you is an essential part of real estate success. This quality is the sixth source of listing power. Please remember that none of the others is more important.

CONVERTING FOR-SALE-BY-OWNERS INTO MONEYMAKING INVENTORY

Sellers of real estate who try to go it alone without professional assistance are one of the top sources for listings. At least once in their lives, a large percentage of owners try to market their own properties. Few succeed. But the myth that it's easy persists. Why? Because that's what many sellers want to believe.

Their purpose, of course, is to save the fee. What they don't face up to is that the buyer also intends to save the fee. Why else should he bother negotiating directly with the owner instead of having a knowledgeable agent do the scouting and bargaining for him? And then there are the complex details to handle and all the pitfalls to avoid.

Few by-owners understand the strength of the fears that grip many people facing the problem of selecting a home. The reality is that most buyers aren't decisive enough to go through with the purchase of a home without the emotional support of a capable salesperson. By-owners don't give much thought to another reality: that the "buyers" they're most likely to get an offer from are people whose credit won't carry the purchase. These so-called buyers usually have been told by several real estate offices that they can't qualify for the necessary financing. Do they go home and start saving their money and improving their credit rating? No. First they try their luck on the by-owners.

Most real estate transactions hit snags at some point between a qualified buyer's first visit and the day he assumes ownership. Unless a skilled real estate professional is constantly monitoring the transaction, any of these snags can hold the transaction up and then destroy it. By-owners don't realize how often problems arise during the time transactions are open. Nor do they realize how difficult it will be for them to resolve matters directly with the buyer.

Why? Because the problems generally boil down to one thing: who pays for curing this new difficulty?

By-owners also underestimate the difficulties of financing the sale of their home. They don't know about title insurance, prorations of taxes, and a host of other questions that a strong agent is well-informed on and can cope with. For-sale-by-owners often enter into transactions that "fall out of escrow" (fall out of the closing or settlement) and are never completed. Such fallouts usually are a disaster for the by-owner. Fallouts often tie the sellers' property up during the best selling season; they often cause the sellers to default on the purchase of their next home; they often force the sellers into costly double-moves or into making payments on two houses at the same time. What a vital service you render to by-owners when you list them for your highly-skilled professional service!

The reasons why by-owners won't save money add up to a compelling argument, don't they? All you have to do is explain the facts and take the listing. Sounds easy, doesn't it? It is—when you've paid the price for knowing how.

The truth is, listing by-owners demands special skills that come only from special training. We'll give you that training in Chapter 6. If you'll makes these skills yours, you'll find that working with by-owners is one of your most dependable and rewarding activities. Though it's the seventh source of listing power given in this chapter, many high-earning agents consider by-owners to be their primary source of income.

GATHERING LISTINGS ON OPEN HOUSES

When done well, holding houses open is a marvelously effective technique.

It's not done well very often. This provides you with great opportunities, because holding successful open houses is a simple, step-by-step process. Doing it well enough to make big money requires work the week before. Unless you do that work in time, your weekend open houses have little chance of being worthwhile.

Many new or unsuccessful people in real estate don't understand that open houses often are better for listing than for selling. Some of these people have only one thing in mind: to sell the house they're holding open. This attitude puts them in the same position as the by-owner: that of trying to fit just one house to everybody who walks in.

At the opposite extreme, other agents try desperately to hook onto everyone who comes through, giving little thought to protecting their sellers' interests. These experts in nonprofessional conduct are as quick to knock the price of the house they're showing as they are to close it up and take off to look at other property with any possible buyer. The results range from wasted time to calamity.

In Chapter 7, I'll tell you how to avoid calamities and cash in on the exciting opportunities that professional open house techniques offer you. This is your eighth source of listing power, and it's one of the best.

CREATING A PROFITABLE LISTING BANK

Call it a farm if you like. That's a good name. It implies that you work your group of up to 500 houses with the diligence of a successful farmer working his acres. Like him, you prepare the soil, plant the seeds, and nurture the growth of the crop you're raising. You work with people, the farmer works with plants. Your seeds are the words you speak and the notes you write. Both of you have to cope with things like insects and rodents before you can take in your harvest. His crop may be corn or cotton; yours is a steady flow of saleable listings.

But I think it's more inspiring to look on your special territory as a listing bank because every time you go in there and work, you make a deposit. (Don't forget, bank withdrawals must be preceded by bank deposits.) After you've made frequent enough deposits in your listing bank, the value you've built up there will support you in the style you'd like to become accustomed to.

Think of your listing bank as your ninth and last source of listing power. Why last? Because a rich flow of employment agreements (listings) won't surge into your control from your bank until some of the first eight sources are delivering results from your efforts. Your listing bank won't be ninth in terms of income produced for you when that happens. Then it'll be one of your top sources of income. I'll show you exactly how to develop your listing bank into a money gusher in Chapter 9.

For most high-earners, the largest source of listing fees is referrals. This entire book tells you how to get referrals by increasing your professional skill and knowledge.

3
LIQUIDATING YOUR LISTINGS

What do you want more of in your bank?

Both at the bank where you do your checking and in the bank where you do your listing, you want to own more things that can quickly be turned into cash. Liquid assets, that is. Things like saleable listings.

Liquid assets is an interesting term. It reminds us that our earnings are like oil if we invest them wisely, like water poured on the desert's sand if we don't. The wisest investment is in ourselves; money used for self-education sticks to us throughout our lives. True education marries knowledge to skill—their child is power—power is money. Every time we go into our listing bank, we have the opportunity to convert our education into money.

First, we take listings; second, we liquidate those listings by seeing to it that they sell. One hazard is that we'll load ourselves up with five or ten listings priced too high to sell. Then we can work hard, we can take a great amount of abuse from our unrealistic sellers who can't understand why we aren't getting their unreasonable prices—but we can't make any money. Listings are like sirloin steaks. Barbecue them promptly and they're delicious; leave them in the hot sun too long and they're not too pleasant to be around.

HOW TO LOSE BY WINNING

Listing runs so smoothly when your properties are priced right in the beginning. Your clients are happy because their equity money comes fast; you are happy because your fee money comes fast. Fewer problems develop over the shorter time span. Listing the right way means pricing the right way.

Maybe you're getting tired of having this point hammered at. Believe me, you'll get far more tired of hearing from clients whose properties haven't sold. When you're their agent because you won the bidding contest for who'd put the most money on the listing agreement, how much respect can they have for you? Who will they blame when their dreams of extra thousands of dollars go glimmering? How patient will they be when there's no action? Who will they badmouth around town? That's how you lose by winning—by being top poodle in a dogfight over who'll take a listing at the highest price. Your prize is a listing that'll sour your enthusiasm and damage your reputation without paying you a cent. The only way you can come out ahead in a bidding contest is to persuade the sellers to give their listing to another agent—for thirty days only. Then, when the market proves you right by ignoring that property, you have a chance to take the expired listing at a saleable price.*

SERVICING YOUR LISTINGS WITH STYLE AND CONTROL

There are two elements in servicing your listings effectively. One, you must know what to do. Two, you must do each thing when it needs to be done.

In an active market, and when your listings are priced for that market, you won't spend much time servicing listings. You'll spend more time monitoring transactions through to completion and a fee for you. But we aren't always in an active market. And, in any market, there are properties that appeal to only a small percentage of the

---

*Be sure you understand and follow your board's rules for ethical conduct regarding listings held by other agents.

available buyers. So you'll need to know how to service listings over a period of time until the right buyers appear.

The Champion sets the sellers up for a smooth running relationship at the time the listing is taken. He (and of course I'm including all highly-paid women listers in that *he)* tells them what to expect, what the market is doing, and how prospective buyers and the agents working with those buyers will operate. That's the start. Then the Champion plugs himself into his sellers' ears until the listing sells. He never lets a week go by without phoning them, never lets three weeks slip by without stopping for a personal visit. This is his minimum program; some sellers may require more attention. What does he keep telling them with all this communication? Things like:

- How the market for housing is behaving. Changes in the interest rates. Competing properties newly on the market. Comments from people who have seen the house. Similar properties that have sold. (Sellers hate to discover for themselves that a house like theirs just sold two blocks away. They want to hear it from the real estate expert they've employed—that's you.)

- Plans for additional selling efforts.

- And reminders, as required, of how the process works.

An important part—perhaps the most important part—of this communications process is listening. The sellers are living in a changing world too. One of its most changeable parts is their emotions. Many sellers feel that they have plenty of time when they list. The act of listing punctures the balloon of security that their home had given them before. They start looking for a new home to make them feel secure again—and suddenly their nonchalance about timing vanishes. The relaxed, confident seller becomes the tense, worried buyer of another house—a buyer, that is, if he can get his money out of his old home. The tabby becomes a tiger. Every day that goes by feels like a week.

The key, then, to controlling your listings until they can be sold is regular phone calls and frequent visits. That's the key. The lock is action—timely, effective action.

HOW AND WHEN TO GET PRICE REDUCTIONS

Let's agree that we're talking here only about reasonably steady market conditions. If prices are rising rapidly, today's exorbitant price may be tomorrow's bargain. If prices are falling, today's market price listing may be tomorrow's no-action headache.

How

How do you get a price reduction? By setting it up when you take the listing. That's what the people who list with power do. That's what the Champions and Superchampions I've trained do. Set it up going in. Do that every time you take a listing unless you get it at market value when the general outlook and seasonal pattern indicates steady or rising prices.

But suppose you've won all your listings in a who'll-go-highest price competition. Obviously, they're not selling. Obviously, you're in trouble with your sellers. Now, how do you go back for the price reductions you'll have to get if any of those listings are going to sell?

Let's talk about that. By confirming your sellers' unrealistic expectations, you set yourself up for this disaster. Mentally, and maybe even actually, they've spent the money they're not going to get because you let them shove an unobtainable price onto the listing agreement. Keep this in mind: you approved the listing agreement too. You're the real estate expert. Your name on that agreement gives their price the stamp of validity in their eyes. Your credibility as a real estate expert rides on that price. When it gets thrown out, you get thrown out too. If you are in serious trouble from this cause, your best move might be to start over in a new listing bank in another part of town.

Contrast this with the Champion's method of operation. He researches the value and presents his findings. If he agrees to test the market at a higher price, he does so only after making sure that his sellers understand that he is not endorsing that price. He gets the seller to initial a comment to that effect on the CMA while taking the listing. The wise agent also gets a commitment from the sellers to consider a price reduction if no genuine buying interest has developed after an agreed period of time.

When

When should you seek the price reduction?

Just as soon as it's apparent that the seller's price is too high. You want a more specific answer, of course. Establish that answer for each listing with your sellers. When you walk in for the listing presentation, you should have a clear idea of how long property in their price category remains on the market when it's listed at market value. Your Multiple Listing Service* or your office's files will give you this information.

Documenting facts is one of the successful real estate agent's primary methods of impressing his expertise on clients. New agents need aids of this kind more than established agents do. Yet new agents generally have less of it. Here's something you can create in a short time to help impress your clients with your real estate expertise. This study is also a powerful aid in setting the client up for a more realistic price now, or for a significant reduction later.

Keep a running list of the Days On Market for all properties that sell in your office's service area. Break this information down by price categories. Keep it simple. You can handwrite this data on a legal pad. Gather the information only on the hottest selling price categories, and don't bother with unnecessary details.

There are 10 properties on the DOM study. To get the average number of Days On Market, we take the total days all ten were offered for sale (587) and divided by 10. The answer is 58 and 7/10ths days, which we round to 59 days.

This example contains information that will make motivated sellers think. So will the DOM Studies that you compile from the public record of what's happening in your area.

Please remember that *the timing of their sale* is of great importance to most sincere sellers, and timing is the overriding consideration with some. The time factor is so important. In fact, if your sellers say they're in no hurry, be wary. All your selling efforts may go for nothing because they're not emotionally committed to selling.

Of course, whatever you tell your clients must be the absolute truth. Be aware that your MLS* book will often only show the days

---

*A trademark of the National Association of Realtors®

* MLS is a trademark of the NAR and stands for Multiple Listing Service. Many real estate boards that are affiliated with the NAR issue weekly MLS books for the confidential use of their members only. These books give detailed information about properties listed for sale in their service area.

DOM STUDY
(Days on Market)

4 BEDROOMS   UNDER $125,000   SOLD DURING MARCH

Address	Date Sold	Selling Price	Original Asking Price	DOM
2814 Lambert	3/2	$109,500	$109,500	26
302 Konya	3/4	$101,000	$101,000	3
2212 Willow	3/5	$122,000	$150,000	314
2874 Ganado	3/8	$124,500	$124,500	19
906 Knollview	3/12	$118,500	$118,500	7
202 Whiting	3/15	$105,900	$108,500	31
811 Rubido	3/18	$104,300	$106,500	33
892 Elm	3/12	$115,000	$115,000	28
1991 West	3/27	$120,900	$122,500	37
1679 Ashley	3/29	$114,450	$119,500	89
				587

AVERAGE DAYS ON MARKET:

Overall: 59
When 2 longest are disregarded   23
When 2 longest and 2 shortest are disregarded   29

on market of the most recent listing; if the house was previously listed with one or several other offices, that information may not show on the list of sold properties. Sellers need to know the cost in time of testing the market with an unrealistic price. One of the most important services that you can perform as their real estate expert is to advise them how much time they can lose trying to get $21 for a $20 dollar bill.

In Chapter 11, I'll give you the words for using a DOM Study to get your sellers to agree to a realistic price. Do that and you're halfway home to liquidating that listing and adding to your liquid assets in the bank where you keep your checking account.

4

HOW TO BE A WINNER IN LISTING'S KEY HOUR

When you get there, you'll be as good as your preparation. Great preparation lets you give a great presentation; mediocre preparation limits you to a mediocre listing presentation; no preparation dooms you to flounder through what can't really be called a presentation at all. If this book convinces you of only one thing, I hope it's that to make money listing real estate, you must prepare effectively before working with sellers.

Unless you do, the seller knows more about his property than you do. He's in control of your meeting. He sets the price. And you aren't playing a real estate expert's part, you're playing a clerk's part.

To illuminate what you're up against in the usual listing opportunity, let's run through one as it develops. The specific facts differ in every case. But the basic realities are the same, and the emotional responses that people have to those realities fall into the same pattern. As you read the situation that follows, picture the people in your mind. Share their feelings. The more you do, the better you'll understand the feelings of your future clients when they put their homes on the market. Understanding how your clients think and feel is an important step toward mastering the art of listing real estate.

My clients are Mr. and Mrs. Watt. An electrical engineer who's been with the same firm for 20 years, Jack Watt is a tall, skinny fellow with an intense manner. His goal in life is to become a vice-president at his company. Over the years management has given Jack a lot of encouragement, and six times he's moved to different states at their request. But now Jack and his wife Gloria have lived in their present home for five years. They like it and the community. They've put down roots. Taking another transfer is a touchy subject around the house. In fact, Jack promised Gloria that they won't move again—unless it's for a really good promotion.

Then one day that kind of promotion comes through. As is so often the case, Jack's new opportunity is a thousand miles away. So Jack doesn't pick up the phone and call Gloria: "Guess what, honey? You get to move to another strange town." Instead, Jack decides to wait until he's with her.

When he starts home that night, Jack has some bad moments. He wonders if the promotion is worth all the emotional upheaval, all the effort of getting resettled and finding new friends, and he worries about the effect of the move on his family. But he knows he's going. Then he starts thinking about his largest investment, his home. Now he'll have to market it. He's spent a lot of weekends working on the house, getting things just the way he and Gloria like them. Remembering all they've shared in their home, Jack feels resentful. He knows he has to sell, but he doesn't want to do it.

When he reaches his neighborhood, Jack starts seeing things he never paid much attention to before. Turning a corner, he notices a For Sale By Owner sign. Jack has the vague feeling that it's been there for quite a while. "I wonder what that house is worth," he says to himself, and makes a mental note of the phone number on the sign.

The house Jack noticed belongs to Mr. and Mrs. Tweety, and it's been on the market since they moved in eight years ago. Mr. Tweety is a perpetual by-owner. Everything he has is for sale at all times. If he gets his price, he'll be happy to move. Not all by-owners are like that, but in every community there seems to be one *Mr. Tweety*.

On another street Jack takes a close look at the XYZ Realty sign on Herman and Wilma Mildue's front lawn. He and Gloria know the Mildues. When he sees the red SOLD rider on XYZ Realty's sign, Jack feels a stab of excitement. Since Gloria and Wilma bowl on the same team, Jack figures he can get the straight story from the Mildues.

A couple of blocks further on, there's another sign. This is the Simpson home, listed with Pathetic Realty. It's been on the market for seven months now but, since Jack doesn't know the Simpsons, he doesn't remember how long it's been for sale.

When Jack turns into his own driveway, he's feeling a little better about selling his home. Without going out of his way, he's found three houses to base his price on. He starts off with this premise: his home is nicer than the other three. Then Jack goes on to the formula that most sellers use in their appraisal process. This formula is simple and natural:

3 GIGOs plus 1 SWIG equals 1 OPT

(3 pieces of Garbage (bad facts) plus 1 Scientific Wild Guess equals Over Priced Trouble.)

At this point, Jack thinks that OPT means *optimum price*—the most money he can get within a time on the market that's reasonable for him. As I'll show you in a moment, OPT doesn't mean that at all.

Our minds are like a computer. Put *Garbage In* your mind about a specific subject and you'll get *Garbage Out* of your mind on that same subject. If Jack puts the wrong facts about the value of nearby houses in his head, he'll get the wrong answer about the value of his house out of his head. That answer might be right as far as he's concerned, but it's wrong for the market.

After squaring things with Gloria and the kids about the move, Jack gets busy gathering his GIGO's. First, he calls Mr. Tweety. That gentleman now has eight years of experience in handling sign calls, so Mr. Tweety is very persuasive when he says that his home is worth $185,000 if it's worth one thin dime. Jack catches his first sack of garbage. When he gets off the phone, he's bubbling with delight.

"Gloria, if that guy on the corner can get $185,000 for his place, we're going to start at $200,000. I didn't think houses were worth that much around here, but I've been hearing rumors. Honey, XYZ Realty just sold the Mildue's place. Why don't you give Wilma a call and see how much they got."

Gloria says, "Do I have to? Wilma's kind of a loudmouth. She'll yap it to everybody we know that we're moving."

"Don't let on," Jack tells his wife. "Just say that maybe we might be moving sometime in the next few months. Look, we're talking big dollars now. Knowing what property sells for around here can make us several thousand more. It'll be like finding a bundle of money in the street. We need that information."

"Okay, okay," Gloria says, "I'll call her."

She does. (Let's listen.) "We noticed that you've sold your home. How'd you come out?"

"On top like we always do," Wilma says. "We got what we wanted."

When Wilma and Gloria were bowling a few weeks before, somebody asked Wilma how much they had their house listed for. Wilma did what many people do when she answered: she added about fifteen percent to get a better sounding figure. In the bowling center, Gloria had been surprised at how high Wilma said their price was. Now, on the phone, Gloria is thinking a little dubiously about that price, but Wilma's manner keeps her from pressing in to confirm the exact figure the Mildues sold for. She puts the phone down and tells Jack, "I think the Mildues might've sold for about $190,000."

"Wow," says Jack, catching his second sack of garbage. "Aren't you glad you called Wilma? You probably just made us at least ten thousand dollars. I'm almost positive we'll be able to get $200,000." Now Gloria starts getting excited about all the money they're going to make, and she forgets her doubts about Wilma's truthfulness.

Here's what actually happened. When the Mildues decided to sell, Herman called in an agent he respected, but he insisted that their house was worth $165,000. The agent agreed to list their house at $165,000 on condition that the price would be reconsidered if 30 days passed without action. There wasn't any action. After a month the Mildues reduced their price to the market figure recommended by their agent, $149,500. Two weeks later, they accepted an offer of $148,000. That price gave them a profit of $23,000—more than Herman had hoped to make on the house when they moved in three years before. In that sense, Wilma told the truth when she said, "We got what we wanted." But, knowing that she'd spread the $190,000 figure all over town, Wilma isn't about to admit to anyone that they actually were glad to get $148,000.

Jack says, "That one sold for $190,000, and Tweety is selling himself for $185,000. All right! Now let's call Pathetic Realty and find out what the real estate experts can tell us about values in this neighborhood."

Jack gets through to Pathetic the next day. After an hour (because it takes them that long to find the listing) someone calls back and says the Simpson house is beautiful, it's priced at $197,500, and would Jack like to see it sometime?

He says no and gets off the phone quickly. Not realizing that he's just caught his third sack of garbage in two days, Jack is overjoyed. A real estate expert has confirmed his hopes.

The truth about Pathetic's listing wouldn't support Jack's optimism. The Simpson's property has been on the market seven months now because their motivation to sell isn't strong enough to make them realistic about price. They aren't leaving town. Mrs. Simpson wants a larger house. Mr. Simpson will go along with that—if it doesn't mean a larger payment. The only way they'll move is if they can sell well above market and buy well below market.

The Simpsons didn't list their home until they got to talking to Fred Blodgett, who works at the butcher shop where they trade. The Simpsons like the way Fred cuts meat. So, when he told them he'd just received his real estate license, they asked him to come over and list their house. That's been the extent of Blodgett's real estate career. He's still working in the butcher shop for a living. Whenever he thinks about it, Fred wishes the Simpsons' house would sell. If that happens, Fred thinks he might start working at real estate a couple of weekends a month. He doesn't want to rush into anything that might not pay. As it is, Fred figures that real estate already owes him for at least two weeks' work because, if he doesn't round up some of his relatives twice a month and take them through the house as though they were buyers, the Simpsons complain about no action. Sometimes Fred wonders why SOLD signs "always pop up on other people's listings, but never on mine." He thinks it's just dumb luck, and someday his will change. In the meantime, Fred's main worry is that he's running out of relatives.

I've just detailed the general method that most sellers use in pricing their homes. They talk to other sellers in ways that are guaranteed to give them unrealistic values; they listen to every rumor that raises real estate prices; and there's always at least one real estate "adviser" where everybody works. You know the type. He bought a vacant lot once that sold for a profit after nine years. Then he went to real estate school three nights in a row for a whole week. He knows everything about all real estate everywhere.

Here's how the sellers' pricing method works: The average seller contributes three GIGO's when he calls in the average real estate agent. Since that agent hasn't done his homework, he can't hose off the three Garbage-In, Garbage-Outs. So he adds his part of the formula: One Scientific Wild Guess. Then what do they have?

An Over Priced Turkey.

The natural-as-breathing GIGO + SWIG = OPT formula (Garbage plus Scientific Wild Guess equals an Over Priced Turkey) never gives you a fast-selling, priced-at-the-market listing. It never results in the bargain-priced buy-of-the-year. It traps you in the turkey cage every time you let a seller run it off on you.

Please realize that this is not the fault of the sellers. They can't help feeling that their home is worth 10 to 30 percent more than the market will carry. They're not real estate professionals. They don't earn their living with real estate knowledge. But you do—or it's your aim to. The point is that you must know more about the property's value than the owners do.

Some tips will help. What follows isn't a set of handy little hints that you can ignore if you feel like it and still make money. They are the essence of real estate success. Here they are:

1. *Fools rush in.*

My friend, every time you rush over to take a listing before you've prepared adequately, you guarantee that you'll lose money instead of making money. The seller will set the price, and he'll always set it too high. It won't sell, so there'll be no income. But there will be expense—which you'll pay; there'll be time spent servicing that listing—which you'll put in for free. Doesn't it make more sense to put in a few hours preparing, and then take the listing at a price that will sell? The alternative is to put in a lot more hours servicing an overpriced listing that won't sell until they get disgusted with you, go to another agent, and reduce the price.

"I must know more about the property than the owners do." Make that commitment to yourself and it will make important money for you.

2. *Set a top price first.*

Before you go in for the listing appointment, know the top figure at which you'll take the listing. If they insist on going above that price, you'll walk away without the listing. Setting a top price demands confidence in your own powers. If you don't develop that confidence, you'll have a tough time making it in real estate.

3. *"I will structure my presentation first, and* then I will learn it word for word."

I know this might seem like an awesome challenge right now. It isn't. Trust me on this, will you? If you've made the commitment to succeed, it won't be too difficult to memorize your presentation. Can you spare an hour a day to make sure that your dreams of success will come true? If you want them to come true faster, do like Tom Korinko did. (His story is at the end of this chapter.) Spend more than an hour a day making it happen. Tremendous improvement in selling skill comes when you follow a daily program for repetitive learning. In what will seem like a very short time after you've done it, the words will flow from you with convincing power.

Now, please, open up your mind for this next step that the successful professional lister always follows to insure his or her continuing success:

4. *"Everything I do must primarily be good for my seller."*

You must go into every listing performance with this attitude firmly in mind. Again, I ask you to trust me that this is in your best interest. Insisting that what you do must always be for the good of the seller will frequently cause you to pass up what seems like a good chance at a fast buck. All too often, those chances aren't really there. Even more often, they lead to reputation-destroying problems. One of the most powerful ways to make people like and trust you is to be committed to doing what is best for them. To be convincing in your fiduciary relationship as their agent, you must believe in your own integrity. If you know you aren't trustworthy, how can you convince others that you are? It all starts with your own internal commitment to giving honorable service.

I wish I could be at your elbow as you read these words. Even though I'm not physically with you, I hope you'll realize that I'm with you in spirit. I want you to succeed as a true professional who serves his or her clients well and, as a result of doing that, is well-paid. If it's not good for the seller, promise yourself that you won't do it.

They used to say to me at the office, "Tom, you can really close."

But I'd never agree. It seemed they were implying that I could talk people into bad decisions with closing tricks. I'd answer, "If it's good for the sellers, they need it. So I didn't close them, I simply helped them understand what their true interests are. Leading people to the decisions that are primarily good for them is what my profession is all about. So when you said that I can really close, you're actually telling me that I give professional service by showing my sellers what's best for them. I agree with that statement.''

USING YOUR LISTING TOOLS WITH FLAIR

This book contains more techniques for listing than you'll have time to use effectively. First, select the listing techniques you want to begin with. Then develop a professional level of skill with those techniques. How? By practicing, drilling, and rehearsing every aspect of them. Practice every question you plan to ask; drill yourself on how you'll handle every response you're likely to get; rehearse every statement, gesture, and movement you expect to make. Practice, drill, and rehearse how and when you'll use your tools.

In Part Two (immediately following this chapter) I'll show you how it's done. But if you give Part Two nothing more than a quick skim, it won't give your earning power a lasting lift. Moving yourself into professional earning power takes a professional level of practice, drill, and rehearsal. That, in real estate, requires very little except time and effort. You can do it all in the privacy of your home.

HOW TO CONVINCE SELLERS BY SIGHT

Do you know that many agents lose all chance to take the listing before they even open their mouths? You might feel that this is rather hard to do. It's easy. Happens all the time. How is this feat managed?

By arriving for appointments sloppily dressed, poorly groomed, and empty handed. Some losers aren't content with taking three strikes; they get themselves thrown out of the game by being late.

The successful agent not only gets there on time, he or she is professionally dressed and well-groomed. Adding to these subtle but powerful indications of competence, the successful agent has the tools for getting the job done right there in his or her hand. By favorably impressing the seller at first glance, the successful agent lays the foundation for a productive session before a word is spoken.

In many areas, professional dress for men is a suit and tie in a pleasing blend of fabrics that are quiet rather than loud in color and pattern. The professional's shoes don't yell for attention either. If you want your clients to trust you, if you want them to listen to what you're saying, don't fascinate or frighten them with your footgear. The same holds true for your entire outfit. Loud ties, bright shirts, clashing colors, and bold patterns are associated with the huckster kind of salesman in many people's minds. Most salesmen who dress this way feel the need to bolster their appearance of aggressiveness. Others do it out of ignorance. A few have a desperate need to show individuality. The winner doesn't let any of these considerations enter into his professional clothing decisions. He indulges his individuality and preferences during non-working hours only. For business, he chooses clothing that will help him make money.

When there are ensembles for business wear that project authority, stability, and competence, why put on clothing that projects eccentricity, instability, and incompetence? You are, after all, asking them to trust you to market what is probably their largest investment. If you're unsure of your wardrobe, visit the nearest large financial center and notice how the men who work there dress. Window shop the best men's clothiers in that area. Then make the best choices you can afford.

On the question of women's professional dress, I have just two suggestions: (a) when in doubt as to what to wear for a listing appointment, choose the conservative alternative; (b) avoid anything below the knee that will compete for attention with your face and what it's saying.

Now let's talk about the things you should carry in for a listing presentation, not only because you'll need them, but also to help convey that you possess a high degree of professional expertise.

THE TOOLS FOR GETTING THE JOB DONE

The doctor has his little black bag, the repairman his tool box, the accountant his calculator and forms. The successful lister carries:

1. *The Comparable Market Analysis.* Take my word for it, you're only 25 to 50 percent effective if you don't use one. Later, I'll show you precisely how to make this powerful persuader work.

2. *The Assumptive Listing Folder.* The CMA and a partially filled out listing form are the two most important ingredients in this effective listing tool.

3. *Presentation Manual.* Like the doctor's black bag, the listing presentation manual enhances credibility. Champion listers always carry them into their presentations, and they almost always use them.

4. *A Clipboard.* This shows the sellers that you're planning to take lots of notes, that you're organized, that you're efficient. Every note you take is a subtle compliment to them.

5. *A Measuring Tape.* (Get the cloth kind that won't scratch furniture.) If you're one of several agents competing for the listing, you'll probably be the only one who takes a tape in and measures the rooms. What does this demonstrate? That you're competent, that you're painstaking, that you get your facts straight.

6. *A Calculator.* Today, people believe numbers displayed by pocket calculators more readily than computations scribbled on paper. A small, thin calculator takes up hardly any space and adds a firm touch of professionalism for very little cost or trouble. When you reach the money part of your presentation, put it on the table and take control.

Chapter 10 will give you detailed techniques for using all these tools for greatest effect. Sellers want to work with an agent who takes his business seriously, who is knowledgeable and effective, and who cares about them and their property. The tools you bring to the listing appointment demonstrate that you have these qualities—or the lack of them shows that you don't.

BALANCED RESEARCH

You can do so much research that you never get out there and put it to use. You can do so little research that you aren't effective when you are working with people. Strike the balance between these extremes that results in effective, well-paid performances.

The exciting thing about the research approach to strong listing is that it gets easier as you go along. When you're the champion lister in your listing bank, you'll already know many of the facts that a beginner would have to dig out because they're about your sold listings. When you're the superchampion, you'll fill out some of your CMA's from memory. Why do superchampions write out CMA's when they have all the facts memorized? For the same reasons you should: written numbers have more impact; they are more readily believed. When clients look at the figures you're talking about instead of just hearing you say them, they're more easily convinced.

When you're well prepared and well rehearsed, you'll use your listing tools with power. The words to lead your clients smoothly toward the listing will flow out of your mouth smoothly and at the right time. You'll ask the right questions, respond effectively to their objections, quiet their fears, gain their trust, and cause them to like you. You'll put on a polished performance that will have a high success rate. You will, in a word, be a professional.

If you'll learn how to use your listing techniques and tools with flair—and then if you'll go out and put them to use—you'll succeed in the real estate business.

How can I be so sure?

Let me explain why. First of all, the average person who enters the real estate business never puts much effort into acquiring expertise. He may work hard at doing the wrong things. He may put in long hours of busy time doing very little. But he doesn't work effectively at becoming an expert lister and seller. Since the average new person is out of the business in less than a year, he isn't much competition to someone like yourself who's resolved to succeed. (I know that because you're reading these words.)

Then what is your competition?

Usually, it's a collection of people who are satisfied if they get by. When any of them go out on a listing presentation, what they put on is not a practiced, polished, professional performance. Your average, hanging-in-there real estate agent gets to the appointment late, wings his way through what he's pleased to call his listing presentation, and gets by because most of the time he's only competing against other come-late wingers.

If you'll practice, drill, and rehearse these techniques, it's not a question of whether or not you'll succeed in real estate, it's only a question of how great your success will be. And that decision, too, you make for yourself. It's all in your hands and mind. The more I travel and speak and train salespeople, the more convinced I become that the most important element of success is your will. It's not good health, looks, education, or connections that decide who succeeds and who fails—it's determination. You may think that you're weak in this area, that you lack drive and stick-to-it willpower. You don't. Any time you choose to do so, you can stop drifting and start succeeding in a big way. You can change. Maybe it won't be easy. But I can guarantee you this: after you change, after you become a highly-paid professional, the pain of the change will be forgotten. And you'll know that it was worth the work many times over. Success, my friend, is more fun than anything else you can name because everything else can flow from it.

Here's the success story Tom Korinko sent me from Amherst, Ohio: His letter was dated October 30.

"Thank you for turning my career around. In April of this year, I attended your seminar. At the time I really was not sure if I was going to stay in real estate. Disillusioned with the lack of accomplishment, I had given my manager notice that I was looking for a new job.

"At the seminar you radiated so much enthusiasm and confidence that I was convinced I could be a great salesman if I would work. So I invested in your tapes and started getting up early (4 A.M.) and practicing for a couple of hours each day. I was amazed at the results. My attitude really changed; so did my confidence and abilities.

"I have become the top salesman of our company's 140 associates . . . I have revised my goals upward . . . I know I will do even better."

Mr. Korinko turned his career around between April and October. Will you devote a similar length of time to turning yours around? I hope you'll say yes because every technique that you'll need to do it listing real estate is given in the following chapters. Please turn to them now.

PART TWO

THE TOM HOPKINS METHOD OF HIGH-VOLUME LISTING

5
REFLEXIVE LISTING TECHNIQUES

A *reflex* is something you do without thinking. A *trained reflex* is something you do fast and well without thinking. In sports, in business, in almost all areas of active life, if you have to think before doing it, you're too late most of the time.

All professionals have trained reflexes, and it is the speed and accuracy of those reflexes that determines how successful each professional will be. When a boxer's reflexes slow down, he's through. The same thing is true of all professional athletes, but there's an exciting difference between the eye-and-hand coordination required in sports and the eye-and-mouth coordination required in real estate listing and selling: our reflexes get faster as time passes.

My goal is to give you the same reflexes that allow a football player to catch a pass and score a touchdown. The action is different, but the underlying situation is the same when we face sellers or buyers in real estate. When the seller says certain things, the strong lister instantly says the right thing—and moves closer to success with that seller. When your reflexes are trained, you'll be a strong lister. It's that simple.

Using reflexive listing techniques means communicating effectively with your sellers. Communicating effectively means leading your sellers to the conclusion that listing with you is the wisest decision they can make. When you lead them by using reflexive listing techniques, they arrive where you want them to go; when you try to force them without using skillful technique, they squirt off in some other direction. After you've trained yourself until your technique is reflexive, it's fast, sure, and overpowering.

THE ASKING SECRET

A listing is nothing more than a major decision that's reached through a series of minor agreements. The big YES is the listing. How do you get it? By first getting a lot of little yeses. The professional athlete doesn't expect to win the game on the first play. He has a plan. His game plan calls for reaching victory through winning a series of plays. The big YES is the game win, reached through a lot of small yeses *won over the entire period of the game.* In real estate, the beginner often fails to realize that there is a game period involved in taking each listing. Not realizing that, he gets overly anxious. He presses too hard too soon. And he starts off telling the seller things. Let's listen to some of the things beginners tell sellers. (Year after year, some old strugglers in the business keep on beating themselves with this approach too.)

"We are the finest real estate company in town."
"I'm the most professional salesperson there is."
"I know more about the real estate around here than anybody."
"By-owners can't sell homes now—and if they do, they always get less." (If you want people to believe you, don't call yourself a liar.)
"You better list with me 'cause we're the best."
"We've got the biggest signs in town."

Obviously, strong listers get a lot of information across to their sellers. How do they do it unless they tell them things?

By asking. Let's try it. We'll begin with the *automatic yes* technique:

- "You'd like to do business with a professional, wouldn't you?" What are they going to say to that? "Oh, no, I'd like to work with the dumbest jerk in town.'' Of course they won't say that; they'll agree that they want to work with a professional. And as they give you that minor yes, aren't they also accepting the fact—telling themselves in reality—that you are a professional of the type they want to work with?

Here's a variation on that statement:

- ''A reputation for professionalism is important, isn't it?'' When you say that, they aren't going to come back with, ''If you've built up a fine professional reputation, we're not talking to you any more.''

- Use these two with sellers who've just been transferred: ''Wouldn't it be convenient to move as a family?'' Most of them will agree with that, just as they will with, ''Today, double moves are expensive, aren't they? As always, sensitivity counts. Sometimes the husband wouldn't mind looking the new town over by himself for a month. If you suspect that he has an adventurous spirit, it might be better not to get into the question of them moving together.

- ''As a specialist in this area, I could better serve you folks, couldn't I?'' If you've already displayed an impressive knowledge of the real estate in their neighborhood, what's their natural conclusion? That it's a good decision to give you the listing and benefit from your knowledgeable service.

If you've decided to turn pro in real estate, I hope that you'll make a small but important promise to me right now. You have two ears and one mouth. Please promise me that you'll remember to use each of them equally every time you're in front of sellers. This means that you listen twice as much as you talk. Do that and you'll double your effectiveness. Go a step further and double your effectiveness again: ask the right questions.

Keep on asking. And listen to the answers. They give you direction-pointers for further questions. For further minor yeses. For staying on the broad open path to taking the listing.

Let's get back to specific questions. Watch how I handle it as I'm sitting across the kitchen table from a couple who needs to sell their home, Don and Helen Lohman:

"Mr. and Mrs. Lohman, before we really even get started this evening, I'd like to—if I might—ask you some questions to see if our firm is the kind of firm that you'd like to represent you. Because, you see, if we don't have what you're looking for, then you should call another firm.

"May I ask, would you like a firm that is known in this community to have a reputation for professionalism?"

When they nod or say yes, I go on to the next question:

"Would you also like a firm that invests a considerable amount of time and money advertising and exposing real estate to attract qualified purchasers?"

The Lohmans don't argue with that idea either.

"Would you also like the firm that serves you to have hundreds of different financing sources at its fingertips to assure that qualified buyers can obtain the funds they need to purchase your house at the least amount of expense to you?"

Again I wait for the Lohmans to indicate agreement before proceeding to the next question.

"Would you like your real estate representatives to screen possible buyers so that only those who are qualified, that is, who can afford and have the money to buy your house, are shown your property?"

The Lohmans nod assent, so I ask the next question in my sequence:

"And would you also like a salesperson who is full time?" When I say that, I hand each of them one of my cards. "As you can see, my card has three phone numbers: my home, my office, and the phone in my car (my answering service, my beeper). Would you like to be able to contact your representative 24 hours a day?—six days a week?"

Am I making them feel important? Certainly. Mr. and Mrs. Lohman have been giving me a lot of small yeses, haven't they?

"And my last question is, do you want as much money out of your home as you can possibly get?"

Believe me, they're going to say yes to that one. So we're certain to end on a yes. That's when I go in for my wrap-up:

"Mr. and Mrs. Lohman, this is exciting. Based on what you've told me, I truly believe that we'll be able to do business because the things you've asked for are the things my firm offers. And now I'd like to at least go over my comparable market analysis with you."

I didn't tell the Lohmans. They told me—because I asked the right questions. By asking the right questions, I pulled out the right answers, answers that turned them around to the *Yes, let's go* mood.

Here's an essential quality that all right questions for listing or selling real estate must have:

They Must Know The Answer.

Don't laugh. If you ask them a question they can't answer, they feel stupid. If you make them feel stupid, will they want to work with you? No, they won't. A truism, yet many real estate salespeople ignore its reality. They feel that if they can just make their prospects feel stupid enough, they'll also make them feel dependent. It doesn't work very often. Ninety-eight percent of the people want you to make them feel smart; only two percent want you to make them feel stupid. Remember that the next time you're tempted to ask a possible client something like, "Mr. and Mrs. Curtis, do you think we should offer FHA financing, VA financing, or the new 4245 graduated program? What are your feelings about financing?"

The average seller doesn't know what you're talking about, but he isn't about to say, "Hey, I'm a dummy; you tell me what financing we should offer." Instead, he'll try to muddle through without admitting his ignorance. But now he's insecure. He knows why. You made him feel that way by implying that he isn't very sharp. So he wants you out of there. Is that any way to get a listing?

In the listing interview with the Lohmans, I asked them six questions that all had only one answer, the automatic yes. But overuse makes any technique abrasive. So, before you rub them raw, switch smoothly to another technique. Here's one of the most dynamic listing techniques ever devised:

THE ALTERNATE OF CHOICE SYSTEM FOR SUCCESS

First I'll give you the definition of this method, and then I'll show you how listing champions use it.

An alternate of choice is any question that has two answers, either of which confirms that they're going ahead.

Each minor yes leads to another small yes, and finally to the big yes. That's why the strong lister doesn't ask, "Can I come by and see you folks tonight?" Why not?

Because it's too easy for them to say no. Here's what the pro, the Champion, asks:

"I'll be in the neighborhood this evening. Would it be more convenient if I stopped by at 6:00, or would you prefer 8:00?"

Give them two choices, either of which confirms that you have the appointment. This works beautifully on an ad call:

"I have an appointment open this morning, or would this afternoon be more convenient?"

If the caller says, "Oh, no, we won't have any free time until the weekend," the Champion is ready with another alternate of choice.

"I have some time open on Saturday and also on Sunday. Which would you prefer?"

"Well, we'll have to wait until Sunday."

Noon divides each day into two parts, doesn't it? So the pro asks the next alternate of choice question:

"Would you like to make it in the morning, or would the afternoon be better for you?"

"The afternoon, I think."

"Shall we say one o'clock, or would you rather see the house around three p.m.?"

"We can be there at one," says the caller. After just four smooth alternate of choice questions, the pro has the appointment. In the same situation, the average salesperson will ask questions that suggest a negative answer until he gets a final *no*. Here's how he drives his car into the wall:

"Can you come out to see the house today?"

"No, I can't."

"Er, uh, do you know when you can make it?"

"Well, that's hard to say. I'm kinda busy this week."

"How about on the weekend. You can come down here then, can't you?"

"No, I'm afraid not. I think we're going away this weekend. Tell you what, I'll give you a call when we have some free time." And, of course, you never hear from them again.

LOGICAL LISTING

It never happens. People list their homes emotionally, and then they justify what they've done with logic. We're all the same on this. The cars we drive, the clothes we wear, the houses we live in—all of them are the result of emotional buying decisions. Many of us would like to think that we used careful analysis and cold logic when we bought—but we didn't. We bought what we wanted. The emotional decision was made quickly; the logic to support that decision took longer to fabricate. But you did it. As you work through the game period of the listing, seize every opportunity to bring legitimate emotions into play. Do it with alternate of choice questions:

"Helen, you know your home better than anyone. If you were marketing your home, would you bring buyers in through the front door or the back door?"

Either answer helps you, doesn't it?

"I love our entry hall, Tom. I'd bring them in from the front."

"Then that's where we should put the lockbox, don't you agree? Let me make a note of that." Look how far toward winning the listing a small yes here takes you. Now watch this one:

Don Lohman is a landscaping fanatic. When I walk outside with him, I see every container plant, I praise every flower bed, I admire every fig tree. Then I say, "Mr. Lohman, you know your home and area better than anybody. One of the keys to a good, fast sale is to catch the eye of the possible buyers—or of their friends—who drive past your home. Do you think it would be wise to place the sign this way (I indicate with my hands) or this way?"

Mr. Lohman says, "Well, Tom, the way the traffic moves by here, I think I'd place it both ways."

"Then you'd like two signs. Okay, that's a good idea. We'll do it. Let me make a note of that." If I can get them to agree to a sign in their yard, I'm halfway to taking the listing, isn't that right?

YOUR BIGGEST PROBLEM WITH THE
LISTING FORM

The biggest problem most salespeople have with the listing form is that they never fill it out. Why don't they? Because they're afraid the seller will tell them not to. So they hide the form, planning to whip it out after they've somehow talked the sellers into saying, "Okay, write it up." The trouble with this theory is that most sellers will never say that unless they are handled skillfully. They'll procrastinate, they'll wait to talk to the next Realtor®, they'll sleep on it—anything to keep from making the decision.

Nearly all strong listers use the listing form as an integral part of their listing sequence. Simply by learning how to use the listing form during listing interviews, you'll acquire more real estate expertise than most people entering the profession ever do.

Let's start with the basic assumption that it's almost impossible to take a listing without writing on the form. And it's equally difficult to write on a form that's locked inside your attaché case. So the first essential for using the form effectively is to expose it to the air of the room.

Have the form in your assumptive listing folder. Before you get there, fill in the information that you're sure of. The address. Their full legal names if you know them. Month and year. Your name, phone numbers, office address. It's more impressive—and more assumptive—if you neatly type this known data in. Then you're ready to quickly and nicely use the minor closes at the right times.

Right now let's take a moment to review a vital point: Minor closes are an essential part of successful listing. Learn the two that follow word for word, and work them into your standard listing scenario. While we're studying them, let's suppose that you're at a listing interview with Chuck and Midge Jones. Here are the two closes:

"Mrs. Jones, would you want us to call for an appointment before showing the home, or shall we just stop by?"

"Mr. Jones, which do you feel would better suit your plans—a 30 or a 60 day possession date and close of escrow?"

They don't sound like much, do they? That's part of their strength: they're non-threatening. Actually, those simple words are dynamite when they're used right. But if you must pop them off whenever they occur to you and then grunt at whatever they answer, the effect is lost. Here's how you use them to take a long step toward nailing down the listing: when they answer—and it doesn't matter which alternative they choose—say this:

"Let me make a note of that."

And then write their answer *on the listing form.* If you can picture yourself doing that in real life, you may get a queasy feeling right now because you're thinking, "But they'll jump all over me if I try that. Couldn't I just scratch a note on a legal pad—so they'll know I'm not using the listing form—and copy it later when the heat's off?"

That's not what the strong listers think. They're hoping the sellers will try to stop them when they slide the listing form out and start writing on it.

HOW STRONG LISTERS KEEP MOVING WHEN THE SELLERS TRY TO STOP THEM

A strong lister is ready when the seller sees him writing on the listing form and says, "What are you doing? We're not ready to give anyone the listing yet."

Listing Champions move forward instead of being stopped cold when this happens. You can too. Memorize the following words. Practice, drill, and rehearse until you can deliver them smoothly and with conviction.

"I organize my thoughts and keep everything in the proper perspective. I do that on the paperwork so I don't forget anything, particularly anything that might cost you money."

Are they excited that you won't forget anything that might cost them money? You bet they are. A lot of them will say, "Keep on writing, man." Are you projecting competence when you respond confidently like that? You bet you are. This is why the pro thinks the listing form is a nice place to write notes. Notice that we don't talk about the listing form to the seller. We call it the "paperwork." Why? Because paperwork is a non-threatening detail; a listing form is a contract, and contracts are frightening.

Let's go through that again. "Mrs. Jones, would you want us to call for an appointment before showing the home, or shall we just stop by?"

"You can just stop by," Mrs. Jones says.

"Let me make a note of that," you say, and write your note on the listing form.

"What are you doing?" Mr. Jones says.

"I organize my thoughts and keep everything in proper perspective," you say. "I do that on the paperwork so I don't forget anything, particularly anything that might cost you money."

"All right," Mr. Jones says, "Go ahead. But we haven't decided to list with you yet."

"I know," you say, "but I want to be sure of my facts in case you do decide to employ my professional skills and let me serve you."

Isn't that easy? And are you miles closer to taking the listing after that exchange? You can count on it.

HOW TO TIE THE MINOR YESES DOWN

Listing is the process of building up minor yeses in the minds of your sellers. When the total weight of your minor yeses exceeds the total weight of your sellers' indecision and built-in negative feelings, their resistance crumbles. Then you can close for the listing and walk away with it every time. On your way to that critical point, you must win many minor yeses, but unless you nail those yeses down, much of their weight is lost. Why? Because, in order to get from indecision to decision and choose to list with you, the sellers must undergo a complex series of emotional changes.

This means that they're preoccupied, doesn't it? They have a lot on their minds, don't they? You'd like to break through their emotional stress and score solid points with them, wouldn't you?

Isn't it true that, if you can get your sellers to voice their agreement with the points you're making, they'll be far more likely to remember and believe those facts? Won't knowing how to do that make your success easier and more certain? Shouldn't you incorporate this technique into your listing sequence right away?

And, by this time, haven't you noticed the tie-down technique that I'm using on you right now? Now that you have the feel of tie-downs, can't you see yourself using them frequently? Because they're so simple, isn't it obvious that you can work them into almost any situation?

THE FOUR STYLES OF TIE-DOWNS

The standard style places the tie-down last; the inverted style places it first; the internal style uses the tie-down in the middle of the sentence; and the tag-on is a tie-down that you hook onto the positive statements your seller makes. Let's review examples of all these styles.

Look back four paragraphs to the one beginning with, "This means." That paragraph contains three standard tie-downs: *doesn't it, don't they, wouldn't you*. Note that they all come at the end of their sentences.

Turn a standard tie-down around and you get the inverted form: "Don't they have a lot on their minds?" The paragraph after the standard tie-downs gives three samples of the inverted style, in which the tie-downs come at the beginning of each sentence: *Isn't it true, won't knowing, shouldn't you*.

Put the tie-down in the middle and you have the internal form: "If you can get your sellers to voice their agreement with the points you're making, isn't it true that they're far more likely to remember those facts?" Three models of the internal form are given in the paragraph beginning, "And, by this time." The tie-downs used internally are *haven't you, can't you, isn't it*.

There are more than twenty common tie-downs such as *won't he, didn't it, shouldn't she*. All of them can easily be worked into any of the four tie-down styles.

The fourth form of the tie-down is the tag-on. Use this whenever your sellers say something you want to reinforce in their minds, usually something that's positive to the idea of their listing with you. Simply tag your tie-down onto what they just said.

Seller: "I see your company's sign all over town."
Lister: "There certainly are a lot of them around, aren't there?"

But you don't have to stop there. Why not tag-on a second booster and double the reinforcing effect? Here's how it's done: (We'll use the same example; the seller has just made the positive statement about seeing your signs all over town.)

"There certainly are a lot of them around, aren't there? Many of my clients have told me that. By the way, doesn't all this heavy sign activity tell you a great deal about our company's effectiveness and reputation?" Wham, and double wham.

Memorize the following tie-down zingers. You need to have them ready for instant use in your toolbag.

"A reputation for professionalism is important, isn't it?"

"You have noticed our signs and activity in your area, haven't you?"

"You're interested in your home having complete exposure, aren't you?"

"It would be convenient to move as a family, wouldn't it?"

"Double moves are expensive, aren't they?"

"As a specialist in this area, I could better serve you, couldn't I?"

The six zingers above can be used word for word during most interviews. When you can honestly say nice things about the sellers' property, tailor comments such as the following to fit the situation. If possible, use these tie-downs to the other spouse when the husband or wife being praised can hear you.

"She's done a lovely job of decorating, hasn't she?"

"He's created a beautiful landscape here, hasn't he?"

At this point you're probably beginning to think there's a tremendous amount to know in real estate before you can call yourself a professional and earn a professional's income. There is. It's like a jigsaw puzzle. A tough puzzle might take you thirty hours to put together the first time, and less than three hours the second time. The tenth time, it'll take you less than fifteen minutes—the reason, of course, is that you've practiced, drilled, and rehearsed your performance. All the elements of strong listing, when you practice, drill, and rehearse them, become part of a developed performance that you'll then find is ridiculously easy to run through. You'll also find that it's fun—for two powerful and basic reasons: Achieving anything worthwhile by using great skill is one of life's greatest pleasures, and so is the knowledge that you'll be well-paid for doing it.

Some final thoughts about tie-downs. Mix the four styles up as you say them. Most of us tend to overuse the standard form, don't we? It easily becomes a habit that annoys our listeners, doesn't it? But we have the other forms, don't we?

Shouldn't we use the inverted style just as often? Isn't the inverted form worth practicing? And, while we're rehearsing our tie-downs, wouldn't it be better if we blended in a few of the internal style to give our speech variety?

When you've practiced the tie-down technique adequately, don't you agree that you'll use the internal form as often as the other two? As soon as you reach that stage of development, won't mixing all three add a great deal to the interest and eloquence of your words? And, in order to make these points, haven't I had to overuse the tie-down technique? Certainly. When your technique is obvious and abrasive, it hurts you more than it helps you. So use the tie-downs liberally, mix them well, but don't overuse them. Now let's move right on to the next reflexive listing technique.

THE FEEDBACK MINOR CLOSE

The unskilled salesperson isn't aware of an important fact: most people don't bother objecting to minor issues unless they're approaching a major decision.

Think about it. What I'm saying is that you won't get objections about details until you're on third base ready to score a run. Since getting specific objections about minor issues is a sign that success is both near and obtainable, why don't more salespeople look forward to getting objections?

Salespeople? That's right. Listing is a form of selling. Never forget that. Taking a listing requires you to sell your competence and your company's reputation to people who own property they want to market.

Why do so many salespeople fear objections when objections really are nothing more than a sign that success is within grasp? The answer can only be that they don't understand how people arrive at major decisions. This is selling's worst no-win trap. How can you succeed if, after doing eighty percent of the sales job well enough to get within striking distance of success, you buckle and quit? Because of what? Because of the usual objections that most people make before committing themselves to a major decision. It's sad when that happens. Many who enter real estate know how to relate to people, and they quickly learn how to create the conditions in which a listing or a sale can take place, but they don't learn how to accept their success. They fold like a suitcase and go home at the first sounds of distress from sellers if they're trying to list, or from buyers if they're showing property. These certain-to-fail types (unless they take the cure) have a fixed and totally wrong idea: they think people enjoy making major decisions. The truth is that major decisions, which by definition involve major changes in the lives of the people who make them, cause anxiety and pain. People have to relieve this pain. They do that with objections. Voicing objections is a way of saying ouch.

Remember that ouch when buyers knock the paint condition, when they squawk about the roof, when they grumble about the water heater. What do they care—unless they're thinking of moving in? On the listing side, most sellers don't fight for a thirty day listing instead of six months unless they're considering giving you the listing. And few sellers worry about having a sign on their property unless they have an idea about employing you to market their property. When you hear an objection, smile. It means that you're getting somewhere.

Then there are the salespeople—some of them come to every one of my seminars—who actually push aside listings that are all but offered to them on a silver platter. Why? Because they're afraid of having to be realistic with the owners about price, of having to be realistic about time, of having to take on responsibility for getting the property sold—because, in other words, they're afraid to do business in the business they're in. Obviously, such people won't last long in the real estate profession unless they learn how to manage their anxieties. In Chapter 12, I'll give you the tools to understand and cope with fear.

And, if objections wipe you out, take heart. Next, I'm going to show you how to receive objections, how to manipulate them, and how to hit them back for winners. It's vital that you learn how to do this, not only for the sake of your own financial success, but for the good of your sellers, of your industry, and of society in general. Your contribution to the well-being of the world is to make a lot of money in real estate by serving the needs of the public honestly and effectively. What happens if you're not strong and don't take a listing from a by-owner? That by-owner will usually have to hold his property too long for his schedule, so he'll lose money. Or he'll wind up in court fighting a buyer because he didn't know what he was doing. All these troubles pour down because a salesperson—let's hope it's not you—was too incompetent to sell the by-owner on the need for professional real estate service.

The day you turn pro is the day you start loving objections. That's right, love 'em. I can hear you now: "Come on, Tom. Don't expect me to believe that you love objections."

I do expect you to believe me on this. It's important that you do. I'll say it again. I love objections. I LOVE THEM.

Why? Because I can't get a *yes* until someone gives me a *no*. In other words, if I can't get any noes, I can't make any money. If they're completely agreeable, if they go along with everything I say, what are they probably doing? Picking my brain. And when I try to close after an hour of that, I can't hook onto anything solid. They keep on smiling and agreeing as they push me out the door.

I don't like it when people pick my brains that way. I want to be of service—and then get paid for it. Being used and then trashed like an empty milk carton is not my idea of fun. When you've made all the skills in this book yours, you'll be a Champion who can say, "I'm not going to be used anymore. I'm not staying away from my family nights without getting the listing."

It's ridiculous to do that. I have a philosophy: *If you keep me away from my family, you're going to pay for it.* Shouldn't that be your philosophy too? I thought so. But, to make that philosophy stick to the walls of reality, you have to know what you're doing. When you learn my material, you will. You'll walk into that listing and be out in an hour and a half—with a six months' exclusive right to sell, with their agreement to have a sign in their front yard, with a saleable price, with realistic terms, with a key for the lockbox. You'll be a pro, who goes on listing appointments to do business and make money, not to fumble around, hope for the best, and get nothing. To be a pro, you have to be able to put the whole jigsaw puzzle together in that hour and a half. One of the essential pieces is understanding and getting past objections.

HOW TO HANDLE OBJECTIONS

First of all, most objections are soon forgotten if you don't talk about them. The reason for this is that most objections are thrown out only to slow the process down. Get comfortable with that idea. Then, when the sellers start pitching a few at you, you'll see that you're coming in too fast. All you have to do is shift gears and slow down a bit. Do that and you'll get home quicker.

Now let's talk about one of the finest techniques for handling minor objections.

FEEDBACK

Using this magnificent minor close is a simple process. All it involves is:

Taking the objection and warmly feeding it back in the form of a question, thus demanding amplification.

Let me explain what I'm saying here. When someone tells you, "We don't want a sign on our home," and you agree with that by saying, "Well, we don't need to put a sign on your property if you don't want one," whom have you hurt? The sellers. Do you want to begin your relationship by hurting the people you'll be working for?

When they tell you, "We don't want to give out a key to our home," and you answer, "We don't need it," whose interests are you damaging? The sellers. If there's no sign, the best buyers will drive by and never think of purchasing that listing because they don't know it's available. If there's no lockbox with a key, the selling agents will pull that listing out of their books and take their clients to houses that are quickly and conveniently seen. Why won't they take the time to wrestle with a key problem? Because their experience tells them that if the sellers wouldn't give out a key, they aren't very eager to sell or the listing agent doesn't know his business. Either way it spells trouble. They can find enough trouble on their own without your help. The pro knows that she, or he, has an obligation to the sellers and to the agents representing buyers to get them a key and to put out a sign that identifies the property as being for sale.

So when they hit you with one of these very common and predictable objections, be ready with the right reflexive response for minor objections, which is feedback. Here's how it goes (Add your name after Champion):

Champion: "Quite a few of our clients tell us that our sign is distinguished looking, and that it compliments the community's architecture. Do you agree?"
Seller: "We don't want a sign."
Champion: "You don't want a sign? Can you tell me why?"

As you feed the objection back and ask them if they'd mind telling you why they feel that way, it's vital that your tone and manner be warm and friendly. If there's a trace of argument in your voice, you'll get argument back. You're not trying to win an argument here (you never argue with a client); you're employing professional skills to persuade clients to do what's best for them. You don't really care why they're reluctant to have a sign, of course. Their reasons are certainly trifling compared with their need to do everything reasonable to help get their property sold. Ninety percent of the time, they don't want a sign because of the neighbors.

Let's pick up our example again.

Champion: "You don't want a sign? Can you tell me why?"
Seller: "Well, Midge and I would just as soon the neighbors didn't know right away."
Champion: "We don't require a sign. However, a large percentage of our buyer activity comes from properties with our signs on them. You know—I have an idea—if we're fortunate enough to arrive at the market value based on the comparable market analysis, we may not even need a sign. We may have the home sold in the next—oh—the next three weeks. Now, why don't we hold the sign off for three weeks, and let's just see what happens, shall

we? Let me make a note of that—no sign for three weeks.'' (Writes on the listing form.)

Seller: ''Hey! What are you doing there?''

Champion: ''I'm organizing my thoughts and keeping everything in proper perspective. I do that on the paperwork so I don't forget anything, particularly anything that might cost you money.''

Now let's discuss another emotional problem that people have when they're close to listing: they don't want to give you a key. Why not? Because it pops their balloon to think about strange people coming through. That balloon of security and privacy is precious to everyone. Logically, giving up a key is necessary if the house is to sell; emotionally, doing so violates their innate sense of territory. And they may have other reasons. Part of your job as a professional is to persuade them to break through those emotional barriers and get on with selling the house.

Mr. Jones: ''We don't want to give out a key.''

Champion: ''Oh, you didn't want to give out a key? Can you elaborate on that?'' (Use this wording occasionally to give a pleasant variety to your responses.)

Mrs. Jones: ''We have lots of valuables.''

Champion: ''Fine. It's not mandatory that we have a key. Are you both home most of the time?''

Mr. Jones: ''Well, I'm at work during the day, of course. But Midge is here all the time.''

Champion: ''By the way, Midge, when do you go shopping?''

Mrs. Jones: ''Usually on Monday mornings.''

Champion: ''It would be a shame to have a buyer unable to see the home on Monday, don't you agree? I have an idea. Have you ever seen one of these?'' (Takes a lockbox out of the attache case, or flips to a photo of one in the presentation manual.) ''This is what we in the industry call a lockbox. We have these to assure as much privacy and security as possible. Here's the key. I'd like to open the box up and show you how it works. In fact, Chuck, to prove to Midge how concerned we are with your security, would you take out your house key for me? Chuck, drop it in there. Go on. This will hang on the front door. That's rather secure, isn't it?''

Now, where's his key? In the lockbox. Where's it staying? In the lockbox.

I think I'm reading you right now. You're thinking, "I couldn't do that." Let me tell you something: you can do it easily—very easily—the second time. If you have trouble convincing yourself that this terminology will get the job done, listen to my tapes, or come to my seminar and hear me say these words, warmly, softly, and persuasively. You can say them like that, too. All it takes is practice.

What is the normal reaction when you use the feedback technique?

They sell themselves out of it. Many times I've had the wife say, "Now Tom, we don't want to give out a key."

I'd say, "Okay. It's not mandatory that we have a key. Are you both home most of the time?"

And then the husband, knowing they're both gone a lot, says, "Oh, come on, honey. We can go ahead and give them the key." Who sold whom? Spouses will close each other if you'll let them. Be alert about timing. Wait a few seconds. Give the spouses time to sell each other. If you don't let them do that, you make your job twice as hard.

Here's my favorite technique:

THE PORCUPINE

Let me ask you a question. If I walked in to where you're sitting right now and threw a live, prickly porcupine in your lap, what would you do?

Let me tell you something. You wouldn't cuddle him and say, "Isn't he a cute little fella." Oh, no. You'd throw that procupine right back at me. Why am I conjuring up this scene? Because, when you're asked a question by a seller that's a bit prickly, he's tossed you a porcupine. Toss the porcupine right back. How? By answering the seller's question with one of your own. *Then write his answer on the listing form.*

When you put this technique in gear, it'll go so well that you'll want to jump out of your chair. Let's take it on a sample run.

Have you ever worked with a couple when the husband is the abrupt kind who's in a big hurry to get things over with as fast as possible? I love this type because they'll close themselves if you'll let them.

Here's one of these hurry-up-husbands, Barry Bevier, talking: "All of this that you're telling me is well and good, but what I really want to know is, can you have our home sold in sixty days?"

What did he just throw at us?

A porcupine.

How would you answer him? Would you say something like, "Oh, the market is so good now, I'm positive that we can. We'll do our best; we'll give it our best shot." Say that kind of thing and you've got nothing.

The Champion, the pro, the strong lister, loves that question. He or she just smiles and says, "Barry, are you interested in giving possession in sixty days?"

Barry: "Well, I think we need to be out by then."
Champion: "Fine. Let me make a note of that." You know
                    where the Champion is going to write that note.
Barry: "What are you doing there?"
Champion: "I organize my thoughts and keep things in proper
                    perspective. I do that on the paperwork so I don't
                    forget anything, particularly anything that might cost
                    you money."

If you'll just run Barry Bevier through a few of those minor closes, he'll see that you know what you're doing. When that happens, he'll lose interest in checking further and tell you to write it up. Here's another common opportunity:

Barry: "Will you put a sign on the property?"
Weaklister: "Will we! We've got signs you won't believe. They
                      rise up out of the ground and hang over the
                      house—you can see them for miles."
Barry: "We don't want a sign."
Weaklister: "Duh, well, we don't, uh, actually require a sign."
                      He's dead in the water. Weaklister let the seller

shear his oars off again. Here's how the pro plays
the same scene:

Barry: "Will you put a sign on the property?

Champion: "Would you like a sign?"

If Barry says yes, the pro uses the let-me-make-a-note-of-that *zap it on the listing form* technique again. If Barry says no, the pro uses the sign close given previously.

You see the method: you always end with a close. Contrast that with the usual course of simply answering their question by giving them the information they've asked for. What comes next? They hit you with another question—and then another. On and on it goes. Very quickly that rhythm is established and you unconsciously accept their dominance. You're not leading them. They are leading you. And since there are countless negative turns they can take, they'll lead you away from the listing every time.

Learn all the closes, all the responses, all the leading questions word for word. I hope you're not telling yourself right now that you don't need to do that. I hope you're not thinking "I couldn't say that" every time you read something I want you to memorize. I know the feeling. When I first took training, I fought it. I said, "Those words are not me," when a great salesperson gave me a script that worked. Fortunately, I didn't fight him long. Instead, I learned his words so well that they became me. That's when I stopped resisting, stopped fighting the words, because by that time I'd only be fighting myself.

After you have total control of this material, after you fully understand alternate of choice, let-me-make-a-note, tie-down, feedback, porcupine—and all the other techniques that follow in this book—you have the right to take my material and re-cast it in your own image. You might not want to say, "Mrs. Jones, would you want us to call for an appointment, or shall we just stop by?" Maybe you'd rather say, "Mrs. Jones, we can do one of two things. Either just have people stop by and see your home, or we can instruct the agents to give you a call before coming over. Which would you prefer?" When she replies, you might say, "Fine, I'll just jot that down." This is the same technique. Even though the words have been changed slightly it still works. But beware. Slight changes can send the discussion off in unintended directions. So, before you tinker with the wording, learn the basic form given in these pages. Then use this basic form with several sets of clients until you fully grasp how this precise wording guides their responses.

This is where the practice, drill, and rehearsal comes in. Don't shortcut it: you'll only be shortcutting yourself. Don't avoid acquiring the skills of your profession. Don't fight words that work until you have better ones for you.

Earlier, we spoke about the game period of the listing. Now that you're beginning to see the entire puzzle that taking a listing is, are you beginning to realize the importance of charting out your entire performance in advance? Are you beginning to see that you need to practice, drill, and rehearse your complete presentation *word for word?* A few weeks after I took my first sales training, I found myself in the cockpit of opportunity. I had achieved some success. I wasn't a failure anymore. But, though the negative minded chairwarmers at the office were blinking away their tears at my sudden turnaround, I couldn't get off the ground and really soar.

Then I set out to learn my entire performance word for word and to coordinate every move and gesture in it. Long before I had achieved the perfection of performance that I was seeking, I began setting new records. By that time I knew to the minute how long my listing performance would take. One hour and twenty-two minutes from the instant I sat down with the sellers, I would be heading for the door with the approved paperwork in my fist.

Let's work on four questions you're likely to meet in any listing interview that you should porcupine back to the sellers.

- "Can you have the home sold in eighty days?"

If you answered, "Would you want the home sold in eighty days?" you'd be close. You porcupined it all right, but it sounded like a technique. That's why you learn to say these words: "Mr. Jones, would you be interested in giving possession of your home in sixty days?"

- "Will you put a sign on the property?"
  "Would you like us to install one of our signs for you?"

- "Will you call before showing our home?"

The obvious answer, "Would you like us to call before showing the home?" has the ring of rote learning and slick technique. That's why you should say, "Would you prefer that we call for an appointment before showing your home?"

If she says, "Please do," tell her that you're making a note of her decision. Where? On your friendly listing form.

By the way, while you're practicing, drilling, and rehearsing every word, gesture, and tone change, also work out exactly where you're going to make your notes on the listing form. Then develop a simple set of abbreviations, and get in the habit of writing small so you won't cover the listing with scribbles and have to copy it on a fresh form while they fidget.

Here's another pitfall for the untrained that's an opportunity for the skilled salesperson:

- "Do we have to leave the draperies?"

The professional wants the draperies to stay. Why? Because it'll help sell the home, which is what the sellers really want—far more than they want to keep their old furnishings. But they can't see the mountain from the basement. So the professional works very expertly here to get them to make the right decision for themselves—and for his chances of earning a fee. Here's how he does it:

"They certainly do enhance this room. Would you want to leave the draperies?" (Never say, "your draperies" because *your* reinforces their owning emotions.)

The pro knows that the wife doesn't want to leave the draperies or she wouldn't have asked the question. He also knows better than to slap her down fast.

She says, "No, we'd just as soon put the old ones back up. We just had the new draperies installed."

Here's how the pro achieves his aim of having them stay. "Midge, the new draperies are lovely. They do enhance the room. In fact, I can see a buyer getting emotionally involved in this room because of them. May I ask, why did you replace the old ones?"

Now, what does she have to tell you? You've praised her choice of draperies, and you've put yourself on her side. So now lean forward and listen intently—without saying anything except to prompt her to keep on talking—while she tells you about how Junior used to play Tarzan on the draperies, about what the cat did to them, about the faded spots and the rips. Keep on listening and the husband will jump in and close her on leaving them. "Come on, honey. Leave the draperies if it'll help sell the house. They probably won't fit in our next home anyway."

Isn't that neat? When you're a trained pro, you wave the flag and then get out of the way. You never fight your clients. You never argue with them. The clients are always right. However, sometimes we have to show them what's right for them. That's what reflexive listing technique is all about, because their best decision is to list with you at a saleable figure, isn't that right? They will—if you'll pay the price to make this material yours.

Among the thousands who've paid that price is Gary W. Roberts of Bellaire, Michigan. Here's what Gary wrote to me recently: "February to July I have listed 63 pieces of property by following your method. I could go on and on but all I need to say is that I owe it all to you and your program."

Gary did it. Why don't you?

6
WINNING THE GOOD FIGHT
AGAINST FOR-SALE-BY-OWNERS

For-sale-by-owners are my favorite area of listing.

Why?

Because it's like owning oil wells when you know how to work with by-owners. Without a doubt, they are the easiest avenue to success in the world. Yet so many of us choke up whenever we have an opportunity to work *right now* with a by-owner. Somehow we always find reasons not to. Or, if we do make ourselves meet them face-to-face, we merely visit with the by-owners instead of working with them. By the way, I hope you're not disappointed that even the easiest avenue to success involves some work. But don't despair—I'll show you how to make that work easy and fun. It'll be easy because you're good, fun because you're well-paid.

By-owners rarely are easy or fun for people new to the business. Most newcomers give the we're-selling-it-ourselves crowd a try. One good whack. Three at the outside. Then they're done. Sure, some of them will keep on making feeble attempts to list by-owners from time to time, but for all practical purposes they've joined the ninety-five percent who'd rather kick a beehive over than get into working contact with a by-owner.

That's right—ninety-five percent of us won't accept the by-owner challenge. Take a random sample in any area and you'll discover that no more than five out of a hundred real estate agents really know how to tap the by-owner money tree. This is why for-sale-by-owners are the least-worked gold mine in real estate.

We need a definition of *working with for-sale-by-owners* now because, if you've operated out of the average real estate office for a while, you're beginning to doubt me. Possibly you're thinking something like this:

"Tom, in my office everybody bangs away at by-owners all the time. Well, what I really mean is, about half of us do. Come to think of it, we better make that one-fourth. Yeah, that's pretty close. During any given week, about one out of four people will give the by-owners some hits. Of course, only our tiger lists them regularly; the rest of us mostly push air. By-owners are tough. Anybody can tell you that."

I agree. Anybody can—and they probably will. On this question our profession is sharply divided into the vast majority who make little or nothing on by-owners, and the professional few who make a great deal of money with them. The majority tell you that by-owners are bad news because losers need company; the few tell you the same thing because winners don't need company.

Why do so many real estate people fail to tap the by-owner gold mine? Three reasons: lack of knowledge, fear of rejection, and *no persistence*. This chapter will give you the necessary knowledge. Chapter 12 will show you how to overcome your fear. That's two out of three. But you have to walk the last mile to the for-sale-by-owner gold mine alone. Persistence, the final element of every successful endeavor, doesn't fall out of a book. You have to reach inside yourself to find that precious resource. However, I can give you a secret that, if you'll live it, will put persistence in your action and success in your future. Here it is: *I must do the most productive thing possible at every given moment.* We'll talk more about this vital concept later. Right now, I want to give you my definition of what this chapter is all about:

Working with for-sale-by-owners means that you meet them, you qualify them, you bring down their defense barriers, and then you follow-up, follow-up, and *follow-up* until they list with you or die!

Now do you see why I'm right in saying that only five percent of us work with by-owners? Because they've overcome their fear, because they've learned how, because they persistently do it, the five percent are richly rewarded for their efforts. As they caught sight of that level of income, working with by-owners lost all terror for them. By-owners turned out to be genuine fun, games, and excitement because they were making big money. They discovered that by-owners aren't tough at all. Now, whenever they see a new for-sale-by-owner sign, they see gold nuggets sparkling in the sunshine, ready and waiting to be picked up.

Follow my step-by-step process and you too will find gold under by-owner signs. At this point, let me warn you about one thing: my process won't work overnight. You have to keep at it strongly for three weeks before you see the nuggets start to come out of your personal for-sale-by-owner gold mine. Some of the steps overlap; read them all before you do anything. Here they are:

1. STAKE OUT YOUR CLAIM

Concentrate your efforts by choosing a clearly defined target area in which you'll work with all promising by-owners. Before you begin, clear your plans with your manager. It's vital that you fully understand your office's policies and the rights of other agents.

Since you intend to dig deep enough to strike gold instead of skimming over the treetops, start with a smaller area than you expect to to cover eventually. Sharpen your skills there. Then, as soon as you're working efficiently with by-owners, you'll be able to expand your area of saturation effort without losing power.

2. IDENTIFY THE PREFIXES YOU'RE INTERESTED IN

This is easily done in most places by checking the front information in your telephone directory. Or call your telephone company's business office. All telephones that have the same prefix and area code are in the same vicinity. (The prefix is the first three digits of the seven-digit phone number.)

3. MEMORIZE YOUR PREFIXES

They are the key to instantly recognizing ads for properties within your target area.

4. TRAIN YOURSELF TO LOOK AT THE PREFIX FIRST

When checking by-owner ads, make it a habit to ignore all of them from outside your target area. If you aren't going to work with the by-owners, why waste time reading their ad?

5. CUT OUT BY-OWNER ADS EVERY MORNING

Not once in a while—every morning of the month. Of course, you do this only with ads that have your target prefixes. Paste each ad on a separate three by five inch card.

6. DECIDE ON A PLAN OF ACTION FOR EACH AD-CARD

What have by-owners done when they state "principals only" in their ads? They've just handed you the key to unlocking their listing. Jump for joy when you see that idea expressed in an ad from your target area. Nobody calls on those ads. Yet, if you have the know-how, they are your best opportunity.

Right after the last step in this process, I'll give you some phraseology for principals-only ads that'll put you inside their doors every time. What if they don't say principals only in their ad? Then the message is loud and clear: "We need professional help."

But there are two problems with that message.

First of all, although the by-owners feel a strong need for professional help—even if they won't admit it—they don't want to pay for that service.

Why do by-owners feel this way? Unrealistic expectations. Ignorance of how complex transactions really are. No understanding of the services that competent real estate professionals provide. Perhaps they've had, or think they've had, a bad experience with an incompetent agent. Don't write by-owners off as a greedy bunch of chiselers. Give them credit for trying to do what's best for their families, and assume that their sense of honor and fairness equals yours. You want the by-owners to like and trust you. Doesn't that demand that you have the same attitude toward them?

The second problem with "we need help" messages is that you're not the only one who's reading them. Already, lots of other agents have called on those ads, or soon will. Work this group of ads first; the sooner you reach them, the better your chances are of being the one who lists them.

Here's where that three-week delay that I mentioned earlier comes into effect. It'll take you about that long to perfect your delivery of the new phraseology, and you'll be starting on ads that have been running in the papers for some time. After three weeks, you'll have your new system down pat and you'll be hitting plenty of new ads. Start today. The sooner you practice your new techniques on old by-owners, the sooner you'll list new by-owners. Follow all my steps, work several hours every day at it, and I promise that you'll take by-owner listings in three weeks.

7. ACT ON YOUR PLANS EVERY MORNING OF THE MONTH

Energy is the key element in getting started at listing for-sale-by-owners. One of the major reasons why they eventually go for professional service is that they get tired of giving up their free time evenings and weekends. By-owners look for workers, not players. If you call Monday on their Sunday ad, they'll think you watched the ponies run while they sweated through another open house. You won't become a Champion lister on the forty-hours-a-week plan. Be sure to let the by-owners know that you're making things happen in real estate on the weekend.

8. SEE THE PEOPLE

Will you agree that very few by-owners list with agents they've never met?

There are two ways to get in to see a by-owner. Since either way works beautifully for agents who use good technique, choose the one that gets the job done for you:

Always phone for appointments first.
The advantages are many. You can call earlier in the morning than you can knock. With the time that one unannounced visit will take, you can phone several by-owners. By phoning first, you won't waste so many precious minutes ringing doorbells at empty houses. You can come on more softly. With the phone, you're more in control of the situation; you can use your sophisticated and well-rehearsed techniques to ease your way into their presence.

The disadvantage of calling for appointments first is that Harry Hottrotter may be sitting at their kitchen table writing up the listing before you can make a date to meet with them.

Dash over and see them.
Many of the Champions I've trained never telephone first; they simply go over to the by-owner's house. How do they get the address? They make it their business to have a way. Many telephone companies will, for a fee, supply directories that are arranged by telephone number rather than by surname or street address. All of them have such lists for their own use.

I didn't use the dash-over method because it takes more time. At first, Hank, Mabel, and Pat often knocked on the door before I did. But I kept on using the phone because I believed it was the better strategy for the long term. As the weeks passed, I began closing for more and more appointments. And I began reaching the soft by-owners, the ones most likely to list, before anyone else did. Then, as my skills grew and I started working faster, I widened my territory. With every passing month I heard less and less about the dash-over folks. Finally, one by one, they gave up. By spending my time wisely, I took over the by-owner business in Simi Valley, California, the little town where I started.

However, thousands of Champion listers don't bother with the phone, and they continue to do well year after year. They know their areas. They know how to get the addresses quickly. So they move out fast to knock on every new by-owner's door.

There are several advantages to dashing over. Your appearance in the flesh makes a greater impression than voices over the phone do. You see the property. You can size it and the people up. You'll then form a better opinion of how promising your listing opportunity is than you would by only speaking to them on the phone. This better opinion will allow you to concentrate your follow-up on your best prospects. And, by being there early, you're in a better position to snap up the by-owners who need nothing but a couple of hours with a highly-skilled agent to list *today*.

If you can minimize the chief disadvantage of this method, the time it takes, and if you feel good about charging over in person without an appointment—go for it. An impressive number of very successful Champions are doing that every day.

PHRASEOLOGY FOR THAT ALL-IMPORTANT FIRST CALL TO A BY-OWNER

Right after carding the ads, I'd start phoning the people. By getting to the office early, I usually had all my new by-owners called before anyone else came in. If a woman answered the phone, I opened the conversation like this:

"Good morning, ma'am. My name is Tom Hopkins, representing Champions Unlimited. I noticed your ad in the paper this morning, and was wondering whether you'd be *offended* if I stopped by to see your home."

Look at the power of that question. You're being very polite. If your tone matches the words—and you must carefully rehearse to make sure that it does—you'll sound very cordial and deferential. Not a whiff of pushiness. Yet, in this situation where they want to say no to whatever you ask, you've phrased your question so that a *no* answer actually means *yes, come on by*. When you get a *no* here, go into your close for the appointment.

Now let's work with the other response that a by-owner can make to my opening question. This time a man answers, and he turns out to be tough.

"Good morning, sir. My name is Tom Hopkins, representing Champions Unlimited. I noticed your ad in the paper this morning, and was wondering if you'd be offended if I stopped by to see your home."

"Yes, I would be."

"You would? Is the reason that you're intending to sell the home yourself?"

"That's right."

"Is that also because you'd like to avoid paying a brokerage fee?"

"You've got it."

"My reason for calling is, the first three digits of your phone number put you into my service area, and I wanted to ask you, if I'm driving by your home, and my buyer sees your sign, and I can't satisfy their needs, may I send them directly to you with no fee charged?"

"I don't have to pay a commission?"

"And you're probably wondering why I would do that, aren't you?"

"Yeah."

"You see, if I sent you some qualified purchasers, you probably wouldn't mind sending anyone back to me that didn't purchase your home, would you?"

"And I don't have to pay a commission?"

"If you sell it yourself, not at all. That makes sense, doesn't it?"

"You bet it does."

"To be more intelligent about your property, I would like to see it, and again, let me reiterate (repeat), I know you're selling the home yourself, and because of that, I just want to visit it, see it, so that if I'm working with a buyer I can't find a home for, I can send them to you. Now, I am available this afternoon at around two, or would four be more convenient?"

"No, I'll be busy today."

"I better wait until tomorrow, then?"

"I'll be busy tomorrow too."

"Would you prefer the weekend? That's a better time for you then, isn't it?"

"Saturdays are okay."

"Fine. Morning or afternoon?"

"Morning."

"Good. I have appointment openings at ten, or should I wait until around eleven?"

"Ten."

Now I have the appointment. It's important that I confirm it by repeating the time that the by-owner has agreed to meet me. Also, I repeat my name, saying it slowly and distinctly, because he's probably forgotten it.

And I'm going to move forward now with getting his name and address. With someone as negative as this gentleman was at first, I would've failed to get anything by trying to learn his name and address before making the appointment.

Let's take up this telephone interview again. The by-owner has just said that he'd prefer a ten a.m. meeting.

"Ten is fine. My name is Tom Hopkins. May I ask your name, sir?"

"Dave Shaw."

"Awfully nice talking to you, Mr. Shaw. I'll look forward to seeing you. I'll be prompt. I'll be there at ten Saturday morning. In fact, what I'll do is—let me go ahead now and get your address."

Notice that my words ramble just a little. As you practice, drill, and rehearse your phraseology, don't aim for unnaturally precise speech. Deliberately put in—or rather, leave in—the slight imperfections of sentence structure that are present in everyone's normal conversation. In other words, rehearse so that you'll sound *un*rehearsed when you say the right things at the right times.

Dave Shaw answers my question by giving me his address. As I write it down, I repeat the address out loud so that he can correct me if I get it wrong.

"What I'm also going to do, Mr. Shaw, is send you one of my cards so that when I arrive, you'll know that I'm the person who talked to you. Thank you again, Mr. Shaw. Goodbye."

It's all in the words. Let's do another one, but this time we'll be calling people who've made it very clear in their ad that they don't want professional help.

PHRASEOLOGY FOR CALLING ON PRINCIPALS-ONLY ADS

Your competition doesn't know how to get around the *agents, stay away* admonition. Read on and you'll understand how its done. Rehearse and practice the method and you'll be able to do it successfully. Do it regularly and you'll make a lot of extra money. By the way, I need to say something to you now. If you're sitting there thinking of reasons why none of this material will work for you, none of it will. And you'll be the loser. Don't look for ways to keep it from working, look for ways to make it work.

Here's our study situation: it's about nine in the morning and I'm ready to make my first phone call on a principals-only ad. Why am I beginning so late in the day? Because I've called all the help-me ads before starting to work on the principals-only ads. The help-me's are most likely to get calls from other agents, and I want to be the first one to call as many by-owners as possible. As usual, things are going well. I've made appointments with some of the help-me's; now I'm itching to get at the principals-only ads.

The first family I reach, although I don't find this out until later, consists of a husband who works outside the home, a wife who works inside the home, and some small children. The husband has told the wife: "If any real estate people call, just say that we're not doing business with them." In other words, this is a situation that. you'll encounter often. When I dial the number, the wife answers.

"Hello."

"Good morning, ma'am. My name is Tom Hopkins, representing Champions Unlimited."

"Are you a Realtor®?"

"Yes, were you hoping one of us would call?" I say that warmly, as though I really think she was sitting there wishing a real estate agent would favor her with some attention. Please notice how I said it—no break at all between *yes* and *were*. If you pause after *yes*, some of them will jump in with a fast chopoff, and all·you'll hear is, "We're not interested," click.

But I don't pause. "Yes were you hoping one of us would call." My answer pitches the porcupine right back to her. After a second, she says, "No—"

I don't give her time to gather her thoughts. Just as soon as she gets the *no* out, I come right back, speaking slowly and confidently, my tone warm and friendly. "Ma'am, I don't want you to think that I didn't read the ad. I realize that you and your husband only want principals to call, isn't that right?"

Now she's definitely off balance. What she wants to do, what she's been told very forcefully by her husband to do, is to give real estate people nothing but negatives. But she has to agree with what I just asked her. So she contents herself with putting lots of ice in her voice.

"Yes, it is."

"And the reason for that is, you do *not* want to list the home—am I right in assuming that?"

"You are very definitely right."

"Good." I pause very briefly here because that's the last thing she expected me to say and I want it to sink in.

"Good—you see, I also do invest in real estate from time to time, and there's a possiblity, of course—not without me seeing the home—but I could become a principal. Now if I were a principal, and of course had cash, would you at least be interested in selling your home to me?"

"Yes, we would."

"Fine. Now I don't know if I would be interested; I do have to see the home first. So—I'm available this afternoon, or would you rather that I wait until this evening when your husband's home?"

"Well, I think you'd better call back when my husband is here."

"Fine, in fact, why don't I do this—? What time does he get home?"

"Six."

"Tell you what—you probably eat dinner then, don't you?"

"Yes, we do."

"Well, it might be a better idea—let me wait until after dinner—and on my way home, I'll just kind of stop by and give him a card, take a quick look, and see if I'm interested in being a principal. Now, would eight o'clock be convenient, or should I wait until around nine?"

"Nine o'clock."

"Fine. Now, my name is Tom Hopkins—" I say it slowly and distinctly. If you have any but the most common of surnames, spell your last name out for her at this point. Then immediately say, "And your name, ma'am, is—?"

"Rosetta Tines."

"And your husband's name?"

"Donald."

"Fine. Would you tell Mr. Tines that I promised you I'd stop by, and tell him I'll just drop off my card, take a quick look, and see if I'd like to become a principal. I'll look forward to seeing you at nine o'clock tonight. Thank you again. Goodbye."

Now, are you telling the truth when you say that you could become a principal?

Certainly. If their home is worth $80,000—and these people happen to be asking $16,950—you'd rapidly become a principal, wouldn't you?

So now you'll meet those principals-only by-owners. I hope you realize that all I've been teaching you in the preceeding pages is to use your techniques just to meet the by-owners. When that's done, your aim is to find things in common, to establish rapport, to communicate on a warm, human level, and to create a basis for following up with them in a friendly fashion. You can't do any of those things unless you meet them, can you?

As a side note, one of your personal goals should be to become an avid principal. The true wealth and tax benefits don't come from listing and selling real estate but from owning it. When you show up at the by-owner and the husband says, "Well, the wife said you may be interested in buying the home."

Your reply is, "Mr. _____, since I'm in the real estate business, I'm like most agents, only interested in personal real estate investments that could reflect an immediate profit, and thus are priced somewhat below the market. Most prospective homeowners want to become emotionally involved as an investor. I must remain somewhat objective.

"Let me step through and prepare a Comparable Market Analysis. At that point I can make a decision."

Now it's time for one of the appointments you made calling the help-me ads.

APPROACHING THE BY-OWNER'S HOME

Park across the street.

If you used the techniques to close for the appointment, isn't it reasonable to think she might be a little upset that she asked you to come by at, let's say, two o'clock this afternoon? In fact, if her husband had told her, "Don't even talk to any real estate people," the odds are good that she won't even be there when you arrive. Or she may make her mind up that, "All right, he can come by, but he's not coming in." This is the reason for our next technique. The first step is very important.

Be on time.

I suggest that you get there at 1:59 if your appointment is at two o'clock. She'll be watching for you. Park on the other side. Then walk to the middle of the street, hold up a light meter, and check the light.

Take a color photo.

Do you know how many people move in, move out, and never get a picture of their home with no one in front of it? All their pictures of the house have Uncle Horace or Aunt Olga standing there.

The camera you should get—it doesn't have to be the most expensive model—is the instant-print kind. If you don't know much about photography, get someone in the photo shop to explain what to do when you're shooting into the sun with a camera that has a built-in light meter. Otherwise, when the front of the house is in deep shade and strong sunlight is hitting your meter, the photo will look like a bucket of oil at midnight. Get in the habit of looking carefully at what you're shooting. It only takes a second to notice that you should move sideways, before you press the button, to eliminate a garbage can or keep a tree from seeming to grow out of their chimney. And learn to squeeze the shutter slowly. Jerking the shutter is a popular way of taking poor pictures.

If the woman you have an appointment with is watching you make the photograph, she's thinking, "What the heck is going on?"

Walk up to the door.

After you knock on it, step back, turn, and look up the street. When she opens the door, turn with a big smile to face her and say, "Good afternoon, Mrs. Bricker. We had an appointment at two o'clock. It's right at two. How do you do."

Now, what did you just tell her by saying that? *I'm on time.*

What's that mean? *I do what I say I'll do.* Then, without waiting for anything else, you move into your next phraseology:

"The longer I'm in real estate, the more I find that people live in a home, and move without ever having a picture of it. In appreciation of your showing me your home, I took the liberty of taking a color photo." Hold the photo up where she can see it and say, "It came out rather nicely, didn't it?"

Keep a tight grip on the photo and start it toward the crack in the door as you say, "May I step in?"

If you'll rehearse these words and use them confidently, you'll be delighted at how well they'll work. Here's this woman who was a bit agitated, and there you stand with a big smile on your face and a gift in your hand. If you'll do all this just as I've spelled it out, you'll get in even when she had decided in advance not to let you through the door.

The whole key is to just get in. By the way, the next thing you're going to do is *stay in.* Let me tell you a little story about the value of staying in.

When I went into management, my specialty for many years had been for-sale-by-owners. For a long time I had been taking most of them in our service area through the simple process of perfecting my techniques and applying them vigorously. Most of the salespeople in the area had stopped working by-owners. One who hadn't given up was a young man in our office named Les. After I accepted a managerial position, Les came to me and said, "Tom, I understand that you won't be competing with us from now on. I really want to be effective with by-owners. Will you teach me your secrets?"

I said, "Les, I'll teach you everything I did. But first, I want to see what you do. Find a by-owner and we'll go over there."

He picked out a by-owner. We jumped in the car, drove over to the home, and I said, "Now do what you normally do."

"Okay," Les said. We pulled right in front. He got out—and I drove off. In the rear view mirror I saw Les staring after me with his mouth open. Then he turned and walked up to the by-owner's door. I went down the street and parked.

Thirty minutes later I drove back and honked the horn. As Les came running out of the house he was all smiles. "Tom, I can't believe it. I think I'm going to get the listing. They have friends that we have too, and I know where they're from—" He went on and on about how much he'd found in common with them and how well it was going until I said, "Les, what's so different about this time?"

"Usually, I go in, give them a card, walk through the home, tell them how great our company is, ask if we can serve them, and in five minutes, I'm out of there. But this time I couldn't leave—because you left me, Tom."

I said, "What did you do?"

"We looked at each other for a few minutes." Les said. "Then I remembered what you'd told me, that the key to this entire business is to get people to like you and trust you by asking them the right questions."

Les went on, "I just started asking questions—and I found out all this information. She likes me. I really think I'm going to get the listing."

What's the point of the story? That once you get in, you stay in. And your main goal is to have them like you and trust you. The next technique leads you naturally into that position of strength.

SEEING THE HOME

Learn these words. "Mrs. Tines, would you please show me your home? In fact, why not pretend that I'm a buyer? This will give you some practice, and I'll give you some tips to better demonstrate your property."

It's ideal if you're the first salesperson they meet, which you will be if you cut out the ads every morning. But it won't work for three weeks, remember, because you won't be getting the new ones. By filing your ad-cards by phone number, you'll know when you hit a new one, won't you?

So here you are, walking through the front door, the first agent to get there. Of course, if it's a principals-only situation, you look at the house as a possible buyer, which you certainly could be if the home has everything it takes to qualify for your investment portfolio. And some by-owner houses won't qualify, will they? So you take advantage of the opportunity to hunt for common denominators and build the rapport that'll allow you to keep in touch. But whether it's a principals-only ad, or a help-me ad, follow these tips as you go through the house:

Carry a pad and make notes.

A true Champion carries a notepad and is writing constantly while touring a by-owner's home. If you tell me something and I take the

time to write that fact down, it's obvious to you that I'm really
listening and sincerely interested. Make notes incessantly when you're
on a by-owner home tour.

Compliment her taste and the improvements.
Some real estate people are very, very syrupy. Everything they
see triggers an *Oh, it's lovely; it's beautiful; I just love it.* And the
by-owners know they're being fed the old malarkey. When everything
is terrific, wonderful, and so on, you're getting yourself into trouble.
The by-owners can hear the dollars sing from your hoped-for fee—and
they'll shut your music off every time.

Be sincere. And learn how to compliment people whose taste
differs greatly from your own. The two ideas go together. When you
have the professional attitude, whether or not you like some feature of
a property won't matter. If just one buyer will like it, that's enough.
Once you have this idea firmly lodged in your bones, you'll find that
creating sincere compliments is a whole lot easier.

But it's not enough simply to be sincere. We can really believe
that the lady's taste is terrific; we can feel that everything she's done
to her home is beautiful; we can love it all—and still sound insincere
when we tell her so. Why? Because we're not thinking. Instead of
stretching our minds a little so that our compliments connect with the
value and uniqueness of her property, we merely let the tired old
phrases roll out of our mouths. In other words, we're being mentally
lazy—and she knows it. Will you believe that by-owners aren't
interested in employing mentally-lazy agents to market their homes?

Can compliments demonstrate that you're alert and energetic?
Certainly. Can compliments build rapport? We know they can. But
what gives them these powers?

Thought.

There's the secret ingredient. It's found in every compliment that
works. Unless you think, you'll repeat the worn out words that remind
them you're there to make money. Unless you put your mind to work
on fitting what you say to what they've done, you'll fall back on
false-sounding flattery. Unless you build rapport with thoughtful
compliments, you'll tear it down with thoughtless comments.

Now let's study eight samples of rapport-building praise for
by-owners:

"The drapes certainly enhance your living room."

"I'm impressed with the way your color scheme pulls the whole
house together. You've made a bold statement here and it really

works.'' Use this approach when the floor coverings and walls are the same colors throughout.

"Your color scheme really gives the house a bright and peppy feeling. Just stepping in here raised my spirits. I'm sure that a lot of buyers will like it too." Use something along this line when the colors vary from room to room.

"The built-in bookcase lends an air of dignity to your family room. Was it professionally done, or is being a master woodworker your husband's hobby?"

"The mural creates a mood of warmth and comfort in this part of the house."

"Your treatment of that wall was the right touch to emphasize just how spacious this room really is."

"You've chosen an extraordinary wallpaper—and it certainly brings a sunny feeling inside, doesn't it?"

"I get a very good feeling in here but I can't pinpoint the cause. I wonder if it's the draperies, or the paneling, or that splendid fireplace? Ah, of course, it's the combination of all the elements. Everything here blends wonderfully. Well done, Mrs. McKiff."

When you've learned the knack of thoughtful compliments, you can go through the entire house without dumping a single "It's beautiful" on them.

Look for common denominators.

When a professional walks through a by-owner's house, he's very alert although his manner is casual. He's looking hard for anything that'll help him find common ground and build rapport. Here are five classes of things he's watching for:

a. *Trophies.*

If you see one, ask what the sport or event was, and who in the family won it. You'll be able to talk a bit with them about that happening.

b. *Sports gear.*

Look for golf bags, fishing poles, a rifle on the wall, skiing posters. Anything of this sort gives you a chance to talk about things other than real estate.

c. *Evidence of hobbies or special interests.*

Be careful not to seem nosey as you do so, but notice what books and magazines are lying around. Often they'll tell you what subjects and activities the by-owners are involved in. Enthusiasts and hobbyists are usually eager to talk about their special interests.

d. *Collections.*

Do you know what's rare? A collector who doesn't want to show off his collection of beer cans, shark's teeth, or whatever. Bring a keen, intelligent, and sincere interest to his display and you're well on the way to writing up the listing.

e. *Pictures of their family.*

I used to stop at their pictures wall and say, "You've got three little ones, haven't you? What are their ages? They're really cute. What are their names? I have three as well. I have a Lara and a Tasha. Did you ever see Dr. Zhivago? We saw it twice."

I used these trifles to establish rapport, and to make them laugh a little and be happy. I'd talk a bit about my son Timmy, and say something about my family. We all like people who are like us, isn't that right?

When there's no evidence of children past or present around, or if you're not comfortable talking about children, don't do it. And, if you're having problems with your own offspring, don't tell the by-owners about it. There's no surer way to destroy your chances of listing them than by dumping your troubles on their carpet.

Compliment any creativity.

Many people have things in their homes that they've made—and they're usually tremendously proud of their work. Check every room you see for handcrafted things, and for features they've built into the house. Also scan the garage if you get the chance. A quick look can tell you much about their interests and provide you with more openings for conversation. The same holds true of the outside. Many hobbies are carried on entirely in the backyard, and no evidence of them can be seen inside the house. Be sure to include a fast tour of the grounds in your first daytime visit. When you return in the evening for your meeting with both of them, it's less likely that you'll have a chance to see the rear yard.

Discover their likes.

Ask the wife what she likes best about her home. When you meet the husband later, ask him what he likes best there. These are safe questions that build rapport, give you valuable information, and keep them talking. The more they talk to you, the more they'll like and trust you—and that's what you're there for, isn't it?

Don't discuss two items.

Religion and politics? I don't recommend those subjects either unless you're absolutely certain that you and they share the same opinions. But what I'm referring to now is *price* and *policy*. If you get into a discussion of price with one spouse, you're dead. You're also dead if you talk about policy, that is, about what your manager requires in the way of fee, length and type of listing, and so on. And your reason for not talking about these things with her alone, or with him alone, had better not be that you want them both present in a closing situation before you get into the gritty. In other words, don't even hint anything like, "One of you can say no, but it takes two of you to say yes, so I don't want to risk getting into the sticky issues unless I'm in a position to close you both and get it in writing."

You had better prepare for this sharp-edged moment because it'll come up every time you start to make progress. Handle it badly and you're out; handle it well and you'll move a long way toward listing them. Most agents don't know enough to avoid discussing price and policy when they're alone with one spouse, which means that they always handle the sharp-edged moment badly. Let's work through one of these moments. The wife says, "Well, what do you think we can get for this place?" Here's how you respond:

"You know, I could pick a figure out of thin air, but I'm sure that's not what you want. However, since you've asked, I'll research the facts and compile a comparable market analysis. This will let us know exactly what the value of your property is at the present time. I can drop the comparable market analysis off this evening at six, or do you think it might be better if I wait until eight?"

There are two more ways in which the price question will come up. Here's the second of the three:

"We've set our price at $110,000—and that's firm."

Since she hasn't asked your opinion and you want to avoid all discussion of price, simply don't volunteer any comment. And that means, don't look shocked at how high her price is. But you must make it clear that you understood what she said or she'll probably bring money up again. So you say:

"Yes, I remember seeing that figure in your ad. By the way, the chandelier adds so much to this room—I was wondering—are you planning to leave it?"

If the price wasn't stated in the ad, you need only say, "I'll make a note of that. By the way, the chandelier . . . ?"

The third way that price comes up is another opportunity wrapped in a hazard. This time she wants your opinion:

"We're asking $205,000. Do you think we should go higher?"

If you're knowledgeable about property values in her neighborhood, the odds are that you know their price already is five to twenty percent above market value. Maybe even more. But when she states the number, have your poker face on—or you've just kissed the listing goodbye. You can't gasp when you hear their wild price. You can't let your mouth fall open. You can't even lift an eyebrow or let the ghost of a smile play around the corners of your mouth. If you let any hint escape that you think their price is unrealistic, you'll become a casualty of your own carelessness. That means you lose your chance to list them. Here's how to dodge this danger and move ahead:

"We're asking $205,000. Do you think we should go higher?"

"Thank you for asking for my professional opinion. Of course, I could give you a snap judgement, but I'm sure that's not what you want. However, since you've asked, I'll research the facts and compile a comparable market analysis. This will let us know exactly what the value of your property is at the present time. I can drop the comparable market analysis off this evening at six, or do you think it might be better if I waited until eight?"

Now do you see why I call this moment sharp-edged? It's sad how many unskilled agents cut themselves down here. But you won't, will you? Instead of getting cut, you'll go for an evening appointment to see them both. And at that time, you'll be able to go into your full presentation with every prospect of walking out with the listing because you'll cope with the price at the right time in your listing sequence.

Of course, you won't always get the evening appointment. But at the very least, you'll create respect for your knowledge and professionalism. When they like you and trust your real estate competence, are they likely to list with anyone else?

When you're alone with one spouse, you must also avoid discussing your company's policies and the terms under which your company will market their home if you get the listing. The one spouse you're talking to may throw out a number of cute ideas to see if they'll bounce or stick. Things like a thirty-day open listing. Or a ridiculously low fee arrangement. Don't allow yourself to be maneuvered into discussing such items. Instead, talk about the appointment you're aiming for:

"Most of the things we'll discuss when I come back after I've done my research—and we'll all go over that research very carefully so you both fully understand what validity it has—of course at that time we'll thoroughly cover all the management decisions that will be made."

To sum up, don't go cruising for the big no when you can't get the big yes.

CREATIVE FOLLOW-UP FINDS MORE FEES

People have an enormous capacity to believe what they want to believe. We all do. By-owners want to believe that selling a house is easy: just stick a sign in the lawn, run an ad in the paper, talk to a few people, fill out a form—zap, and it's done. If they're convinced they'll save thousands of dollars with little effort, you won't be able to puncture that idea before the ink dries on their ad. When the by-owners' hopes are rising like a balloon, they're listproof. The only thing that will change their minds is meeting reality. Until they feel the frustration of coping with the homelooking public, until they experience the disappointments that are the by-owners' lot in life,' until their patience is gone and their time is running out, they can't understand why a real estate agent is worthy of his hire. A pair of convinced by-owners can't be listed until some of the gas leaks out of their balloon and they become somewhat unconvinced. Knowing that, the pro positions himself where he can see it happen. Then he's there when they float back to earth. That's what follow-up is: being there when they get down to reality.

And it's one thing more. It's using the time they're floating high on hope to build friendship, trust, and respect for your real estate expertise. If you antagonize them while they're learning that they need professional help, they'll get it elsewhere.

When first putting up the sign, three out of four by-owners are convinced they can successfully market their home. As I've said, for all practical purposes they are unlistable. But not for long. Within three months, nine out of ten of those by-owners have either already listed with a real estate firm, or they've acquired so much respect for the trials and tribulations of by-ownership that they've become listable.*

Lurking in those figures is a concept that can have a substantial impact on your future income. If you're active in real estate, you know that few agents are persistent about by-owner follow-up. They mostly find them, hit them a lick or two, and forget 'em. This means they stop working with each month's new by-owners before three-fourths of them can be listed. No wonder they're discouraged.

The persistent few, on the other hand, work through the time that ninety percent of all by-owners can be listed. No wonder the persistent few are making money. No wonder they're becoming more confident and more effective every day with the by-owners who list quickly as well as with the by-owners who hold out for long periods of time. The discouraged agents with short breath think that by-owners are tough; what they don't realize is that the Champions of persistence are tougher. You can join the tougher group, the high-earning elite, simply by using the effective methods given in the rest of this chapter to follow-up with your by-owners. But you have to keep at it day after day until you succeed. You can do it. To help yourself stay with it, keep in mind that an agent with strong follow-up is at least ten times as successful as the common run of quick-tiring salespeople.

You may doubt that. Yet, in truth, the advantages that effective follow-up will put in your hands are more likely to be greater than ten to one. Consider this: the average real estate agent writes no by-owner listings that sell during his one year in real estate. During that same year, the Champion lists at least one by-owner a month—and we're only counting the listings that sell and create income. I don't know how to put a meaningful multiple on twelve to nothing. Do you?

As we go through the detail of effective follow-up, please bear in mind that the timing given is aimed at the most common situation for homeowners. That situation, of course, is the husband-works-days, wife-keeps-house arrangement. Other circumstances, such as night shifts or the wife works outside the home, will dictate a different follow-up schedule. Be alert for those opportunities, and remember that if they both work, their need for professional help is even greater—and fewer agents will take the trouble to follow-up with them.

---

*These figures will apply in most areas except during runaway sellers' markets or other unusual circumstances.

A. MAIL A THANK-YOU NOTE IMMEDIATELY.

Personalize it as much as possible. This means that you write it out in longhand. Speed is everything here because speed demonstrates energy. Your thank you notes must be in the mail the same day that anything significant takes place: when you first contact them, when you first see their house, after any opportunity they allow you to give them service.

Keep all materials for writing and mailing thank you notes in your car. When you leave a by-owner's house, pull over to the curb a few blocks away, write the note, and drop it in the first mailbox you pass. Do it now or you'll never do it.

B. CALL EVERY FRIDAY AFTERNOON

As your minimum program, call every by-owner you're working with every Friday between 3 and 5 p.m. Very few agents will do that because they don't know what to say to the people. Or they just call now and then and bug the by-owners. Failing to keep in touch, or keeping in touch by bugging people, are two equally good ways of not listing by-owners. There are words that don't bug them, that keep you in their minds, that demonstrate your professionalism. These words give you frequent opportunities to be on hand when they begin to see the light about listing for professional assistance. Here are the words to use on Friday afternoons:

"Hello, Mrs. Putnam. Tom Hopkins with Champions Unlimited. I'm updating my inventory for what looks like an unbelievable weekend. Is your home still available?"

"Yes, it is."

"Fine. Well, I'll stop by and say hello before the weekend's over. Thanks—nice talking to you."

You can make calls like that to a dozen by-owners in a few minutes—but your object isn't to get through those calls in the shortest possible time. Pause briefly after each of their answers to give them a chance to volunteer information. Sooner or later, the strain of going it alone will begin to tell and, if you've been building rapport with each call instead of bugging them, you'll be all set to move in for the listing.

Let's go over that last vital bit of phraseology. Here's what you say:

"Hello, Mr., Mrs., Miss, or Ms. whoever you're calling. (No pause.) This is *your name* with *your company.* (Still no pause.) I'm calling to update my inventory for what looks like an excellent real estate weekend. (Use a different adjective each time. First, it might be an unbelievable real estate weekend, then it's terrific, exciting, tremendous, wonderful—and by that time you'll probably have them listed.)

Again you don't pause for a discussion. Instead you go right into: "Is your home still available?"

Now you wait for their answer and, if they want to talk—and especially if they show signs of beginning to realize how tough by-ownerland really is—you make the appropriate move: you go for a listing appointment to give your full presentation.

However, they'll usually say something like, "Yes, it is, but we're still not ready to list."

"Oh, I know that, but, as I said before, if I have a buyer I can't satisfy, I want to be able to send them to you."

Then you say without pausing, "I'll be in the neighborhood Sunday, and may stop by just to answer any questions that you may have."

All of this must be said very warmly. You're always being so nice. A lot of us don't realize something that I believe from the bottom of my heart: the average American is a nice person. A lot of us expect everyone to be nasty, but there are millions of wonderful people out there. Give them honest service; demonstrate integrity; help them—and many of them will let you serve them.

C. STOP BY SUNDAY

Sunday afternoon is the best time. It took me five hours to get home on Sundays—and I only lived four miles from the office. Why?

I was always on my way home when I stopped in to see all my by-owners.

When they answer your knock, the important thing is for you to act enthusiastic about how good your real estate weekend was. Let me give you the psychology of the situation. Most by-owners, like most real estate agents, aren't persistent. They only try to sell their home for a short time. After that sign goes up, they don't get in the recreational vehicle on the weekends anymore. He might not be able to play golf the way he used to all day Sunday. If she doesn't work, the chances are that she was home all week with the little sweethearts, their darling children, and she's ready to get o-u-t. People like to move around on the weekend, do you agree? Here's another factor. When people start thinking about selling their home, they stop being able to really enjoy it.

If you'll knock on their door when the shadows are long on Sunday, and if you'll tell them how active your office is finding the real estate market, you'll score some psychological points. Your by-owners stayed home all weekend when they'd much rather have been elsewhere. And what did they accomplish? Zilch.

At such moments, people often have sudden flashes of insight—things like, "We're never going to sell this place by ourselves." So don't miss a single one of your by-owners "on your way home" Sunday afternoon. Here's what you say:

"Hi, Mrs. Putnam. Tom Hopkins—just stopping by to say hello. Did you have any luck this weekend?"

"No."

"We had a beautiful weekend. Booming. Five transactions. Did any questions arise that I can answer for you? Did your buyer ask you any questions?"

"No."

"Okay. Well, everybody's okay?"

"Yes."

"Well, here's another card."

That's a sample of tough conversation. Usually, you'll get an opening for a few minutes' discussion of the real estate market, during which time you'll have an opportunity to demonstrate your local knowledge.

Persistence pays plenty. So keep at it.

Here are some follow-up ideas that I try my best to get salespeople to do because I know they pay off. How do I know? Because the first two paid off for me, and I've seen the third pay off for people I've managed. The first is simple, doesn't cost much, and pays tremendous dividends.

YOUR OWN FOR-SALE-BY-OWNER SIGNS

Committed by-owners spend money on fancy signs and large ads. The less committed use a piece of cardboard on a stick. This means that the by-owners who'll be the quickest to list with someone are the most likely to welcome your sign. Have three or four made up to begin with and rotate them among your by-owners. You'll find they work so well that you'll want to have more of them. The quality and appearance of these signs is important. You won't look professional unless they look professional.

CHECKLIST FOR SIGNS TO HELP YOU LIST BY-OWNERS:

1. Size as specified by your board's rules.
2. Colors to match your office's regular for sale signs.
3. Front legend:
   FOR SALE BY OWNER
   in large block letters.
4. Blackboard area below front legend to be large enough so that a by-owner's phone number can be chalked in and read from the street. (You can save a little money here by writing the phone numbers on white cards with a broad tip marker pen and taping them to the signs.)
5. Back legend:
   COMPLIMENTS OF YOUR NAME,
   YOUR PHONE NUMBER
   in small, cursive letters no more than half-an-inch high.

The way you get them to take the sign is critical. Imagine that I'm talking with a nice young couple. They seem to like and trust me.

Because their emotional responses are good, and because I'm with both of them, I decide to try the sign technique. As you can see from his comment, I'm not having it all my way. This phraseology, incidently, should be memorized.

"Tom, we may call you later, but really—we're selling it ourselves."

"Mr. and Mrs. Willis, one way of obtaining a buyer is having people stop when they see your sign. The color of our signs, for some reason, stops people. There's something I'd like to do for you—I'd like to let you use a for-sale-by-owner sign that I really feel will stop their eyes. Now you're probably wondering, Mr. Willis, why I would do that. I'm doing that, not so much to obligate you to give me the listing, more importantly, in hopes that if you sell your home yourself thanks to any of my efforts, you'll be kind enough to refer anyone else that I can serve to me."

Let's talk about this approach. You may be wondering: Is he telling me to help them sell it themselves? Does that make any sense?

The sign isn't going to make the sale—don't worry about that. But if you can get your sign stuck in their yard, what will they see every time they leave the front door? *Compliments of your name.* If you can get a sign in their front yard, they won't listen to anyone else. That's the whole reason you try to do it.

I kept my signs working. Yours won't do you any good holding up spider webs in your garage. After one of my signs was in someone's yard for a few days, I'd often hear something like this: "You know, Tom, we've had more people call and stop by since you gave us that sign—but nothing's happened. Come on over and let's see what else you can do for us." You know what else I could do for them.

Using by-owner signs is great technique. Don't be afraid to try it. A sign will cost you less than a tank of gas—and it'll take you a whole lot further.

FOR-SALE-BY-OWNER FIRST AID KIT

The results of this technique, if you'll learn and use it, will thrill you. But you have to follow my instructions closely to make it work. Take one of the folders you put listings in, one of the legal size manila folders your office has, and print the name of this technique in big black letters. The reason you want FOR-SALE-BY-OWNER FIRST AID KIT printed large is that the by-owner must be able to read it when you hold the folder up. If it were me, I'd make up twenty-five of these first aid kits—that way you'll have to use them, won't you? Here's what you put in the kits: (All of the forms can be blanks, or copies of actual documents on which you've blacked out the names and dates.)

1. Purchase Agreement.

This document might be called the deposit receipt, the earnest money receipt, the binder—whatever it's called where you work, it's the original document expressing the buyer's agreement to buy. Don't use your office's form in the kit. Get a standard form from a title company or from a large stationery store.

2. Escrow, settlement, or closing instructions

Again, they go by different names in different parts of the country but, whether the title company, an attorney, or an escrow officer does it, somebody has to get written instructions on how to complete the transaction. These instructions must be prepared by trained people. Get all the blank forms you can.

3. Title insurance policy.

In some states, it's called an abstract. Whatever it's called, get some blanks.

4. Settlement (or closing) statement.

If VA, FHA, or other government insured or guaranteed loans are common in your service area, use one of those forms in your kit. There's so much stuff on those forms—you'll love it. All you need, of course, is one form that you can run copies of.

5. Deeds.

You need four different kinds. Go to a large stationery store and ask for Wolcotts forms. There are other acceptable brands, but Wolcotts has good ones for this purpose. You need four deeds for your kits:
General Warranty Deed
Special Warranty Deed
Bargain and Sale Deed
Quit-Claim Deed

Here's what you should do to put a high gloss on your ability to use this technique successfully: talk to a representative of a title or abstract company and arrange for a tour of their plant. When you're there, have one of the title people fully explain why title insurance is necessary, how it works, and who pays for it. Learn the difference between the ALTA and the ATA, the owner's policy and the lender's policy.

When you've done that, you're ready to rehearse your phraseology. Remember that it's important to give your first aid kit performances to both the husband and the wife at the same time. If you give it to only one of them, you'll lose almost all of the impact of this technique. Let's imagine this scene: you're talking with Jerry and Marge Ferris, a young couple trying to sell their home themselves and, as usual, having no success.

Hold up the folder as you begin to talk so they can see its name. As soon as you start talking about the first form, take it out and hand it to them. Work your way through the kit, handing them more and more forms as you continue to tell them about each of the documents. You need to have the words rehearsed so that they'll flow smoothly, as they should coming from a professional talking about his or her profession.

One set of names has been shown for the forms and procedures. If the names used in your area are different, say them instead. Here's the phraseology:

"Mr. and Mrs. Ferris, I've prepared something for you. This is what I call my for-sale-by-owner first aid kit. I find that if I give people service, they may not list with me, but they will refer other people to me. I'd like to go through the kit with you, and review the forms and the complexities that I, hopefully as your agent, will handle for you. But if not, this should make you much more aware of what you get to do.

"The first form, Mr. and Mrs. Ferris, is the purchase contract, and it's the first document you'll want your buyers to sign. It's also a receipt for their deposit, which is why it's often called the earnest money receipt, the deposit receipt, or the binder.

"I would suggest that you ask them for a large deposit. The larger the deposit you get, the firmer your sale. We always get the largest deposit possible.

"The second form I have in here is a standard escrow instruction to the third impartial party, that is, the attorney, the escrow company, or the title company. It will instruct them exactly what to do with all your money that's involved in the transaction.

"The third document is the standard title insurance policy. Now, there are different types of title insurance. First, there's the title insurance that you as the owner will obtain, under which you'll insure the title for the new purchaser. Then there's the mortgagee's policy. If a new loan is put on the property, the mortgagee, the lender—or of course the beneficiary if a trust deed is used—will be the one who'll determine if you'll need the owner's and the mortgagee's policy. There are samples of the policies; you can kind of look through them.

"The next form is the standard closing statement, or the settlement statement. This is a copy of an actual transaction and, of course, to protect my clients' privacy, I've blocked out anything that could identify them. On this statement, you'll see two columns, the debits, and the credits, representing the liabilities and the assets of the buyers and the sellers. I've made some notes here on the prorations of your interest and your taxes. Notice that this transaction involved what we call points, the loan discount fee, also known as the loan origination fee. And, as you can see, the charges were quite extensive.

"Lastly, let's talk about what in many ways is the most important document in any real estate transaction, the deed. Four different kinds are used, depending on the circumstances—and to make sure we'd have the right one, I've obtained blank copies of all four deed forms for you. The deed is the document of conveyance whereby you two, as the grantors, convey your interest to the grantee, that is, to the buyer.

"Now, the most commonly used deed is the general warranty deed. The second deed is the special warranty deed. It has limited warranties and is very seldom used with title insurance, or when a new loan is obtained. The third deed is the bargain and sale deed. A bargain and sale deed is normally only used in a trust deed sale when there's a probate and it's handled through the courts. And then I have a deed here that is a dangerous kind of deed. It is known as the quit-claim deed. In a quit-claim deed, the grantor, which remember was you, is in no way warranting to the grantee any more than as stated on the deed, which may not be valid, and this is why very few people use it, and I would advise you to avoid it. There have been so many people, Mr. and Mrs. Ferris, who become involved in court proceedings because of the quit-claim deed. I would *stay away from it.*

"Now, do you have any questions?"

I know. It seems like a lot to learn. Maybe you think it's far too much. But before you decide that this isn't for you, listen while I tell you how easy it is to rehearse the first aid kit speech so that you can give a convincing performance with it every chance you get.

You only need to memorize the first three paragraphs, from "I've prepared something" through "largest deposit possible." After that, you just talk about the complexity and importance of each form, using the forms as cue cards. As a real estate professional, you already know enough (or soon will know enough if you're a determined beginner) to talk about the basic forms of your profession.

Begin your drill by copying what you'll say out of this book. Then sit down in front of a mirror with one of your first aid kits in hand, and give your performance to the face looking back at you. Run through that drill three times a day for a week and your performance will be as smooth as Bo Derek's smile.

One final tip: always have the forms arranged in the same order in your kit. Then introduce them with the same key words: *first, second, third, fourth* or *next,* and *fifth* or *lastly.*

What we've got to act on is this fact: a for-sale-by-owner must be convinced that the fee we charge is definitely not out of line. Real estate people sometimes don't realize it, but what they do is a very difficult thing. Or, if they realize it, they do so only in a negative way. Focus on the difficulties in a positive way. How? By making your prospective clients aware of the legal, economic, and emotional complexities that must be overcome before any real estate transaction can close.

FOR-SALE-BY-OWNER SQUAD

Here's where two (or more) of you work by-owners together. If you decide to use this technique, team up with a Champion, a top producer, a highly-motivated individual. Otherwise it won't work. But when a pair of Champions pull together with this technique, great things happen. Here's how it works—and it must be done exactly like this:

1. Pick someone you feel you can work enthusiastically with, someone you like, someone who's a winner.

2. There are two roles in the squad technique: scout and clean-up. Maybe you'll switch roles back and forth, maybe you'll both prefer not to switch. The scout cuts out the ads, makes the calls, gets the appointments, and sees the people first. When he's done everything in our program to list the by-owner, the scout notifies his partner to go in for the clean-up.

3. Let's say that you're running clean-up this week. Your partner, Bob Brophy, has been scouting. For example, at nine this morning, he was out to see the Johnsons. They are new by-owners, and Bob was the first agent to reach them.

Your partner performed eloquently. Now it's your turn. At five o'clock today, you knock on the Johnson's door. When Mrs. Johnson answers, here's how it goes:

"Hello, Mrs. Johnson. Tom Hopkins with Champions Unlimited. I talked to a gentleman in our office who came by to see you earlier, Bob Brophy. Now, Bob and I work together." (Since you're splitting all brokerages received from converted by-owners, you must say, "Bob and I work together." Why? Most importantly, to be honest—also to build trust, to avoid disaster when friends compare notes, and to stay out of trouble with your board's ethics committee. Always say, "Bob and I work together," and take pride in yourself.)

"I only stopped by to let you know that you've really picked a winner in Bob. He'll do a great job for you. He's one of the top people in our company. You really don't need to look further for a salesperson if and when you ever decide to list your home. Bob will give you such great service. He's one of our top listers. Been in the business now for—let's see, more than five years. He's a veteran—and he's full time by the way. You'll like Bob. He's very involved in the community. And he's a very honest man as well. So, I wanted to let you know that. I, of course, will also be serving you along with Bob, and we both thank you so much.''

Here's the psychology: if you've praised the third party, they must be good. But you must let them know clearly that you're working together. You can say lots of good things about your partner and not sound as though you're bragging—but in effect, what you're saying is: we're both knowledgeable, energetic, and honest. This point brings the whole issue of honesty into focus: it's only fair to tell the truth—and it's also greatly to your advantage to tell the truth about your partner's abilities, accomplishments, and enthusiasm—and also that you work together.

"In fact, I'll be representing you as well. We're partners, and we help a lot of for-sale-by-owners who eventually let us get them moved.''

SUMMING UP

Close for the listing as soon as you have both of them together and they're responding to your minor closes. Don't think that you have to go through every technique in this book with every by-owner. You don't have to hand them all a sign, or become half of a F.S.B.O. squad, or give them all the first aid kit. You only do those things if you're not getting the listing. Many times I've gone over to see a couple on a Saturday morning. After an hour and a half, while chatting over a cup of coffee and acting like I don't want the listing, I've had them start to ask me questions. The questions made me take out one of my for-sale-by-owner first aid kits to help them. Then, after that, I've had some of them say, "You know, we were going to try it, but now we're not so sure. The only thing is, we've put the ad in the paper—and it doesn't come out for a week.''

Do you know what I'd say then? "Well, that's certainly no problem,'' and I'd give them the money for the ad just to show my good faith that I'll serve them well. I've done that. I've also written into the listing, "This listing has no effect until _____,'' the date their ad runs out. Or if they say, "We have two couples who're interested," I again tell them it's no problem. I get the names of those two couples and put in the listing, "No fee if sold to name number one or name number two."

Follow-up by-owners. Call them. See them. Write them. See them. That's how it's done. Are you going to get them all if you use all my techniques?

No.

You're going to have some people who wouldn't list with you no matter what you do. Working with by-owners will give you plenty of chances to say, "I never see failure as failure, but only as the opportunity to practice my technique and perfect my performance."

Working with by-owners will also give you plenty of chances to be paid well for performing well. But, again, how long will it take before this starts to happen?

Three weeks.

Expect no results for twenty-one days. Please, review every step. Practice, drill, and rehearse every technique. Then put them into effect vigorously, and watch what happens! You'll be more than delighted with the results you'll achieve.

I think it's safe to say that Joan Huette, of Peoria, Illinois, is more than delighted. Here's what she wrote recently: "I memorized Tom's FSBO section in my workbook, picked up the phone, and had four appointments in a half hour on my first attempt. As I became more confident on the phone, I scheduled as many as nine appointments at one time. Within four months I have eight listings. Knowing what to say and how to say it is so critical!"

7

HOW TO CASH IN ON OPEN HOUSE OPPORTUNITIES

Now let's hold an open house.

Maybe you're thinking, "Just a minute—isn't this a book on listing, not selling?" It is, and that's why I've included this chapter—because open houses create more opportunities to list than they do to sell.

If you're a licensee, do you remember your first open house? Wasn't it exciting? Let me tell you about my first one.

It took place about three weeks after my start in the business. I hadn't done anything yet, hadn't received any training yet, didn't know what to do. So I was getting a little down. I went in to see my broker and said, "I've got to make some money. What do I do?"

He picked up a message on his desk. In fact, there were two or three from this same person. He said, "I have an idea. Why don't you hold an open house."

I said, "A what?"

"An open house. Here's a seller who would love you to hold an open house."

"What's an open house?"

"You go over to the house on the weekend and put a sign in the front yard. The sign says open house. Then all these people come in to see the house—and someone gets to buy it."

I said, "Why have you waited so long to tell me about open houses? This is exciting!"

Knowing that my sales were going to start because of holding an open house, I couldn't sleep well that night. But, in spite of that, I was really feeling pretty sharp when I went over to the home. And I was there early—to be ready before the mobs. I thought about getting some of the numbers stores use so I could handle everybody strictly on a first come, first served basis. After all, if two or three couples wanted the house, I had to be sure the right people got it. Anyway, I drove over there, put my sign in the yard, went in, and practiced opening the door a few times. Then I sat down. Seven hours later no one had come by.

That's when I realized that the open house is like everything else in real estate: it's a waste of time unless done right. I hope you'll realize that you can't do every single thing I teach you. No one can build a listing farm, work the for sale by owners, canvass, go around the new-home-on-the-market techniques, hit the sold signs, do the mail outs, and hold houses open too.

My purpose is to offer you a variety of techniques to choose from. Whether you reach decisions like this quickly or only after careful study, at some point in this book I want you to say, "That's me. That's going to be my specialty."

If you become an open house specialist, you can make a lot of money—if you'll change some of the things you've been doing. Start by realizing that open houses should be held to generate listings. A lot of us, when we're new salespeople, hold open houses because we want to sell the home. That's not the main reason you hold the open house. The main reason should be to get listings.

THE PHILOSOPHY OF A REWARDING OPEN HOUSE

In order to have a productive open house, you have to invest time and effort, which is the same thing as money. Before you commit yourself to such an investment, make sure that the property you want to hold open has what it takes. Here are the five things you need:

1.   Priced right.

Please don't hold an overpriced turkey open. There are two reasons why you shouldn't. Holding overpriced listing open ruins you with buyers. It also ruins you with sellers. Who's left?

When buyers come into an open house, normally they are familiar with the area. So there you stand, in the entry hall of a home worth $100,000—and you've got it at $120,000. Do you radiate a tremendous degree of confidence in the home? When they ask how much it is, you sheepishly say, "Well, the folks are hoping to get $120,000." Are they going to let you show them other homes? Of course not. They think you specialize in over-priced turkeys.

I'm going to ask you to invite the neighbors to your open house. Those who come probably have some idea of selling in the not too distant future. When these neighbors, or other sellers, come to your open house, they often have a good idea of the values in that area. When they see your over-priced turkey, what happens? Before you know it, you have two over-priced turkeys. Remember—your time is money. Please trust me on this. If a property isn't at market value, don't waste your time holding it open.

2.   Traffic flow.

The first thing that successful corporations do when they think about establishing a new retail outlet, a new profit center, is to look at traffic flow. Often they put in traffic counting devices to find out how many people go by each site they are considering. They know that a percentage of people who pass by will stop in. What they want to discover is, will enough people pass by to justify being there. Your business is no different than theirs: you must have traffic.

On many properties, of course, you can create a good traffic flow with directional signs off a main thoroughfare. But it doesn't make sense to hold an open house where no one can find it.

3.   Within your service area

Some agents take a listing outside their service area. When the seller gets upset, they start driving forty miles to hold an open house. They aren't going to get more listings there—the sellers who come in soon realize that the out-of-area agent doesn't know the neighborhood.

For the same reason, that agent can't do anything with buyers either. If you have the chance to take a listing outside your service area, do yourself a favor—and do the sellers a favor at the same time. Refer them to a strong agent in that neighborhood. The only way you can make money from a listing outside your service area is to collect a referral fee.

4.   The sellers must be gone.

Please notice that I didn't say "should" be gone. The sellers *must* be gone when you hold an open house. Tell them that when you originally set up the open house. Say, "No buyer will relax in your home if you're there. They only go to open houses to avoid contact with either owners or salespeople who are too pushy. So please be away, and let me be alone in the house." Now if they won't leave for your open house, I'd say, "I'm sorry." Then do something else that day. You can't waste your time. And you can't succeed by letting your sellers prevent you from doing your job. Ask them to be away from 12 to 5 p.m., and tell them that you'll take care of everything.

5.   The sellers must brighten up the home

Most sellers know that unmade beds, unwashed dishes, and unmowed lawns won't help to sell the house. Sometimes they don't realize how much a little paint and polish and elbow grease will enhance the value of their homes. Here's where a few tactful suggestions can make them and you a lot of money.

The above five items are your ticket to a rewarding open house. But the ticket only gets you in—and that's where most agents stop. The day comes, they put in their time, and nothing happens. If you want to make a payday happen, you've got to do more.

ADVANCE PREPARATION

It's a rare house that's so well situated that you can depend on traffic flow alone to create a profitable open house. Much can be accomplished with advertising and other forms of promotion, but the Champion always finds time for the following method. It's a powerful listing technique that's personal, immediate, and inexpensive. Here it is:

1.   Hand deliver at least twenty invitations.

The form is given in Chapter 14. Don't mail them; put them in the neighbors' hands. What an opportunity this is to meet people in your service area. And what an opportunity this is to demonstrate your energy and professionalism.

Who gets the invitations? The people living closest to your open house. I recommend that you deliver the invitations the day before your big event.

When you walk up to the door, have your open house invitation in your hand. Here's the phraseology to use then:

"Hello. My name is Tom Hopkins, representing Champions Unlimited. As you know, we have a home up the street that we're helping the people to market. Tomorrow, between twelve and five, we're going to have an open house. Now the Smith's will be gone for the day, and I'll have refreshments. If you'd like to stop by, it's an exciting value. You may have a friend or relative who's looking for a great investment, so I wanted to be sure to invite you and your husband to see it."

What are the key phrases? "The Smith's will be gone for the day" is the most important thought to get across. Next in power is, "I'll have refreshments." Then comes, "You may have a friend or relative who is looking for a great investment." Those three ideas are what you want to put in their minds.

Now what are they going to be thinking? "Terrific. I'll go by and see what they're getting, and then I'll know what mine's worth. And the Smith's are gone, so they won't even know I've been there. In fact, we won't even let on that we live in this area." But you'll remember them, won't you?

Many sellers don't want the neighbors coming into their homes. You can usually get around this by saying, "You know an interesting phenomenon? A large percentage of the people who buy in a given area already have friends or relatives living in the neighborhood. A neighbor of yours may have a friend who's just waiting for a home in this area. That's why I'd like to have your neighbors in while you're gone. Of course, you're going to be moving in about thirty days, and when I get you happily moved, it won't matter anyway.''

But a few sellers won't have it. They insist that they don't want the neighbors in. Then don't invite the neighbors.

2.   Put the signs in good locations.

Always ask permission to place your directional arrows on someone's private property. Never be in too much of a hurry to do that. Some people live on a corner for five years and find signs stuck in their turf without their permission nearly every weekend. Go to that door and say, ''Good morning, sir. My name is Tom Hopkins, with Champions Unlimited. A family in the neighborhood is employing us to professionally market their home. I'll be having an open house today from twelve to five, and I'd like to ask you a favor. Could I use just a small portion of your lot to put my arrow in directing people to the home? When I'm done, I'll replace the sod and you'll never know it was there. Would you mind?''

What will they say? Very few will reject you if you ask them like that. But if you don't ask, they might turn the sign around or lay it down.

Then what do you do your first free moment while you're at the open house? You sit down and send a thank you note: ''Dear Mr. Stinson, I want to thank you for letting me stick my sign in your yard. We had a tremendous amount of activity at my open house. If I can ever serve you or any of your friends with a real estate need, please feel free to call.''

Is that a little different than the average real estate agent's action? You bet it is. That's what you have to do to be great. Be a little different. Do more.

3.   Prepare to serve refreshments.

What's the one thing people coming through your open house don't want to do?

They don't want to slow down and meet you. They want to come in, take a quick look, and keep moving. They don't want to give you a name. They don't want to talk to you. So you have refreshments to slow them down.

What slows them down most? Coffee that's almost boiling. The way you get them to take it is critical. Don't ask this 'say-no' question: "Would you like a cup of coffee?" Here's how to do it:

Smile and say, "You now, I'll bet you'd enjoy a nice, fresh hot cup of coffee. Do you take it black or with cream and sugar?"

What is that? It's an alternate of choice, isn't it? I've had people who don't even drink coffee take it with cream and sugar! And there they are, holding the seller's cup, trying to cool it off so they can leave.

One of my top Champions in Arizona has a nice little technique for open house. Whenever he qualifies some buyers and discovers that they're motivated to buy soon, he gives them two quarts of ice cream on their way out. Why? To get them off the streets until his open house is over and he can start working with them. You see, not too many people drive around in Arizona with two quarts of ice cream when it's 115 degrees outside.

4. Plan ahead to have work materials with you.

Even at a highly successful open house, you're likely to have periods when no one is there. Keep a set of work materials in your car so that you can use any spare time at open houses productively.

5. Guest directory.

The sellers like to see signs of activity, so get a nice little guest directory that you can have for people to write their names in.

OPEN HOUSE PREPARATION

1. Start early.

If you are an open house specialist, the most important thing you do during the week is holding open house. This means that you arrange your schedule so there's plenty of time to do what you have to do and still get your open house set up and operating at the appointed hour. Remember that many sellers won't leave until you get there.

2. Put the signs in the best locations.

Sometimes you'll have to get out a map of the area to work it out, but be sure you put your signs in the right locations. If there's a turn you don't have marked, your buyers will go right on, get interested in something else, and you'll lose them forever. They'll never come back.

3. Turn the house on.

Switch all the house lights on and open all the drapes. If the house is air conditioned, set the thermostat where the people coming in will notice the air conditioning. You want them to be aware, not chilled.

Especially in the summer, light a small fire in the fireplace. If you want to join the five percent, you'll have to be different. I'm not suggesting that you have a roaring fire. A little flame is all you need.

First of all, will they visit many open houses that have a small fire going when it's hot outside? No, they won't. When they walk in and see the fire, will they become somewhat curious? And will they doubt your sanity?

Yes, they will. That's why a Champion, when he or she sees them notice the fire, will warmly say, "I'll bet you're somewhat surprised to see a fire in the fireplace, aren't you?"

When they agree that they are, a Champion smiles and cordially says, "We wanted the people who would be moving into this home to experience all the emotions of the seasons, and all of the feelings of being home. And you know, we really enjoy a fireplace on a winter's night, don't you?"

Do that and they won't forget you.

4. Two heads are better than one.

If you do everything right, you'll need another agent at your open houses. Let me explain why.

When your property is priced at the market, you've issued the personal invitations, and the traffic flow is good, you're going to have activity. But, since only a few people are interested in any one property, most of the qualified buyers who come in will want something else. Your best chance to take control of a buyer is to show them some interesting homes that day. But you can't leave if you're working the open house alone.

A good open house has two agents on duty. One can leave with qualified buyers. The second agent stays at the open house until the first agent returns.

If you've been holding open houses, the chances are you've been doing it for the usual reason. Which is to appease an angry seller. It's bad enough to waste one salesperson's time on such an open house, let alone two. Most agents haven't learned that they should never put themselves in the position of having to hold an open house to appease a seller. You should hold open houses only if you're an open house specialist, and then primarily to get more listings. If you do everything I tell you to, you'll take listings at market price. Then you don't have to hold open houses at all. I've told people, "I won't hold an open house unless I haven't got you happily moved in thirty days. Then I'll consider an open house."

I hope you're not one of those agents who promises everything. The trouble with doing so is that you can't deliver. A pro promises only one thing: to get the seller as much money as possible, to get it in the shortest time possible, and to get them happily moved together as a family. That's all they really want. Everything else you throw in is what you try to close them with.

I used to carry an average of thirty active listings. I've had people say to me, "How can any human being service thirty or forty active listings?" I hope you realize that I held very few open houses. You don't service a listing that sells within two weeks..Which ones do you service? The listing you've had for ninety days. The listing no one shows. The listing where the seller wasn't in a hurry—suddenly he's in a hurry. The listing where a friend is now their real estate adviser. What's the common denominator of every one of those listings? The price is too high. If you learn to take them right in the first place, as I'm going to show you how to do, you'll only be servicing listings that are in closing.

OPEN HOUSE LISTING AND SELLING POWER

We're at your open house. It's priced right and has good traffic potential. The sellers shined it up beautifully before leaving; you've delivered your invitations around the neighborhood; your signs are out. You're all set for a strong showing. In other words, you've already invested heavily in this project.

So don't blow it now. Have the right techniques practiced so you can start using them the moment anyone approaches your open house door. Your body movements are just as crucial as the manner and words you use. While you read the techniques that follow, see yourself making the movements in timing with the words.

Let's set the mood. The people coming in want to see the property fast; they don't want to get involved with a salesperson; and they don't want to give out any information. If you let them set a new record for the hundred-yard dash when they go through your open house, what are your chances of doing business with them?

So you want to slow them down. Nicely. Here's how you go about it: when they knock, or when they come in through the door you've left open, use these words:

"Hello. Won't you folks step in and make yourselves at home?"

Here's the important part. As you say that, back up. That's right, take several steps backward. You'll have to think ahead to place yourself where you can be backing up as you greet them. Whatever you do, don't charge forward as they come in.

Keep withdrawing until they're well inside. Then stop. Look them straight in the eyes, smile warmly, and say, "My name is _____, with XYZ Realty."

Now you're standing there right in front of them, smiling warmly. Hold your ground. They've committed themselves by entering the house. They won't turn and leave now. You're smiling warmly, so they aren't going to trample over you to get at the house. Since you're after a name, not a shake, don't offer your hand. Only if one of them initiates the ritual do you shake hands at this point.

What'll happen if you just keep on standing there, smiling?

It'll force their names out of them.

After you do it, you'll love it. Don't be afraid of the silence. Keep on smiling; keep on looking them in the eye. You've got to do both or it won't work.

As you get their names and say your nice-to-see-you's, execute another strategic withdrawal by stepping aside. It's critical that you get out of their way promptly now. If you come back at them with more pressure right after getting their names, they're going to feel pushed. They won't like you for making them uncomfortable.

Avoid that by stepping aside and saying, "Why don't you folks just walk through the home by yourselves. If you have any questions regarding the construction, real estate in this area, or the general market, please feel free to ask."

Let's discuss this situation. It occurs every time people go in an open house, and all too often the way the agent on duty handles them is all wrong. You see, the average agent is scared to death that they won't buy the property because they'll miss seeing the extra shelf in the hall closet. What these untrained agents don't realize is that potential buyers can't sense their feelings about the house if someone is showing it like a baboon having a nervous breakdown. Buyers hate that. When they want to feel the house, anything you say is just irritating noise pounding on their eardrums. So let them go through by themselves. They'll respect you, and they'll like you, for doing that.

Avoid hovering over them, but when you have the opportunity, ask some unthreatening questions as if you're just doing it to have something to say. Here they are. I've numbered the sequence:

1. "Do you folks live in the area?"

I want to know whether they're potential sellers or potential buyers. Where are they from? Do they live next door, or around the corner? Or are they here from out-of-state?

2. "How long have you been looking for a home?"

I want to know if these people are professional open house visitors. I want to know if they've been in the marketplace for three months. If they say, "Only a couple of days," and if I find out that they're motivated, I know I usually have only five more days to work with them before they'll buy through someone.

3. "How many are in your family?"

A pro never asks, "How many children do you have?" Lots of average agents do. Maybe the couple are not married, or maybe this morning they had a knock down drag out fight about having another child, and here you go, "How many chidldren do you have?" It's possible that they could have lost a child, or they may be remarried parents with child custody problems. This can be a very sensitive area. A pro always says, "How many are in your family."

When they say, "There's five." You respond with, "Oh, then you have three children." If you make a mistake now, whose fault is it? Theirs.

4.　"Have you seen any homes you like yet?"

Do you know that some of them have already purchased a home and now they're going to let you use all your talents to justify why they got a good buy. Everyone buys first with emotion; then they find the logic to justify it. Looking at all the homes that are available in the area is looking for logic.

Some of them have made an offer on a home that didn't go through; now they're out looking for another one on their own. Let's go with this one. Suppose they say this to you: "Well, as a matter of fact, we found one in the neighborhood that we love, but we didn't get it." If the answer is "Yes, we found one we liked," here's what I ask: "What prevented you from owning that one?" I want to know, did they get blown out of the saddle because of another offer? Or was it more than they could afford?

5.　"Are you looking for a good investment as well as a good location to live?"

Speak slowly when you ask this one. You're fishing for more than just a positive response. I've had the husband jump in and say, "I'm really concerned with the investment opportunity. I'm happy where we live, but I'm finding out my equity is so large right now that we should move up."

See the kind of things you'll learn with that question?

THE PERFECT HOUSE CLOSE

If I didn't even get their name, I'd say: "Would you folks do me a favor? Would you mind commenting on this home so I may gather some data for the seller?"

I want them to comment about the house they're in because what does that make them do? Tell me their likes and dislikes. So, while they're giving me all this valuable information, I'm taking it into the real estate computer in my head and matching it with my inventory of available houses. What I'm trying to do is come up with the perfect house close.

Let me list the three key ingredients for this powerful close first.
1. "It's nearby."
2. "We have a key."
3. "You can follow me by it."
Now we'll run through the entire phraseology:

"Mr. and Mrs. Weber, based on what you've told me, I can't help but see in my mind's eye a home that might have everything you're looking for. The amenities are beautiful, the location is excellent, quality carpets, quality draperies. Now it does have the four bedrooms, and you mentioned that you wanted a fourth bedroom. It's one of the most exciting homes I know of."

You must sound excited yourself as you ad lib words like the above that fit the situation. Enthusiasm and excitement are contagious. They'll catch some of your mood and start thinking to themselves, "This may be it."

You continue with, "You know, it's nearby, and we have a key. You might like to just follow me by it." Did you notice how I wrapped it up with the three key ingredients? They have to feel that it's like the one they're standing in: you have the key so no one will be there. They want to know that it's very close, so they won't spend much time seeing it. And they want to feel that there won't be any problem about getting involved because they're going to follow you in their car.

Please keep one vital thing in mind: you must have the home. Use the perfect home close only when you have a property that fits their description. Otherwise, you will have gone to a lot of trouble to lose them, and there are easier ways to do that.

If you can't leave the open house because you're the only one there, you can use the perfect home technique as an appointment close. But your best chance is to take them there right away, which is why you organize your open house so that two of you work it together.

BRIDGING TO THE SAME CAR

If they say, "Yes, we could run by that house and take a quick look at it," your next goal is to ride over there in the same car. Ideally, all of you go in yours. Here's how you bring that about:

Keep the chit chat flying as you walk ahead of them to the sidewalk. Go straight to your car—which you'll have conveniently parked for this purpose. Open the car door, smile, and say, "Won't you step in?"

That's an assumptive close, and usually they'll climb into your car. But suppose the husband says, "Oh, no, we'll follow you."

Slam the door of your car, and say, firmly and pleasantly, "Fine. I'll go ahead and ride with you."

That'll work ninety percent of the time. But if he now says, "Look, we just want to go ahead and drive," don't fold up. Tell him, "I've had such good luck showing my people the schools, the shopping, the amenities—please let me serve you. Besides, I'm sure you'll agree that we're all concerned with our natural resources. Let's not waste gas by taking two cars, shall we?" Sell or you'll be sold. More sales are lost because we lose control than from any other cause.

Now, let's suppose you're talking with some people and you don't have the perfect home for them, or they don't want to see it. You've got their names, but that's all you have. What you need now is my next technique.

THE DOUBLE-REVERSE PHONE NUMBER CLOSE

I stumbled onto this one by mistake. It worked so well that I made this technique an important part of my open house routine. Here's the kind of situation I'd use it in: We've looked through the entire home. I can't leave with them. They like me and trust me. I have their names. In fact, they were kind enough, when walking out, to give me their address for the seller so she could know what area they were coming from. Now I want to be able to get in touch with them. Have your cards available for this phone number close. My cards are in my left hand coat pocket.

"Mr. and Mrs. Clinard, some of the finest values come on the market and are sold before the signs are even put on them." (Now is that true? Of course it is. We've all seen this happen. But few buyers realize this, and we want to let them know that they might not even get a chance at the best values without our help.)

As you go on, get some excitement into your voice. "If a fantastic value comes to my attention—"

They brace themselves for what's coming next, which they're sure will be: "—how can I get hold of you?" They've heard that tired old approach too many times already. But you don't say that. Watch how it goes:

"If a fantastic value comes to my attention—(pause)—*let me give you my card*. Here is my office phone and let me circle my home phone. You can reach me twenty-four hours a day for service. How do I reach you?"

The psychology behind this close is devastating. They'll give you their number when you go through it just like that.

Do these techniques really work?

Read what Mark Duncan of San Bernardino, California wrote:

"I used to be one of the agents who was happy if five people came through an open house. Now I'm upset if I have less than thirty visitors. Back in those days I avoided open houses like the plague. Then I got help from Champions Unlimited, and held my first productive open house.

"It was the first weekend after I attended Tom's three day seminar. I was informed and I was enthusiastic. I decided to hold open a vacant house I had been employed to market, and I asked another agent in my office to help me. Together we distributed almost two thousand flyers, and made one hundred personal contacts inviting neighbors. We worked hard, and the neighborhood was impressed. It was the biggest effort anybody had ever made in that area to sell a house.

"The work was nothing compared to the return. As extra incentive for people to come, we offered refreshments, gifts, and copies of our company magazine.

"The turnout was great. Luckily , not everyone is a football fan or we would not have had any guests. We inadvertently scheduled the open house on Super Bowl Sunday. I don't remember exactly how many people came, but it was more than I had ever known to come to an open house in our city. I met enough people to keep me busy for most of the next week showing them houses that better suited their needs. As a bonus to our efforts, the first couple that walked through the door bought. Cash to existing loan, full price, thirty day escrow.

"That day started me using my greatest real estate tool, the open house. Today I spend most of my time promoting my next one, and working with the clients that come to me at my open houses."

Yes, the techniques work if you make them work. If you want to be an open house specialist, create your own checklists for all the things you must do to make them a smashing success. I ask just one thing: don't go halfway. The only way to win is to run hard over the whole course.

8

REAL ESTATE'S ROYAL ROAD TO RICHES IS CALLED PROSPECTING

It's amazing, but that road isn't crowded. There's plenty of room on it for you. And it runs right past your office's front door. Once you're pounding along on it, you'll love the results of taking the fast track to success called prospecting.

But you'll have trouble making yourself get out there on the road where the money is. Sure, you can glide effortlessly out to the street for caravan or lunch. Have you noticed a definite difference in your ability to leave the office for a session of knocking on strange doors?

Why the difference?

Do you enjoy having someone interrupt you at home by knocking on the door and trying to sell you something? Probably not. Can you remember the most irritating person who ever stood on your step and pushed something unwanted at you? Your troubles with the idea of door-knocking started then; you don't want anyone to feel about you the way you felt about that person.

Your feeling is a hangup. Most of us treasure our hangups. We take good care of them. The fact is, it's scary even to think about changing them. Grit your teeth and think seriously about changing this one, though, because your hangup about knocking on doors is a major barrier to your success. And what is that barrier made of? Nothing but your own undisciplined emotions. Since you put that hangup in your head, you can curb its power—if you choose to. So think scary thoughts. You don't really want to pay the cost of carrying that hangup around, do you? Unless you get rid of it, here's what'll happen in every year of your real estate career: a large sum of hard cash that would otherwise find its way into your pocket, won't.

Hangups start to become manageable when we stop feeding them the emotions that brought them on in the first place. It's a slow process. Here's a quicker one: pour positive new emotional concrete over your old hangup. I guarantee that this four step method will destroy your hangup about knocking on strange doors:

1. Practice, drill, and rehearse the effective techniques in this chapter.
2. Get out on the street and use them.
3. Think long and hard about the good doors you go to, and little or not at all about the bad ones.
4. Make enough money prospecting to impress yourself.

All of those steps are vital to your success. The one that's usually overlooked—so it's the most common cause of failure—is number three. If you knock on doors, you'll have two kinds of results every day you do it. At some doors you'll have good conversations, you'll go away encouraged, and you'll approach the next door with increased enthusiasm. At other doors the opposite will happen. This brings us to the factor that will determine whether or not you'll succeed at canvassing. That factor is how you control your thoughts about the results you get each day.

Which doors will you think about? The good ones or the bad ones?

If you allow yourself to think only about the good doors, you'll soon be making lots of money through your canvassing contacts because you'll learn and use effective technique. From every session of prospecting, you'll gain enthusiasm and confidence. But if you allow yourself to think mostly about the bad doors, you'll never cure yourself of the hangup about prospecting that most of us bring to real estate. You'll never make any money canvassing. And you won't do much of it either.

You see, the fear you have at the door doesn't hurt you, it's the fear keeping you from getting out on the street that does the damage.

Have you noticed how much fun it is, and how easy it is, once you get there?

The problem is getting there. Turning doorbells into dollars is simple: learn the easy methods of prospecting that follow, and then go out and do them.

EASIER WAYS TO GET YOURSELF OUT ON THE STREET

Don't ever forget that real estate is a percentage business. I don't care what your natural abilities are. No matter how much or little you have of charm, personality, and wit, the person that sees the most people *who could say yes* will make the most money. That's the way real estate is. Not the fastest talker, not the one with the most charisma, but the one who gets out there and sees more qualified people will reap the richest rewards. Don't ever forget to make the percentages work for you. If you don't, those same percentages will push you right out of the business.

I live by the belief that everything we want is behind a door. When you put down this book and go out to make your fortune in real estate, you'll walk out your front door, open your car door, and drive yourself to another door. Your life is punctuated by going through doors. When you come home, your loved ones are behind doors. Possibly you've heard someone in real estate say, "Knocking on doors is unprofessional." Whoever told you that is chicken. Knocking on doors is unprofessional if it's done unprofessionally.

When it's done professionally, it's fun. And people will often thank you for stopping by. Perhaps you've been getting different results. Learn my techniques for making prospecting fun. Try them. If you still have a hangup about doors, that problem took many years to develop. You won't change it overnight. But you can do it if you are determined to. Everyone can become a strong prospector if they'll pay the price of learning and doing. We all succeed in direct proportion to our ability to handle failure and keep on trying. Even the most experienced and effective prospectors continue to fail and get rejected much of the time. But they don't let that prevent them from getting the success and the acceptance that only prospecting can give them.

Remember that you'll never fail unless you make yourself try. Neither will you succeed. If you're willing to put yourself in an uncomfortable situation, you can overcome your fear of that discomfort. When you do that, you will succeed.

I've watched salespeople become very successful before they developed any deep knowledge of real estate. They did it through prospecting. They just left the office, went out and knocked on doors, and put the following phraseology to work. And it did work. Then they were highly inspired to acquire the deeper knowledge of their profession that would keep their income growing rapidly.

THE FUNDAMENTALS

Let's begin our study of prospecting with a quick look at the fundamental steps. Then we'll get into specific phraseology for three special situations. You can always go out and work on one of them. But, no matter what opportunity you're prospecting, success depends on sound fundamental technique.

1. Work around the block.

If you work up one side of the street and down the other, or cross over from side to side as you go, more people will see you. Many of them will phone one of their neighbors. The conversation will go like this:

"Who was that at your door?"

"Oh, just a real estate person."

That's one less door that'll open for you. Play the numbers. In today's world, you'll find less than half of them home anyway. Don't cut your percentages further. The pro works entirely around the block. It might open just three more doors a day for you, but that's enough to make a great difference.

2. Walk enthusiastically.

Do you know that successful people take five steps while the average person is taking only four? Do you know why? They always have somewhere to go. Walk like you have a purpose, somewhere to go, and a reason for getting there.

3. Knock enthusiastically.

Everyone rings the doorbell. You're different—so you knock. You can't ring a doorbell enthusiastically. Every time, it'll give them the same old ding dong. When you walk up and knock on that door with excitement, you'll be amazed at how curious they get.

4. Stand back.

After you knock, take a few steps back. If you're standing right on top of the door, they won't open it. It's too easy for you to leap in! So back up three or four paces.

5. Face up the street.

Turn your body and head so the person behind the door will see your profile as you look up the street. Your presence is less threatening if eye contact doesn't hit her the instant she opens the door.

6. If you're a man, whistle.

If you don't know how, learn. Always trill a few cheerful notes as you wait. If a woman is alone in the home when another woman knocks, there's not much fear. That's not the case when a man knocks. If you're whistling merrily, it lets her know that you're happy and harmless.

7. Wait until she acknowledges you.

Whether you're a man or a woman, don't turn to face the homeowner until she speaks. You want the person inside to begin the conversation—if they'll do it within a few seconds after you hear the door creak open. She'll say, "Yes," "Hello," "What can I do for you," or whatever. When you hear that, go to the next step.

8. Face her and smile.

Some salespeople have stopped smiling. They've forgotten how. Maybe you should practice. Stand in front of a mirror and smile until

you've got the knack of it. Being able to put on a smile when you
need one is a valuable prospecting skill. Although you can't prospect
without interrupting people, you can certainly ease their shock by
smiling. But if you put on the old "I just ran over your cat"
expression when they open the door, you'll be coming to bat with two
strikes against you.

9. Bring their defense barriers down.

Let's think about the feelings that the person behind the door will
have. What goes through the mind of a lady who's alone at home
during the day when there's a sudden strange knock at the door?
- She feels interrupted. "Oh, who could that be? The kids? I
told them to use the back door."
- She feels curiosity. "I wonder if that's Jean again. I haven't
time to talk to her today."
- She feels fear. "I'm not expecting anybody—I better find out
who it is before I open the door."

If they think you're a salesperson, some of them won't open the
door. That's why you back up. That's why you look up the street.
That's why you're dressed as a professional. It's all to show that you
have a purpose in being there.

I've had people open a little window and talk to me through it.
You can give the same performance right through the window! Don't
feel like they must open the door. Don't let their fear make you
uncomfortable. You see, it's all a numbers game. The more people
you meet, the luckier you get.

On the average, you have just thirty seconds (after they first
speak) to bring their defense barriers down. When they realize you're
in sales, many people decide, "I'm getting rid of you as fast as
possible." Expect that whoever answers your knock will have some
defense barriers up. Break through those barriers and catch a little of
that person's interest quickly. In each of the phraseologies given
below, notice how I do that with my first statement.

10. Don't hesitate to use crutches to get yourself out there.

Knocking on doors is easy. The tough part is getting yourself out
on a street where you can't do anything but prospect.

There were days when I didn't want to go door-knocking. I mean, I really didn't want to do it. So I'd sit in my office and squirm. Why was I uncomfortable? Because it was looking at me. It had a way of glowering at me when I wasn't listening to it. I'm talking about my framed motto. Finally, I'd look up and read these words: I must do the most productive thing possible at every given moment.

And I'd promised myself that I always would. So I'd get up, shuffle out to my car, and drive someplace where I could prospect. By the time I came to the third or fourth door, I'd have my enthusiasm back. It never failed. I'd tell myself, "I did it again. I'm out here again. And I'm really glad I came."

Now let's study the phraseologies for the three special canvassing situations. In each one, we'll start after you've run through the fundamentals. That is, we'll pick up the action right after the lady of the house has opened the door, said something, and you've turned, smiling easily, to face her.

THE WARM CANVASS DOOR

This can be the door of any property that doesn't have a sign on it. She says yes and I begin:

"Good afternoon. My name is Tom Hopkins representing Champions Unlimited. There's been a tremendous amount of real estate activity in this area, and I was wondering if you'd thought of making a move in the near future."

Notice the phraseology. Every word is important. "There's been a tremendous amount of real estate activity in this area." Isn't that true of every area? Throughout this country, real estate is booming. So you can honestly say that.

"And I was wondering if you'd thought of making a *move* in the near future." I didn't say ". . . if you'd thought of *selling* the home." Use "making a move." And when? Not *now*, but "in the near future." Drill yourself on using these softer phrases that make you sound more likeable and less pushy. Expect a no here. They'll follow their lines if you'll learn yours. But once in a while they'll say yes—so pay attention. Don't assume a no. Don't hurry it out of her. And don't lose your composure if she answers yes to any of your questions. You won't—if you've rehearsed what you'll say when you get a yes. (Also drill yourself on not looking dumbfounded, on not sputtering, and especially on not acting like you've just stumbled onto several thousand dollars—which you may have. But it's too early to spend the money.)

She says, "No."

That first no is, psychologically, one rejection. She's rejected you. She knows it, and she feels it.

You keep smiling and say, "Do you know of anyone in the neighborhood who might be interested in moving?"

You'll usually get a nice big no here too. Then you warmly say, "Well, thanks so much for your time." That causes her to think you're about to leave. But you're not done yet. Then, with a cordial manner, you go on, "When I find a home today, would you know of any friends or relatives who might be interested in living here?"

Notice that you don't ask, "*If* I find someone who wants to sell." A pro operates with confidence: "*When* I find a home." It's as if there's no question about it at all.

"No," she says, giving you *no* number three. Back up so she's sure you're leaving. Then smile and say, "By the way, may I ask your name, please?"

Now you've let her reject you three times. If you're smiling as you ask for her name, she's going to give it to you. Why? Because she wants to show she's not a grouch.

"I'm Mrs. Johnson."

Repeat her name immediately, and speak pleasantly. "Mrs. Johnson, when will you be moving?"

Do you know what's exciting? If you let her reject you the three times, and if you've been radiating warmth and professionalism, many times they'll tell you the truth.

I've had the woman say, "Oh, we wouldn't probably be moving for at least three years."

Do you know what a pro says here? "May I keep in touch, and come back in three years?"

What'll she say? "Sure," because she doesn't believe you will. But you will, won't you?

If she mentions any reason for, or possibility of, moving within one year, start asking more questions. Let's suppose she says, "Well, uh, no—we've thought about moving. In fact, my husband's talked to the people on the job, but they don't think it's possible for at least a year."

"I see. Your husband—where does he work?"

"Well, he works at Northside."

"Oh, how long has he been there?"

"Seven years."

"Oh, really? So you'd kind of like to move—kind of like to transfer to another area? What kind of an area were you looking for?"

And you keep on asking her questions until she starts to get a little restless. What do you do now?

Three things. Smile. Warmly say, "Thank you so much." And then give her your card.

Please note that the home owner doesn't get your card until the end of your performance—unless she asks for it sooner.

Some agents canvass like this: "Hi. I'm so-and-so. Here's my card." The prospect takes the card, looks at it while the agent goes on talking, and doesn't hear a word that's said. Give them the card last.

If you represent a company that uses *realty* in its name, I suggest you omit that word when you introduce yourself. In other words, if I'm with Champions Unlimited Realty, I would introduce myself as "Tom Hopkins, representing Champions Unlimited." Why? So that word doesn't trigger "He's a real estate salesperson" before I'm into my performance and she's listening to me. Of course, she'll realize what I am within a few seconds, but by that time I've had a chance to communicate with her as one human being to another. This is not a critical step. If your broker wants you to use the entire name, do so. Your broker is always right.

That's what I call a warm canvass door. You had no special reason to go there. You just said, "I'm going to work this neighborhood because I haven't seen any listings show up from here for a while."

But the next door *is* special. It's a fun door to knock on. And you're there for a specific reason. One of my top Champions developed his entire listing bank around this door.

THE MOST BEAUTIFUL HOME ON THE BLOCK DOOR

When do you schedule this canvassing knock? On your way to an unimportant appointment. Don't do this door right before you present an offer, do a listing presentation, or have an important meeting of any kind. This door could unpsyche you. So schedule it before unimportant meetings.

How do you qualify this home? It must really be the nicest home on the block. Drive up and down the street until there's no doubt that this one is the nicest house.

Park in front. Whoever is in that home should see your car. Go through your prospecting fundamentals. When you hear a woman say, "Can I help you," turn with a smile and use this phraseology:

"Good morning. My name is Tom Hopkins, representing Champions Unlimited. I was driving by and just decided to stop and say thank you. (Pause.) Thank you for the pride of ownership you've shown in your home. As a professional in the area, I'm always proud of people like yourself, who take such pride in their home."

Turn now, and look at the front yard. Continue with, "Did you do the landscaping yourself, or was it professionally done?"

That question is an alternate of choice designed to give you something to start talking about. She'll answer, "My husband and I did it," or "We had it done." Then you say—and I hope you can see the effectiveness of the phraseology:

"I sincerely believe you have the loveliest home on the block." Then hand her your card, smile, and say, "I only have a moment." Look at your watch. Go on in your most agreeable manner, "Is the inside as nice as the outside?" Lean forward.

Then say, "I do specialize in this area, and really enjoy knowing and seeing the nicest homes in the neighborhood."

After the word *neighborhood,* I'd say, "Could I take a quick peek?" I used these words because that was my personality. You might want to put it another way. Of course, I only said that if her reaction was good, as it almost always was. But if it wasn't, I'd say, "Well, I just wanted to stop by to thank you." Then I'd leave.

Here's what's exciting: I've had both men and women tell me, "It's awfully nice of you to say that. We work hard on this place. And if you want to take a quick look inside, come on in. But we aren't interested in selling."

"Oh, I know that," I'd say. "No one is—till they do."

Then they sometimes said, "Well, uh, what do you think our home is worth?"

A lot of people you'll encounter on canvassing will ask that. Of course, they'll phrase it in many different ways, but it's still the same opportunity-loaded question. Always answer in this way:

"Mrs. Coolier, I could pick a figure out of thin air, but I'm sure that's not what you'd want. Since you've asked, I'd be more than happy to prepare a comparable market analysis of the area. No obligation, of course. And I can drop it by, well, I'm available this evening, or would tomorrow night be better?"

Now I've closed for an appointment, haven't I? She might say, "Oh, no, you don't need to go to all that trouble."

"There's no trouble."

Practice that phraseology before a full length mirror. You may want to work some body language into it. I did, and I felt strong doing it. Maybe you'll just want to use a subtle gesture or two. Practice them.

Don't pause after the word *want,* or she'll say, "Yes, it is." Time it like this: "I'm sure that's not what you want SINCE you've asked . . ." Raise your voice, intensify your tone, and speak quickly when you say SINCE. Drill yourself until you can do it smoothly and retain control through that point without startling them. After SINCE, slow down to finish the phraseology so that you can give emphasis to your words and allow them time to understand each one.

Add four important words with a smile, "No obligation, of course," so she doesn't feel that they have to list the home, or that they'll have any problems with you.

Follow-up for the most-beautiful-home canvass.

1. *Same day.*

Send a thank-you note to every most-beautiful-home-on-the-block you visit. You'll find suggested wording in Chapter 14.

2. *One week later.*

Deliver the Most Beautiful Home on the Block Award. The wording and format for the award are also given in Chapter 14. All the details about the award are citical, so follow them carefully.

a. You must remember her name when you present the award.

b. It doesn't matter whether you were admitted to the home or not on your first visit. Give her the award anyway.

c. Reproduce the award on parchment, or on some other fine quality paper such as is used for diplomas. A small letterpress printer (rather than offset) will probably be most economical.

d. Have someone skilled at calligraphy do a beautiful job of handwriting the name and address on the award.

e. Get some notary seals from a stationery store, put one on the inscribed award, roll it up, and tie it with red ribbon.

f. Use this phraseology when you present the award one week after you first knock on their door. (Go through all the canvassing fundamentals again, of course. Knock, whistle, step back, turn, smile warmly.)

She opens the door and you begin by immediately using her name:

"Mrs. Coolier, Tom Hopkins. I was by last week and you know—"

She might interrupt you and say, "Oh, yes, I got your thank-you note."

"Wonderful. I stopped by because I really feel that you folks deserve this. We in real estate are concerned with doing our best not only to increase the value of property, but also to make our areas nicer. And you're doing that. Thank you."

Hand her the award. There'll be a little bit of nervousness now. She'll be thinking, "What on earth is this?" When she opens it, watch what'll happen. She'll look at it, she'll read it, and she won't even believe that anyone in today's world is that nice. Guess what she'll do with that award? It's not going in a drawer, is it? That's why the workmanship on your awards must be *suitable for framing*.

One of my top Champions went a step further. He ordered one hundred small walnut plaques from a trophy company. By investing in that quantity, he got each one of them for about the price of a good hamburger. His goal was to find the hundred nicest homes within a five mile radius of his office, and then to make those properties his listing bank.

After locating the homes and giving out the awards, he began a program of steady follow-up with those owners. Every month they got his newsletter, and every three months he called or visited them all. Why? Because this Champion knew that, based on the averages, there'd be a turnover of one hundred percent on those homes within five years.

And guess who they've been calling? This top Champion is well on his way to converting the cost of one hundred hamburgers into one hundred large fees.

If you can do that, they'll call you. Find one hundred of the finest homes within easy driving distance of your office. Twenty of them will come on the market every year—and they'll keep on turning over at that rate for as long as any of us can see into the future.

g. In the next chapter, we're going to talk about how you create a profitable listing farm, or listing bank. If you're going to have a farm, don't use the most-beautiful-home-on-the-block award there. Here's what'll happen if you do: over coffee with the neighbors, Mrs. Coolier will bring out your award, and everyone else will think, "Where's mine?" They'll all hate you.

A special aside to brokers and managers:

No good manager lets a new salesperson go out alone to canvass for the first time. It's a traumatic experience; the new salesperson doesn't know what to expect. In my seminars, I get managers who say, "I never canvassed myself. Why should I start now?"

Some managers tell me, "Tom, I love the *most beautiful* door. I can take a new person out on it." And that, by the way, is one of the things I did when I hired a new salesperson. I'd take them out before they even came to the office. I told them, "This is all I expect you to do—just once a day, for a couple of hours—get out and prospect."

You know, I had some people not want to work in my office because they didn't want to prospect. And that's just as good, isn't it?

Management, this door has tremendous training potential. Take new people out on it; let them get the physical feel of canvassing here. And get the lowest producing four-fifths of your veterans out on these doors too. They'll all thank you for it with more listings.

Maybe you're sitting there thinking, "Canvassing isn't me. I'm just not that kind of person." You may not want to go to the last door. That's your privilege—and it's your problem too. But if you're not going to the next *two* doors, your decision will cost you a bundle.

THE NEW HOME ON THE MARKET DOOR

After doing some effective work, you take a listing. What homes are most influenced when your sign goes up?

The five homes on either side, and the ten homes facing them across the street.

Timing is vital on this door. When should you knock on those twenty doors? Within forty-eight hours after you take the listing, and before you put your sign up on the listing you just took.

Now you can't always do that. Some people want your sign up the moment you take the listing. If so, don't fight it. Put your sign up. Other people will want you to hold off for a week or two.

I wanted to knock on those twenty doors fast, before they heard the news on the backfence hotline. The morning after taking the new listing—if at all possible—I'd start hittings those twenty homes. If they were curious about what house was involved when I started talking, it went better. Stale news is not news—so be fast with the knocks. Then put up your sign.

However, it didn't always work out that way for me. Please realize that I'm outlining many ideal situations in this book. But is everything always ideal? So adapt yourself to the circumstances you find yourself in, and do the most productive thing possible at every given moment. My goal is to up your percentages. If you're not rapping on the twenty critical doors near your new listing the next morning, a very pressing, income-producing activity should have preempted your time.

Your approach to each door is exactly the same as to all the others—meaning that you run through all the fundamentals. Then, when you hear a hello, you begin with your usual warm smile:

"Good morning. My name is _____,˙representing (name of your company.) A family in this area has employed us to help them sell their home."

Notice the exact phraseology. You don't say, "We just took a listing up the street." Doesn't that sound cold, commercial, and calculating? The pro says, "A family—in this area—has employed us . . ." Most people don't know that the listing is an employment agreement, do they?

You then say, "We feel it's an excellent value." Why do you

say that? And why do you pause when you do? So they can ask you how much their home is worth. Whenever that happens, go into your comparable market analysis appointment close.

"We feel it's an excellent value, so I stopped by to find out if you know anyone who'd be interested in living here."

Many people today would like to buy a single family residence as a rental and hold it for appreciation. Where would a lot of them like to own it? Two doors from their own home. Not only that, many people have friends and relatives who've become interested in their area. These friends and relatives have told them, "Find us a place."

That's why you then say, "This home should definitely generate much activity." Doesn't everyone want something that's good, something that lots of other people will want?

I hope you realize that you must rehearse speaking these lines slowly, confidently, and with emphasis. If you say them too fast, or if you slur your words, they'll tune you out.

Make your next point by continuing the previous sentence. We'll take it from the top: "This home should definitely generate much activity, and produce a lot of qualified buyers." Go on in your warm and positive manner, "When we sell it, we'll have a surplus of people seeking homes. Would you happen to know of anyone who may be interested in moving in the near future?"

They say no.

"Well, I sure thank you for your time. By the way, when' will you be moving?"

I hope you see the psychology in those words. It wasn't luck that permitted me to take an average of eighteen listings a month. It was words. My confident, rehearsed delivery of the right words to the right people at the right time did it.

Follow-up for the new-home-on-the-market door

Send a thank-you note to the nicest five people. You saw twenty of them. Choose the five who were the most pleasant to you; they get a little thank-you note.

Add those five people to your general file. Send them your newsletter, and keep in touch with regular phone calls and an occasional visit.

THE MOST PRODUCTIVE DOOR IN THE WORLD

Now you're going to canvass where the streets are paved with gold. When you sell a piece of real estate, please realize that you've put a big one in the record books. You've scored a victory for the sellers—and for the buyers too. You deserve the top grade: A+, ten on the ten scale, 4.0. You've done what you're paid for. You've come through. And people have respect for you. That's why the professional knows that his odds are best around the scene of his latest selling success.

When you canvass the twenty doors closest to your sale, carry your sold sign. Get out there fast. Do this within forty-eight hours too. If you don't, the neighbors will leak the fact that it's sold, and some other broker will get the listing next door.

Watch the phraseology on this one. I've got a little change in it, so watch closely. Of course, you go through the fundamental approach first.

"Good morning. My name is Tom Hopkins, and I represent Champions Unlimited. We just sold the home up the street to a lovely couple." (There are times when you don't say *lovely.*)

Hold up the sold sign so she can see that you're there to put it up. Had I just knocked on their door for the new-home-on-the-market canvass a week earlier, I'd change the phraseology, as I'll show you later. Let's do it now as though I hadn't knocked on their door before. Perhaps I've sold someone else's listing.*

"We just sold the home up the street to a lovely couple. They have two children, about six and ten, and he's employed by the Salt River Project."

Before saying that, get the sellers' approval to talk about them. Never disclose personal information about anybody without permission. If you do, what might happen? You could get sued for invasion of privacy. That's why a pro doesn't divulge personal data unless he has their okay. But you can give this kind of information:

"While selling the home, we generated so much activity for the area that I wondered if you'd thought of making a move in the near future."

*Check your board's rules on what you can say about selling another broker's listing.

"No."

"Would you happen to know of anyone else in the neighborhood who might be thinking of moving?"

"No."

"Thank you again." Then give them your standard, "By the way, when *will* you be moving?" Of course, you wouldn't use this last question if, three days earlier, you'd been there doing the new-home-on-the-market routine.

Watch how I do it if the listing sold fast. When I show up at that door, believe me, I'll be radiating enthusiasm. Here's what I'd say:

"Good morning. Forgive me for not remembering your last name, but I was by three days ago, telling you about the property up the street—the exciting value."

Pause. Look at them. Then say, "Sold."

"And I'll tell you, we need inventory in this area, so I just came by to tell you that we at Champions Unlimited, we don't just list real estate, we get families moved. Have you folks thought of making a move? Please, I'd love to help you."

· "Well, what are they going for?" is an answer that you're very likely to get.

"You know, I could pick a figure out of thin air . . ." And you know the rest.

Isn't that fun?

But you have to follow your local board's rules, the code of ethics, and your broker's instructions. Some brokers have certain instructions about the canvassing. I'd also like you to realize that your city may not allow soliciting door-to-door. If you're new to real estate, or reading this book before you get your license, you may not know if there are ordinances about canvassing in your area. Here and there around the country, communities are enacting these ordinances—and the courts are throwing some of them out as being unconstitutional. But you're not soliciting with this phraseology, you're informing people. You told them about the new property for sale. Then you told them it was sold.

If I were in a city with a non-solicitation law, I'd come up with phraseology so that I would not be soliciting. So if you live in one of those places and are sitting there thinking, "None of this canvassing applies to me," you're lazy. Because there's a way to create a method for seeing people. It's your obligation—to your company, to your family, and to yourself—to find it.

However, if you want to sit in the office all day, and if you're happy being average, then stay happy, won't you? Others want and will take the business you're not willing to go out and get.

One of the Champions going after the business—and getting it—is Michael Fuller in Gresham, Oregon. Mike writes: "I'm twenty-four years old . . . over a million closed in my first year . . . over $3 million in my second year . . . on target now for my third year goals. There's no way I would have done this without your help.

"The fact is, I did nothing but listen to Hopkins tapes my first year . . . ." (and close over $1 million—T.H.) ". . . as I still do. Practice, practice, practice has made the difference for me.

"One morning I knocked on a door and said, 'Do you know of anyone in the neighborhood who might be interested in moving?'

"The lady said, 'No, but I do know that Don and Millie up the street have four houses they're trying to sell, and they haven't had much luck. They're looking for a good Realtor® to help them, but don't say I sent you.' To make a long story short, I listed all four houses, and sold three within a month. Since then, I've sold two more of their homes and have had several profitable referrals from them. All from asking one question the way Tom told me to."

Mike said everything that needs to be heard about the value of using sound canvassing techniques, didn't he?

So what are you waiting for?

9

DEVELOPING YOUR LISTING BANK INTO AN INCOME GUSHER

"What do I do now?"

Most new agents ask themselves this question as soon as their real estate license arrives. It's a question of paramount importance to every newcomer. Only those who find a good answer quickly will remain in the business. All the others lose their most valuable asset, original enthusiasm, before they gain much knowlege or make any money. Without knowledge, enthusiasm, or monetary reward, motivation evaporates. Hope dies. They leave the business.

That's why I emphasize step-by-step processes in my seminars, on my video and cassette tapes, and in my books. New agents need a plan that pays off with certainty. They can't afford to experiment. They can't afford to flounder in the swamp of newness season after season.

To follow a proven plan demands energy. In fact, it'll take all your energy until you're established. Save your experiments until you can afford to lose the time and money they'll eat up.

This book is a distillation of step-by-step processes that will enable you to earn fees in spite of your newness, your inexperience, and your lack of in-depth real estate knowledge.

Farming a listing bank is the next such process that we're going to study. This is the queen of prospecting methods. It's the most gratifying and the most profitable system for creating brokerage fees that I know of. This is the method that really changed my career. With it, I went from average performance to outstanding results in a very short time.

So I've proven that this method works with my own efforts in my own career. But, as any scientist will tell you, unless anyone in similar circumstances can achieve similar results using the method in the same way, nothing is proven.

I agree. That's why I refer you to the vast host of Champions who learned this method, put it to the test, and achieved great things. Every day, new Champions and old Champions are re-proving that this method works. Tomorrow morning, thousands of Champions will be using this step-by-step farming process to rise to a higher level of outstanding performance and income.

You may be wondering, "Is it too late? Has it already been overdone? Can I achieve the same results?"

Certainly. One thing never changes: for every doer, there are twenty wishers. For every person who works a program through to success, twenty stop trying long before their efforts have a chance to succeed. If you're a doer, the way is clear. Your success is certain.

After my first six months of failure in this business, I took some training and began to earn a few fees. At that time I came to an important conclusion. I realized that I had a very low threshold for rejection. So I thought, "Tom, if you're so sensitive and emotional that you can't handle rejection, then you'd better develop ways of prospecting where you won't get rejected very much."

So I began with the concept of growing listings on a low rejection diet. After about a year, I had developed my concept to the point where I was harvesting eight to ten listings a month with the method. A trainer heard about it and put my system into his training program. We came up with the name *listing farm.**

Now I call it the *listing bank.** All your efforts there have the same effect as deposits at a bank. Those efforts are time-deposits. You have to let some weeks go by before you can withdraw them. Please remember a business axiom that we have in this country: bank

---

*Listing bank and listing farm are two names for the same thing. I use both names throughout this book with no difference in meaning intended.

withdrawals must be preceded by bank deposits. That's what you do with a listing bank; you work effectively and methodically there to build a clientele that will provide you with four to ten listings a month from the one area. The method has proven itself, and it continues to prove itself, every day in thousands of listing banks that agents trained in my systems have created in urban areas all over Canada and the United States.

The facts don't lie. This program works. It pays off. And it does that reliably and well. The day I started developing this system is the day that everything started happening in my real estate career. Now I'm going to take you, step by step, through the entire program. Here's the beginning:

STEP 1: CHOOSE THE RIGHT AREA

Don't think about the real estate, think about the families. To become a Champion lister, please realize that you can't think about property. The people come first. With this system, you decide to become the family real estate agent for lots of people living in a certain area. If you think of the program this way, your listing bank will become something you'll be excited about building.

The figures really are exciting. They are accurate. I've proven that myself in my own listing bank.

In my opinion, the ideal number for a listing bank is five hundred families. But I have to realize that not everybody is a workaholic. To take on five hundred families demands strong commitment. Maybe you'll say, "I don't want to work that hard; I'm only going to work with two hundred families."

Then two hundred is right for you. One hundred? You can make money working a one-hundred-family listing bank—if you'll do it thoroughly. Whatever number of families you choose to work with, you must teach them to think of you when they think of real estate. If it's farmed methodically, a one-hundred-family listing bank will give you one listing a month on the average. Want two listings a month? Farm two hundred families. Five listings a month? Then go for the five hundred family farm.

But you have to do it thoroughly. Work one hundred families consistently and they'll give you consistent production; neglect five hundred families and they'll give you nothing. "What could be more obvious?'' you may be thinking. Yet the average agent will fight for a listing bank that's so large the thought of working it overwhelms him. But he won't give up a single house. Pick a number that you can and will farm effectively.

Let's work out the numbers for a five hundred family listing bank. Nationally, we move once every 3.7 years. In our calculations, we'll use five years to give us a margin of safety. This means that one hundred of your five hundred families will move every year.

Let's say that eighty percent of them employ professional services to help them market their homes. That gives us eighty listings per year.

Can you get all eighty of those listings? Impossible. Some are committed to another agent. Others have friends or relatives in the business. Things happen. But if you do everything I tell you to do with warmth and enthusiasm, you'll get eighty percent of the listings that come out of the bank.

How many is that?

Sixty-four. In one year. That's more than five a month.

But those are unsold listings. If you do everything I tell you to do with the professional skill that practice, drill, and rehearsal can give you, how many of your sixty-four listings will sell per year?

Ninety percent. That's fifty-eight. But let's play safe again and say that only eighty percent of your listings sell. That gives you fifty sold listings a year from your five-hundred-family listing bank.

Now you should put this book down, and take a moment to figure something out. What is the average net fee that you'll put in your checking account for each listing sold?

If you're not in the business yet, you may not have a clue. Rather than quote percentages, which certain governmental agencies frown on, let me suggest that you call a local broker. Tell him you're thinking of entering the business, and ask how an agent's compensation is calculated in his office.

Arrive at the figure for one average listing sold, and then multiply that amount by fifty. This will be your yearly income from skillful and dedicated service to a five-hundred-family listing bank.

Before we move on, let's give a thought to one additional idea. If you want to achieve the best results that you can reasonably expect to achieve, you won't spend all your time taking listings in your bank. Farming should require no more than a third of your time. And you should earn as much with the rest of your time as you do farming. In other words, your total real estate income should be three times what your listings-sold-in-farm income is. That's right. Multiply by three. I did. It's fun to work that out on paper. It's even more fun to do it in reality. There's no reason why you can't.

Where will the other two incomes be earned? Besides farming for listings, you can sell your own listings, sell property outside your farm, and take listings outside your farm.

You can work for-sale-by-owners, open houses, expired listings, to name only a few of the techniques that you can specialize in to get additional business. And let's not forget the emperor of real estate income: referrals.

During my last year in real estate prior to going into management, I earned $52,000 just on listings sold in my listing bank. That doesn't sound terribly impressive today, does it? But it was a record-setting performance in those pre-inflation days. To grasp the significance of that figure, consider what the dollar was worth then. I began listing and selling real estate in Simi Valley when the average home there sold for $20,000. Gas was about 32¢ a gallon. Today's dollar is not the same dollar I farmed for. However, since I sold most of my own listings, and was also listing more by-owners than anyone else in the city, I was earning three substantial incomes at the same time. You can do the same thing—if you have a full time commitment.

There's another exciting aspect to building a profitable listing bank: it's yours to sell when you retire from the business. Maybe you'll move on from listing and selling in a few years, as I did. When I left California for Arizona, I found a young man who was smart enough to invest in this business. I sold him my real estate practice, my listing bank and referrals, for twenty-five percent of all fees generated. It was a wise move on his part because he acquired a very successful going business with no cash outlay. What leverage! It was a wise move for me too. Over a period of time, I received a substantial amount for something I could no longer use.

Doctors serve families, and they sell their practices when they retire. So do attorneys, architects, real estate agents, dentists, insurance agents, engineers, and all other licensed professionals whose work creates a flow of fees. As you set up your records and work your listing bank, keep in mind that you're developing a valuable and highly marketable asset in addition to your primary goal of increasing current income.

What will you eventually sell? Your recommendation and introduction of your successor. Your reputation for honest, expert, and faithful service. Your neat, readable, and detailed records. Your knowledge of the families and properties in your listing bank and referral files. Your emotional rapport with your clients and the probability that they'll work with your purchaser. All these factors combine to make your real estate practice a property of considerable worth.

Now let me warn you about the greatest danger that faces the agent who is beginning to develop a listing bank. Many newcomers to this industry start off strong. They swiftly build up a following. They start to make some exciting money. And then they quit farming. Some of them think they've got it made; some keep themselves tied up with busywork; some simply forget about farming. Many of these agents know they should keep on farming. Maybe they worry about it now and then. But they just don't get out there. I hope you'll go all the way with this program. Only a few agents do, and those few, the strong listers and the Champions, are very well paid for their persistence.

It's sad how few people keep up their farming after they get started and make a little money at it. Farming gets easier, and it gets more profitable per hour spent doing it, as you go along. Your second half-year of intense farming benefits enormously from your first half-year's intense farming. And the benefits continue to compound rapidly.

If you'll do the whole program, every year you'll make far more money in much less time. If you continue the full program for several years, you'll be unbeatable. Nobody can touch you. No other agent can afford to fight you for your listing bank because you know everything and everyone in it. And the people there not only know you, they like and trust you. Who can break your grip on your listing bank now? Nobody—except you, yourself, and the face in the mirror. Arrogance, neglect, and forgetting that you're in a service business can do it, but the competition can't. As long as you keep on doing what gave you the bank in the first place, it's yours until you choose to retire and sell it. You still won't get it all. But when you're sticking in four green pins for every red one, who cares?

If you're a veteran of the business and have already built up a clientele, you may not want to start all over with this program. You may be too active and successful with other techniques to take on a five-hundred-family listing bank. Or you may already have a strong position—but not a dominant one—in your listing bank. If so, adapt parts of this program to your circumstances.

If you've been active in the business for less than six months, my advice is to make this program the cornerstone of your real estate success. Base your entire real estate career on your listing bank.

Now that you've decided how large a listing bank you can and will work, let's talk about what area to choose. The first consideration is that you must like the people who live there. If you don't like the families, you won't work them. Stay in your comfort zone. If you try to farm with people who make you uncomfortable, they'll sense your unease and return your dislike. You'll build rejection, not rapport, that way. And your listing bank will go bankrupt. Avoid all that pain by putting your energies into building your bank where you feel comfortable.

Today, I would be uncomfortable building a listing farm in Simi Valley. When I started there at nineteen, I was comfortable. However, don't think that the listing bank concept only works in areas where the houses are inexpensive. Some top salespeople in Beverly Hills follow every single step of this program, and their average selling price would buy a block in many other areas.

So forget about the real estate and pick the families that you want to work with.

By the way, you may want to spread yourself around—taking a hundred homes here, another hundred there. One fine Champion I know decided that he'd be better off with plenty of variety. So he went for a four-part farm. He started off with a hundred most-beautiful-homes-on-the-block. These were located in areas beyond where the other agents in his office had their listing banks. For low-priced property, he chose a group of blocks near an industrial park that contained a hundred homes. Another neighborhood, this one with two hundred homes, provides him with a wide selection of housing in the middle price ranges. He completed his five-hundred-family listing bank by selecting an area with a hundred executive homes. His farm gives him listings in every price range. He's a gregarious fellow with an unusually broad comfort zone who's doing very well with his diversified listing bank. It doesn't matter that his farm is scattered—he can't work it all in one day anyhow.

STEP 2: GET YOUR LISTING BANK NOTEBOOK SET UP

Buy a strong, attractive three-ring binder. Then reproduce the listing bank control sheet in Chapter 14. You'll need one copy for each family in your listing bank. Five hundred families, five hundred control sheets.

Organize your listing bank notebook in the order that you'll walk your farm. Begin by numbering all five hundred pages from 1 through 500. Then decide how you'll work through your farm—a look at the map might help—and proceed with putting one property's address on each page. The first house in your listing bank, let's say, is 2603 Glade Street. Write the address on page number 1. That's where you'll accumulate information about the family that lives at 2603 Glade Street. The next house is 2607 Glade; it's address goes on page 2.

Reinforce the page holes with stick-on reinforcements. If you don't, in a few months a page will fall out. Then what will you lose? A family. You don't want to let that happen, do you?

Getting a listing bank fully organized in one notebook takes quite a bit of time. Doing that job took me ten days of steady work. But it's worth it.

STEP 3: OBTAIN THE OWNERS' NAMES

The street address directory is your best place to start. This publication, often called the criss-cross or by-street directory, gives you the addresses, names, and telephone numbers at the same time. Unfortunately, not all areas have one. Check with your telephone company. Because of the changes that occur after its deadline, the street address directory will be about seventy percent accurate. You may be tempted to organize your notebook right out of it and skip walking your farm to get the addresses as suggested in Step 1. Don't. You'll miss all the families that have unpublished phone numbers, and you won't be able to put your notebook in the order that you'll farm your listing bank.

The tax rolls are another source for names. You can inspect these public records in your county courthouse.

In many areas, there's a more convenient way to get this information: title companies. If you find the right title representative, one who's eager to help a new Champion start developing a lot of title business, that representative will supply you with the names and addresses you want on a complimentary basis.

When you complete this Step 3, every family in your listing bank will have its own page in your notebook, complete with name, address, and phone number.

STEP 4: SET UP A VISUAL CONTROL BOARD

Use a map, an aerial photo, or a plot plan of your entire listing bank. Where do you put this control board?

That depends on whether you're committed to becoming the top lister in your farm. If you're serious about doing that, you'll put the control board on the wall opposite your bed. Why? So you'll see it first in the morning.

That's where I put the map of my listing bank in Simi Valley. It was the first thing I'd see when I woke up. My control board was a title company plot plan that I had a photo shop blow up to the size I wanted.

I put colored pins in it. *Red for danger* highlighted other brokers' listings; *black for emphasis* gave the location of for-sale-by-owners; *money-green* showed my listings.

There was no kidding myself with that map hitting me in the face every morning. I knew when someone else was making inroads on my area. Oh, the delight of sticking a green pin in—the pain of adding a red pin! The pin went in the map the first time I entered the bedroom after getting the news, whether the news was good or bad.

If you'll use your visual control board this way, it'll be worth thousands of dollars a year to you. It was one of my main motivators, one of the important sources of my continuous drive to conquer my listing bank. You see the facts at a glance, and they don't lie. You always know where you stand.

STEP 5: USE LETTERS OF INTRODUCTION

Most salespeople don't plan ahead, and they won't commit themselves to an organized program. That's the entire reason why they're average. That's why the homeowner immediately recognizes them as being average when they show up on the doorstep without notice or introduction. "Just another real estate salesperson," the homeowner thinks, instantly forgetting the face briefly seen. At least ninety-eight times out of a hundred, they're right: they'll never see that face at their door again. One shot is the whole program.

You want to be a strong lister. Maybe you plan to be a Champion. Perhaps you even aspire to become a Super-Champion. You'll get where you want to go faster if you start off being different. Send a letter of introduction.

But don't do it the average way. Most agents who get this far whip out a letter at the local fast-print and have a teenager run around hanging them on doorknobs. Then it's months before they knock on every door—if they ever do. That's no letter of introduction. That's just a flyer, and not a very good one, either.

A sample letter of introduction is given in Chapter 14. Notice that it isn't fancy. The words are simple, friendly, and easily understood.

Handwrite the letter. If you'll use a good quality black felt pen, an offset printer can shoot your letter and run off enough copies for your whole listing bank. They'll look like you wrote them all out.

Mail these letters in groups of twenty-five. Use blank envelopes, or envelopes with only your name on the return. No company envelopes. Why? Because it's more personal. And don't get overorganized with a label mailing system for your farm. If what you send looks like junk mail, it'll get ashcanned like junk mail. Hand address everything you send to your listing bank.

If you have children old enough to write, get them involved in your business. Timmy, my oldest, was too young when I started, but his babysitter was fifteen. She loved to make extra money while being paid to babysit and watch TV. A lot of kids would love the responsibility of a job, and some of them write a beautiful hand. Back in those days, the babysitter was delighted with a penny an envelope. I think you'll have to pay more today. Do it yourself if you have to, but get them hand addressed.

Psychologists have established that it takes an average of six meetings for people to remember you. For a meeting to count toward the six, they have to be aware of you, of your name, and of your business. For example, if I had knocked on your door yesterday, and today we ran into each other at the drugstore, you probably wouldn't remember. And the drugstore meeting wouldn't be number two of the necessary six unless I spoke to you, re-introduced myself, stated my business, and we talked a bit.

But after six meetings, during each of which the prospect hears your name, sees you, and understands what your business is, that person will associate you with that business. In other words, after six meetings, when the subject of real estate comes up, they'll think of you.

So now you see our purpose in farming a listing bank: it's to meet five hundred homeowners six times each. That means we've reduced our farming goal to three thousand meetings.

Does that make you swallow hard?

Before you get discouraged, think of it this way: those three thousand meetings are your fifty-week goal. Farm five days a week. So now you only need twelve meetings each farming day to achieve that great goal. If you allow ten minutes per meeting, you can do it in two hours a day. Ten hours a week. If you don't want to spend ten hours a week building a tremendous income gusher like a listing bank, you should stop reading this chapter right now. You're wasting your time. Farming isn't for you. But if you really want to move out, and if you're determined to have that gusher going in six months, hit twenty-four families every twenty-four hours, five days a week, rain or shine. The money's there. All you have to do is go get it.

Remember that about one out of five families in your listing bank will move during the next twelve months. Many of them will move because of a sudden happening: an unexpected transfer or job change, for example. Less than one out of ten pick their Realtor® with great care. Most homeowners call the first agent they think of that they like and trust—if they know anyone who meets those requirements. Only a few do, because so few of us have the personal discipline to farm persistently.

Not everyone will require six meetings to remember you. When you farm vigorously, you start having all kinds of good luck. You knock on the door the day after somebody was offered a better job in another city; you strike up a good conversation with someone who tells you that the people up the street are selling out and moving south; you find a grandmother who wants to buy a house nearby for her married daughter. That's the gravy. The entree is dominating your listing bank. Six months of twenty-four families a day and you'll own the area. The facts don't lie, as you will see.

Now let's integrate our letters of introduction into the farming concept. Six meetings is the means by which you reach your goal of becoming a family's real estate agent when they need service. But some people will move before you can see them six times. That's why you want to make as favorable an impression as you can with every meeting, and especially the first. So you start with a letter of introduction. What is the essence of that letter? That you, Mr. and Mrs. Homeowner, are important enough to be treated with respect, and I am a professional who is also worthy of respect.

Find out the mailing time lag. Strike up a conversation with the postman when you re walking your farm, or mail a few sample letters to friends in the area. Know when your letters will be delivered to the day and hour. Your goal is to show up at the door right after your letter gets there.

You may learn that letters mailed by 5 p.m. Monday will be delivered on Tuesday about 2 p.m. Find out if some parts of your farm get their mail in the morning, and other parts in the afternoon. Then set your schedule so that you hit their door right after your letters are delivered. Doing that requires some planning, some attention to detail. In other words, it requires some professional-level work.

STEP 6: KNOCK ON THE DOOR

It's Tuesday. You're getting next day delivery. The twenty-five letters of introduction you mailed yesterday were just delivered a few minutes ago to the families that are on pages 1 through 25 in your listing bank notebook. We'll start at house number one, which is page number one of your listing bank notebook. The family's name is Wagner. Here's the phraseology. Use all the fundamental door-knocking steps given in Chapter 8, of course. Notice that you being by using her name:

"Good afternoon, Mrs. Wagner. My name is Tom Hopkins. Did you receive my letter of introduction?"

It doesn't matter whether she's opened your letter or not. Just the fact that you say "Did you receive my letter of introduction" raises you to a level far above the average.

After she responds, continue with: "I just stopped by to personally make your acquaintance, as I will be the firm's representative in this area. I'm in the process of conducting a market survey to establish market projections for the coming year. Would you please help me by answering a few questions on my survey?'' Then immediately ask the first question.

This technique is beautifully effective when it's done right. If you're planning on becoming a Champion, watch every detail carefully. It's based on the psychology that would affect a lady on a business trip who returns to her hotel at one o'clock in the morning after an evening with friends. No one is in the lobby as she walks to the elevator and pushes the button. Then someone taps her on the shoulder. She turns around to find a man standing next to her saying, ''You're really goodlooking. I'd sure like to get to know your better, sweetheart. What's your phone number?''

The average woman would be alienated, do you agree? But if the same thing happened, except that the man, when she turns, takes a step back, smiles, and says, ''Excuse me, but could you do me a favor? Could you tell me the time, please?''

If you were that lady, you wouldn't refuse that request, would you? No, you'd tell him the time because the question is normal and unthreatening.

Unthreatening questions are the psychological foundation for the next technique that will take you twice around your entire farm. This one step allows you to go a full third of the way toward controlling it.

Let's go back to door number one, where we're using the survey technique with Mrs. Wagner:

''. . . please help me by answering a few questions on my survey?'' Hold up the survey form as you continue talking without waiting for a reply. ''Do you feel the area is improving?''

STEP 7: SET UP A MARKET SURVEY

Don't tense up. It's all done for you. In Chapter 14 you'll find the whole thing laid out. Here's how you go about putting this technique to work:

a. Type the questions on a sheet of plain paper. Leave space for the heading and for the answer columns.

b. Get a 4 by 10 inch sheet of transfer lettering. Art stores sell them for the price of a bag of popcorn at the movies. A good style is

Helvetica Italic 24 Pt. Look for Adletter 521-24, or pick another style that pleases you. There'll be plenty of letters left over for your first house flyers.

   c. Transfer the letters to make headings of the words: MARKET SURVEY, name, yes, no. To do this, position each letter where you want it on the survey and rub it off with a pencil. Nothing to it. Anyone in the art store can show you how in ten seconds.

   Work carefully. It only takes an extra five minutes to do a neat job. If you've never used transfer lettering before, practice on a separate piece of paper first. Drawing blue lines helps you keep the letters straight. Use the special non-reproducing blue pencil that's also available in art stores for these lines.

   d. The MARKET SURVEY heading must be large enough for the people to read it when you hold the survey up. And the neater it is, the more credibility it'll instantly confer on you.

   e. Before you set out for a day's door-knocking with the survey, write the name of each family you plan to see on one of the forms. Then, at Mrs. Wagner's doorstep, when you hold up the market survey, she sees her name written large there. What does that tell her? That you're organized. That you came there expressly to talk to her, Mrs. Wagner, not just to whoever answers whatever door you knock on. In other words, you have a serious reason for seeing her. All these details not only build impact and interest, they also tear down fear and apathy.

   Maybe you're thinking, "I like the idea of farming, but I hate paperwork. I'm going to skip all that stuff and just go out and see the people. That's where the money is."

   This idea destroys most attempts to build a successful listing bank. To make money farming for listings, you have to build rapport with large numbers of people. Unless you do that efficiently, there won't be enough hours in the day.

   Unless you work methodically with step-by-step processes that you can keep track of, you'll soon lose your farming drive in a fog of confusion. You'll remember a few good doors and a few bad doors, but the mass of ordinary doors will run together in your mind. You'll forget who lives where and what their names and interests are. All the minor details that are of major importance in building rapport will be a jumble in your brain. You won't be sure who's hot and who's cold this week. You'll have trouble recalling which families might be moving ninety days from three months ago. In other words, you'll be an unnecessary amateur in your listing bank instead of a necessary professional. A farm that isn't farmed professionally isn't farmed at all.

The survey technique is a plan that gives you reasons for at least two of the six meetings you need. Always remember that it takes six meetings to fix yourself in their minds as a real estate expert with special knowledge of their neighborhood. With the survey, one call gathers the information, another passes the results back to them. More importantly this technique puts flesh and blood on your skeleton wish to create a listing bank. Unless you set your sights on knocking on every door in your farm at least six times during the next year, you're not going to make farming pay.

Lack of method or plan is the most common reason why the few agents willing to doorknock mostly stop doing it. The usual pattern is this: the new agent overcomes the fear of getting out there and knocks on some doors willy-nilly. It goes well. Some leads develop. Then the agent happily spends all his time working on those few leads and, when they've run their course, has nothing. The listing bank doesn't exist. Very often, the agent is now discouraged with the idea of farming because the first leads took four months to finally pay off, and now he or she doesn't have anything in the pipeline. So they have a revelation: "I'm going to concentrate on buyers because they pay off faster."

That decision generally sends them straight out of the business. At the least, it plunges them deeper into trouble. The whole idea of building a listing bank is to create a sustained and steady flow of income. You can't do that with a little spurt of doorknocking twice a year. You can create a listing bank only by methodically working an area until you become a power there. You don't have to dominate it. But you're always safer—and richer—if you do.

STEP 8: PUT THE MARKET SURVEY TO WORK

In Step 6, we showed you how to use the letter of introduction to swing right into your market survey. Now we're going to give you information about every question on the survey.

Question 1: "Do you feel that the area is improving?"

If she's unhappy with the area, it means she probably wants to get out. That's good for listings, isn't it? If she likes the area, she'll probably encourage other people to live there. That's good for sales, isn't it? So your purpose is to get her talking and to find out how she feels. You're not there to argue the area's merits. This is a pearl of a question. Non-threatening. Flattering because it asks for an opinion. Not a bit personal. Always open with this one. And pay attention to the answers, because they'll tell you much about how this family fits into your farming future.

Don't let people flounder trying to come up with an answer. That'll make them feel stupid. If the question throws them for a loss, help them. Point to the yes or no. Mrs. Wagner might say, "I have no way of knowing, I don't know."

You could say, "Well, the homes sure have gone up recently. I guess we could say it really has improved. Let's mark yes." Now, you've got number one. Keep on moving to Number 2.

Question 2: "How long have you folks lived in this area?"

I used *folks* quite often. The word came naturally and seemed to help me establish rapport. It worked for me, and it'll work for you—if you like it. If not, don't say *folks*. Say whatever pleases you and your listeners.

This is the key question of the entire survey. You're using it to look for people who've lived there three years or more. Why? Because it's almost time for them to get the itch to move. Work a little harder with the over three. When you find a family that's been there five years or more, make a special effort to get close to them. They need help. They don't realize that it's time for them to be moving along.

I color-coded the pages of my listing bank notebook. A red spot meant they'd lived there less than one year. Blue meant one to three years. Money green called attention to the people who'd been there over three years. Whenever I didn't have time for an entire program, I concentrated on green.

If you can get an answer to question two, you've had a successful meeting. If you're running into short answers and hard looks, say, "Well, I see that you're busy. I won't take up any more of your time today. Thank you so much for your help. Bye."

But if they're not too restless, press on with the survey.

Question 3: "Do you feel that the shopping facilities in this vicinity are adequate for your needs?"

You can ask this question in a variety of ways: "Are you satisfied with the stores in this community?" "Do you feel that the shopping facilities are adequate for the area?" "What do you think of the shopping here—is there enough variety for you?" Use what suits your style, fits the neighborhood, and gets the best response. And you don't have to ask the questions with the exact words that are on the questionnaire. Your goal is to get the people to talk to you, so go with the wording that works for you.

One of the top Champions we've trained is an energetic lady in the San Clemente area. She took this program all the way—with spectacular results. Here's what happened: when she went through her farm for the first time, she used this market survey technique with enthusiasm. She didn't worry about rejection. She didn't waste energy wondering if it was necessary. She didn't tear herself down wishing she was back in the office chitchatting and twiddling her thumbs. She concentrated on working through her entire listing bank—and she'd picked a large one—as quickly as she could without seeming hurried or uncaring to the people there.

By working straight through, she covered her entire farm in just eighteen days. That was a giant step toward achieving the dominance she now enjoys there. In covering her farm that first time, she told me she found enough listing opportunities to give her an excuse to forget about farming for the time being. Every agent who farms vigorously with good technique quickly runs into that temptation. What's interesting about this lady's action is that she didn't want to stop farming. Instead, she was eager to go through her farm again. But her instinct said it was too soon. So she waited.

Although she didn't think much about it at the time, the people in her new farm answered question number three with an emphatic no. Most of them thought the shopping facilities were miserable. Then some great luck popped up—the kind that keeps on coming to all alert, hardworking Champions. A few days after she completed her survey, a firm of developers broke ground for a shopping mall on a huge vacant parcel of land bordering her farm.

So this lady went charging back through her farm for the second of her six meetings. People kept saying, "Thank you so much. We sure need that mall."

She just smiled and said, "You're welcome." And then she proceeded to talk some real estate.

That's not the end of the story. After getting that lucky push, most agents would coast. Why knock yourself out going back six times when so many people remember you after one hit?

This lady knew that people forget very quickly. So she carried on with the entire plan—saw everybody six times—did all the other things. Today, if you have eyes for her listing bank—forget it. You can't make a living there. She has it all locked up.

Question 4:   "Where do you do most of your grocery shopping?"

I hope you realize that some of these questions are designed to keep the people moving with you. If you bore into real estate with every question you ask, they'll tighten up and turn you off. So the last two questions were throwaways. But the next one isn't.

Question 5:   "How many are in your family?"

Before you ask this one, smile warmly. Number five is an important question. First of all, a major reason for moving is a change in family size. Growing families want more space; empty-nesters want less upkeep. So this question can cause them to discuss one of the vital issues that bear on how long they'll live in their present house.

Secondly, this question marks a psychological resistance point. Five questions are a lot to ask at one time. Make a decision here guided by this thought: they aren't likely to get more friendly today than they already are. They're probably getting restless and thinking of other things at this point. If you detect the slightest indication of that now, break off the interview before you erode the rapport you've already built. Tell the person, "I know I've kept you for several minutes now. I'll stop back at some future date and finish my survey. Thank you so much for your help."

You only proceed beyond this point during your first meeting if you've had clear go-ahead signals. The vibes are good. The lady feels like talking. Let's say that she answers this question with, "There are four of us."

Your response is, "Then you have two children?"

Here's the third reason why this question is important; you can make some real progress if she's relaxed as she answers, "Yes, that's right."

"You have two. What are their names?"

"Ricky and Susan."

"Ricky Wagner," you say, writing on your form. "And Susan Wagner. What are their ages?"

"Ricky's nine, and Susan will be seven next week."

"Oh, so Susan has a big day coming up. Wonderful."

You're going to review that information before you come walking up to the Wagner's home the next time, aren't you? You'll have more to talk about with Mrs. Wagner then. How did Susan's birthday party go? How's Ricky doing?

But if Mrs. Wagner was showing signs of getting restless when you asked question five, put her answer down, make your brief thank-you statement, and go.

Question 6:   "Do you folks commute to work alone, or do you both use car pools?"

This one needs to be handled carefully. Women who work outside the home often resent it if you assume they aren't employed. And many homemakers are touchy about their status now. In these days of two-income families, many areas can only be canvassed successfully in the evening; no one is home during the day. There's nothing wrong with canvassing in the evening. Some of our top

Champions are out in their farms between 7:30 and 8:30 nearly every night. That one hour is productive because they find a high percentage of both husbands and wives home.

So you ask if they both commute to work alone or ride in a car pool. Most of them will say they drive their own cars. The purpose of question six is to set up question seven which, had you sprung it without preparation, might not be well received.

Question 7:   "Where are you and husband employed?"

Never ask anyone where they work. That's a four-letter word. Today, everyone is employed.

The answer to this question is one of the most important facts that you can record about a family in your listing bank. It'll tell you a great deal about them, and furnish you with many future conversational openings.

Question 8:   "Do you believe the school system is providing the kind of education you want your children to have?"

In the sense that you don't have any direct use for the answers you'll get, this is another throwaway question. But it does serve four purposes: It relieves the pressure built up by the last two personal questions. It encourages a little discussion of a safe subject. It establishes that your interests aren't limited to real estate and making money, that you're also concerned about community affairs. And it sets up question nine.

That is, it may set up question nine. Or your string may have run out. Be especially alert at this point, and don't ask the next question unless you've had an encouraging interview so far. If you feel yourself slipping, question nine won't pull you up.

Remember that you can't pound through this entire survey like an elephant heading for the river on a hot day. You've got to be responsive to the interviewee. That person is the whole point of the exercise. Be prepared to shut down and shove off for the next door any time they get twitchy. Never forget that the first, last, and only purpose for the survey is to help you become a force in your farm. You can only do that by building rapport with the families who live there. The survey gives you a vehicle for gathering facts about people that will help you continue to build rapport. But it's counter-productive—it hurts you more than it helps you—if you use it to squeeze information from people when they don't want to spend time talking to you. In case of doubt, cut it short and keep moving. When impatient people learn that you don't linger long, they'll be more likely to talk to you for a few minutes the next time.

Question 9: "Do you have a full time real estate agent serving your family's needs?"

Have an answer rehearsed for those who say, "Why should I? We're not selling."

"No one thinks they will—until they do. Lots of people suddenly find themselves with an exciting opportunity that involves moving or some other real estate transaction—and they don't know where to get trustworthy information in strict confidence. I'm an expert in this area, and I can be your confidential source of accurate facts."

Some people answer question nine with, "Yes, we have a friend in the business." Don't let it bother you—that's a technique they learn from each other. Your answer is, "That's wonderful. I'm glad to hear that you appreciate the value of knowledgeable professional service. Since I'm a specialist in this area, I'll keep in touch with you from time to time so that I can be of help if needed."

After you finish with this question, close off the interview with these words:

"Thank you very much for your help. I'll let you know of any interesting developments I find out about our area."

That sets you up for meeting number two, doesn't it? The key to effective farming is to always look ahead. Always keep yourself moving toward stronger positions.

As you work through your farm with the market survey, you'll acquire a large collection of priceless information about the people living there. You've worked hard for this information, so treat it with respect. Every night, transfer the facts you've learned that day onto the control sheets in your listing bank notebook. Don't scribble on the run in that permanent record—it's vital that you be able to read what you've written any time in the future.

Keep your notebook up. The secret of not getting swamped is to do every day's work every day. Of course, if you're out until 3 a.m. with an offer one night, you'll have to play catch-up the next day. Start making your spare moments count. The budding Champion expects to be busy. Time is precious; the Champion doesn't waste it. The busier you get, the more ways you find to make one minute do the work of two. Keep going back to your listing bank. Every time you work there, you make a deposit.

Let me warn you again about the trap that destroys most beginning farmers. They hit the doors, turn up some action, and stop farming. Often it's not a conscious decision; they just feel too busy to think about farming. But they aren't really too busy. I know. There's a tremendous difference between real busy and feel busy.

Be sure to transfer the vital details into your notebook promptly or you'll forget a lot of the things that were said to you. Here are some of the facts you want to record in your listing bank notebook:

a. First names.
b. Children's names.
c. Nicknames, if any, that they want used instead of their real names.
d. Names of any pets they have.
e. Employment information.
f. Length of time in the area.

When you come back, you'll know so much about each family that they'll have to be impressed.

STEP 9: MAKE YOUR FIRST SWEEP IN SIXTY DAYS OR LESS

That's the test. If you can't knock on every door in two months, your farm is bigger than you have the drive to handle. This is the real world you're dealing with now, and in the real world, the only farming that pays is intense farming. You can make money farming one hundred houses intensely; you can only lose money farming five hundred ineffectively. So be straight with your broker; be straight with yourself; and don't let wishful thinking lead you to disaster.

STEP 10: DRIVE YOUR LISTING BANK AT LEAST ONCE EVERY OTHER DAY

Your car and you must become part of the neighborhood's environment. Drive slowly in your farm. Keep your listing bank notebook on the seat to help you memorize names. You'll be able to do this with surprising ease, because you have a reason for learning these facts. Make it a challenge to learn everyone's name. A kid with a paper route knows all the people's names after about three months. You can bat in that league, can't you?

Some of my Champions have their spouses drive. Then they can concentrate on looking at the homes and associating the names and the people with each house. Call each owner-couple to mind as you pass their house. Every trip you make through your farm will imprint more faces and names on your memory. Whenever you drive your farm, have your notebook with you.

If you see a man out watering the lawn, the odds are good that he lives there, aren't they? Start flipping the pages when you see someone doing yard work. Before you get there, you've found the page. Stacey Street, number 2856. Aha.

Down comes the window. "Hi, Mr. Jeffries," you call, giving him a friendly wave.

Mr. Jeffries will wave back. And he'll think, "There's that real estate guy again. Never too busy to say hello. And what a memory!"

It's fun. And it's effective.

Watch for activity in your listing bank. Don't get all the news from other agents. The competition will be taking a lot of listings in your bank for a while, but don't let that upset you. You won't become a force to be reckoned with in your listing bank until you've met the nicest ninety percent of the homeowners there six times.

Are you thinking, "What if everyone does this?"

I wish you could sit down with any one of the top people I've trained and hear their answer to that question. You see, I get plenty of feedback. The other day I received a letter from a man who now owns a half interest in the brokerage firm he started with, as a beginner in real estate, four years ago. Since then, he's been to eleven of my seminars. As you might expect, this man follows my system all the way. He and thousands of other heavy hitters take time off from their high-earning careers to be constant repeaters at my seminars. All of them tell a similar story. It runs like this:

"Tom, after my group went to your seminar, everybody was flying high. They were all going to charge out there and set the world on fire. Three months later, I was the only one still doing your program. And I was starting to make excuses and have doubts. Then it started coming. It was like lined-up dominoes—push one and the whole row falls over. Suddenly I took off. But I remembered what you said. I didn't stop farming; I kept on doing what had made me busy. Pretty soon, it seemed like people were shoveling money at me."

So I hope you realize that you won't be getting fifteen listings out of your farm the first month. If you get one, you're very lucky—which means you worked smart and hard. After your third sweep through your farm, count on one a month. Quite possibly, you'll be doing much better than that. After six meetings, you'll be getting five listings a month from a five-hundred-unit farm—if you've done everything I tell you to do.

Expect to get depressed occasionally. It'll happen. That's as sure as the tides. So, while the sun's still shining, give a few moments' thought to the rainy days that lie ahead. We all have moments of doubt, moments when we're close to giving up, moments when we want to hide. The Champion expects that—and keeps on working when it happens. Think of farming in the same way you might think about running a mile every morning. The first commitment is to improving your financial health, the second to improving your physical health.

You're in trouble the first day you miss your mile run. The second day, it's easier not to run again. Before you know it, a week has disappeared forever and you're thinking, "Why should I start again?"

The same emotion can destroy your farming program. Keep working. Just get out there. Promise yourself anything—that you'll only knock on three doors, for instance. Then, when you've done three doors, you'll always say to yourself, "Well, this isn't so bad. And I'm already out here—so I might as well finish my regular twelve-family-sprint." Once you get moving, the easiest thing to do is to keep on moving.

Why am I so sure that you'll get depressed? Because that's the primary cause of most failure. It isn't skill, brains, or looks—it's the ability to put depression and rejection aside and keep on going that makes winners. Chapter 12 is devoted to methods of defeating rejection and reversing depression. I know these methods work because I could not have achieved success without them.

STEP 11: HAND OUT A SMALL GIFT ON YOUR SECOND VISIT

Again, you make this second sweep in sixty days or less. This time you're reporting the results of the market survey, and you're also dropping off a small gift.

I hope that I can convince you of the value of giving. I believe in gifts as a sound business practice. You give them the gift for helping you with the survey. The gift doesn't have to be expensive, but it shouldn't be too cheap. Some people say, "I got a gift for everyone in my farm. It's a plastic bottle cap!" This is not too impressive.

Spend money to make money. Let me mention the Brown and Bigelow company. You know, I've been very fortunate in my life. Since I stopped carrying steel, things have happened to put me in the right place at the right time. If you knew it all you'd say, "No one could be that lucky."

I anticipate wonderful things. I expect them to happen. Do you know what I say to myself before I go to sleep at night? "Tomorrow, I'll meet the right people at the right place and time for the betterment of all." And I always do.

A young man walked into my office a month after my training with J. Douglas Edwards. I still had no money. I had a lot more enthusiasm, but no money! But I saw that it was going to happen. Some of you reading this book know it's just a matter of time. If you know you'll make it, you're already halfway there.

This young man said, "Tom, I have lots of advertising specialties for handouts." He showed me pot holders and all kinds of things. I really craved some of them. I said, "I'd love to take a few hundred of these two items out in the field and see what I could do with them. But I don't have the money."

Do you know what he did after an hour of talking? I didn't try to sell him on this idea because I didn't know what I was doing. I didn't have enough technique to do that. He finally said, "Tom, anyone that would sell real estate in a black and silver band uniform, anyone that makes $42.00 a month and is still here, needs help!"

I said, "I know."

This young man let me order my first little giveaways, and let me pay three months later. That's why I talk about Brown and Bigelow. I will never forget the people that helped me when I was on the bottom.

By the way, as you climb that ladder of success, don't forget or look down on the people you pass. Because, if you miss a rung, you'll see them on the way down! And you may need their friendship badly.

I ordered some little blackboards for my entire listing bank. My second gift—I passed them out on my third sweep, was chalk for the blackboards. Next, it was little kitchen memos. It can be anything. One of our top people gives kitchen notepads. You can get them through a printer for next to nothing. On the last page it says, "Time to call (your name) for your new pad."

Some give out flower seeds. "Here's something that will make you and your family just a little happier—beautiful flowers." It's inexpensive, but the thought counts.

So you give them a gift the second time through and thank them for their help on the survey and let them know what you found out.

Let me show you what I mean: I knock on a door: "Hi, Mrs. Johnson, Tom Hopkins." I'd only use her first name if it felt right. "When I was by a few weeks ago, you were so kind to help me with my survey. And you know what? Ninety-eight percent of the people I surveyed said the area is improving. Seventy-six point one percent said the shopping facilities are adequate. And do you know that we have eighty-four children on your street?" Give her the information you learned on the survey.

"And here's a little something to thank you for the help. I'm really excited about serving the homeowners in this area. I'll see you in a couple of months. Bye."

You notice there's one thing I'm not even mentioning—real estate. That's why, if you're in a non-soliciting area, you have not solicited with this approach. You made a survey, and now you're giving a gift.

STEP 12: IDENTIFY THE NICEST TEN PERCENT

In a five-hundred-house farm, you'll find fifty friendly families. Really nice people. Send them a special note the second time you sweep your farm. "Dear Ted and Maxine: Just wanted to drop you a quick note to thank you again for your help on my survey. I enjoyed seeing you. Hope the seeds grow beautiful flowers. Regards—"

Cultivate these people with extra attention and they'll respond with all sorts of valuable information about real estate opportunities in your listing bank.

STEP 13: MEET EVERYONE IN YOUR LISTING BANK ONCE EVERY TWO MONTHS FOR ONE YEAR

As I said earlier, if you're really hot, you'll have your six meetings in six months—but this is only for people who've decided to be Super-Champions.

STEP 14: ORGANIZE A SPECIALIZED PROGRAM

This is a promotion program that's coordinated with a holiday or special event. My first specialized program was pumpikins. I went to the source: the pumpkin farms of Ventura County, and bought 518 pumpkins at bargain prices out there. Then I arranged to haul them to my listing farm in a rented three-quarter-ton truck.

But first, I did some advance work. Three weeks before Halloween, a letter went out to every home in my farm. It told them not to buy a pumpkin because I'd be bringing one. Then I painted a sign for the truck that read, HAPPY HALLOWEEN, TOM HOPKINS.

I recruited two little guys to help me and, right before Halloween, the three of us, dressed as ghosts, drove around the listing bank. My two helpers ran the pumpkins to the doors.

I didn't stop promoting, following up, and keeping in touch just because my pumpkin promotion was a tremendous success. But from that day on, I had that farm in my hip pocket. I didn't get every listing there—just most of them. You'll never get them all. You don't need them all. You don't even want them all. Some are rundown, overpriced turkeys dumped on the market by nasty people.

Here's a pumpkin tip for brokers and managers that can be applied to any kind of promotion. When I went into management, I discovered something that astonished me. This won't astonish an experienced manager: my salespeople didn't have enough faith in themselves and in their profession to commit for a farm-wide pumpkin campaign. Not one of them would invest a little to earn a lot, even though they knew about my great success with pumpkins.

So I assessed my salespeople a small sum and, as an office, we bought a thousand pumpkins. The agents each received thirty pumpkins to give out on their farms. The rest we piled in front of our building and told all our clients to drive in and pick up a pumpkin at their convenience. That caused plenty of activity around our office, and brought a lot of people there for the first time. Some of these people who came for a pumpkin, stopped back by later to talk serious real estate.

Do you know that it's physically impossible to go anywhere for the second time until you've been there the first time? The whole secret of this business is activity, isn't it? This is a great way to keep things moving.

Here's another fine program: give a candy bag to the children. You can order these bags with your message printed on them: "Happy Halloween. Get lots of goodies. Compliments of Retsil Gnorts."

This program isn't expensive, but you need to order in time. One of our Champions was late getting his candy bags out the second year and he started getting calls. "My kids are pestering me about the candy bags." "We didn't get ours yet." Tell me they weren't aware of who he was!

Don't just send a Christmas card. They get lost in the card blizzard that hits every house. Another of our top Champions sends a letter on December first that reads: "I'm just writing to say hello, and to remind you not to forget to send me my Christmas card." Is that ever different.

Chocolate Easter bunnies—go out just before the holiday and give them to the kids. This is an excellent promotion.

After my first year in the business, I decided that, once every twelve months, I'd try something in my farm that I'd never heard of anyone doing. Why not have a party for all my clients? That seemed like a great idea. I felt that I should do it right or not at all, so I mailed invitations engraved with gold leaf.

The first year, only thirty-five out of five hundred came to my party. That was fortunate, because I held it at my home. The second year, more than a hundred people came. By the time I put on my sixth annual Tom Hopkins Festival, it had become *the* yearly event in Simi Valley. No one had six hundred people to a party in Simi Valley—except me.

For my last one, I rented a large ballroom. My friends and family helped me decorate it with crepe, banners, and balloons. I always picked an evening between Christmas and New Year's for my reception in order to have it during party time but not be in conflict with everyone's holiday plans. I had two bands: ballroom first, rock second. There were two huge Christmas trees—refreshments—food. When I totaled up all the bills for my last year's gala, I had paid out $3,000.

But I never thought I was out $3,000 for that party. As a matter of fact, at least six dollars came back for every dollar I invested in that promotion. Let me put a new word in your vocabulary: SALTMAL—spend a little to make a lot. You have to build up to it, of course; but be sure to spend a little of the money you make this year to make a lot more next year.

My last party was more than a financial success; it was a gratifying emotional experience too. More than once while it was going on, I remembered how I'd bought my farm's first little promotional gifts not seven years before—nervously—and on ninety days' credit.

Who do people think of when they decide to move after coming to your party for five years since you helped them find their home? You see, after three years, the majority of the people at your party are getting the itch to move. Isn't that exciting?

I made the party formal. Made them all dress up! Here's a secret. Hire a sharp gal, one who'll pay attention to your instructions to greet people warmly at the door and write their names on name tags in big, black letters. Don't let the people write their own names—lots of them will write them too small for you to see. Remember, those name tags are there for the benefit of only one person: you. Pay attention to this detail. If the door person prints large and plain, you can see their names before they know you're looking. You can't remember them all.

This was really a big event. The mayor's office called because they knew the newspaper people were invited. The secretary said, "Mr. Hopkins, we understand you're having your big annual party this year. The mayor would like to stop by."

It would have been fun to say, "Would you advise the mayor that this party is for the people I've served. Luckily, we have two weeks before the party for him to get happily involved!"

Think about all these ideas. I hope you use them, or create exciting new promotions of your own, because specialized programs lift you far above the average. When you get these things rolling, you're not a peddler any more, you're a celebrity. You're not out there begging for business; you're someone whose service is sought out. This is the kind of thing I want you to think seriously about doing. The secret is to give, give, give.

STEP 15:   LOOK FOR TWO SPECIAL TYPES YOUR FOURTH TIME THROUGH

When you go by to say hello for the fourth time, you'll be having many wonderful things happen. Lots of people will know you now. This time through, you're looking for two more special kinds of people. On Step 12, you spotted the nicest ten percent. You've already marked these people for special attention.

This time through, look for the neighborhood snoops. Every street usually has one or two. Once they like and trust you, they'll be delighted to give you the latest update on who's getting divorced, who's having a baby, what's happening in each family.

And also, on your fourth sweep, decide who are the nastiest people in your listing bank.

Then take them out of your book.

You don't need them. Why put up with the pain? Why fight the aggravation? You're a Champion. You'll soon dominate your listing bank. You'll soon know more about the real estate there than anyone else does. It's their loss when you tear them out of your book.

They don't get a pumpkin!

They don't get the gilded invitation to your annual party. Just walk right past their property. But don't put them in the nasty group the first time they're nasty unless it's really bad. Anyone can have a bad day. But if they get you two times running—out. Champions don't accept that kind of treatment.

There's an interesting phenomenon about the rottenest, nastiest people—they still want the best service. But I'll tell you something about many of that kind. The toughest to win over will often be your most loyal supporters once you've done it.

I remember a man I set a goal to list when he was a by-owner. It took me a year. Once I got that listing, I gave him such service that he was amazed. That man then moved out of state. For years afterward, when anyone he knew visited any part of California, they had to come all the way to Simi Valley to meet me. This is what happens.

At my seminars, for example, I have people that are pressured to come by their managers. Or their spouse says, "You're going to hear this guy."

They walk in with the idea, "Okay, Shorty, prove it." Some of the people who come to fight instead of learn wind up being my most loyal students. These hard cases go out, use the material, and prove to themselves that it works.

STEP 16: ASK FOR THE BUSINESS

On your fifth sweep through, you're going to ask for their business. You've earned that right now. You're going to tell them that you have a lot of activity in the area. You want them to know that. If they're thinking of moving in the near future, ask them to think of you. And do they know of any neighbors or friends who are planning to move?

I want to warn you that there are people back in your office right now who have listened to one of my tapes for five minutes—or they've attended one of my seminars and then failed to use the material. In other words, they've lost their enthusiasm. They feel that the business has let them down. Actually, it's the other way around, of course. But they aren't going to admit that. And they really don't want to be reminded of their failure by having you come along, months or years after they didn't have the drive to be successful, and succeed with the material they had first but never used. Do you see their problem? Your success with my material would be another defeat for them. So, if you tell them that you're going to set up a listing bank, they'll scoff. They may laugh in your face.

These people want you to follow their advice, which is, essentially, to work as little as possible, and then to complain as much as possible. If you want to be like them, take their advice. Do as they've done—which is nothing. If you want to be a Champion, take a Champion's advice. Do as countless Champions have done—which is plenty. And from their plentiful efforts, they've earned a great plenty of the things they want.

However, some of the worst complainers actually did work my plan. Here's how they did it. First, they reproduced the control sheets and put them in a binder. (Not much rejection in that, is there?) Then they entered all the addresses. (That doesn't hurt either, does it?) Then they mailed the letters of introduction. (No pain there.)

But they never went to see the people. Maybe they knocked on a few doors—once. Meet them all *six* times? Are you kidding? *No*body does that.

Well, almost nobody. Just the five percent who are doing terrific.

When you start taking listings, please don't quit. Don't let a little success kill your career. During my first three years, I took only one day off a year, Christmas. I had no help. Now people say, "Oh, he had a secretary."

In my fourth year, you bet I had a full-time secretary. She handled the details because my time had become too valuable for paperwork and follow-up that others could do for me. My strength was in closing; I was best in front of buyers and sellers. A pro realizes that he should do what he does best, what he gets paid most for. The secret of building any organization is to find people who like to do what you don't like to do, and then pay them well.

I've said it before, and I'll say it again: if you want to be a winner, do as winners do, not as losers do. Don't listen to the losers. Work through all sixteen of the previous steps, and then go for the last one.

STEP 17: PRESENT EVERYBODY WITH A NICEST FAMILY IN THE STATE GIFT

By this time, you'll be making enough money from your listing bank so you can afford to spend a little money on them. At this point, as you're completing the last of your six sweeps through your listing bank, give everyone who's still in your book (sorry, nasty people) a special gift. You might want to have a card printed that says, "To the nicest family in the state," and sign it in ink. Have this card printed, so they won't be surprised when they discover that their next door neighbor got the same gift.

Give. Give. Give. Some of our top Champions spend more than $10,000 a year on gifts. Of course, they work up to it; they spend money they've already earned. It all comes back.

When you reach that level, you'll walk down the street so proudly. When you go into your listing bank, people on every side will be smiling and waving and greeting you. You'll be a celebrity of service there.

I hope you'll do it all. You can, you know, now that you have the direction.

I wish I could tell you about all the Champions I know of who have achieved their goals through this farming program. Space limitations make that impossible. So I'll tell you about just one such person. Like me, Joan Pate started her career with several dismal months. Joan writes from Salt Lake City:

"At a Tom Hopkins seminar, I learned the true importance of listing . . . I dedicated myself to farming and grew to love it as I saw how farming assured me production. From April when I completed the seminars to the end of that year, I closed a million in residential real estate. The next year I doubled that. The next year I more than doubled that. The next year I closed over six million dollars in residential real estate and earned the title I had set my goals to: "The Six Million Dollar Woman." I have been able to reach personal and financial goals far above my original ones. Part of those goals are to have the home of my dreams, my Mercedes 450 SEL, share my happiness with my husband who I love more every day . . . .

"As my production increased, I did not "give up" farming as many do. Today I farm what I call my "Hidden Gold Mine," my past clients and customers. They already like me and trust me and know how ready, willing and able I am to work for them. I don't ever forget them, but instead, build loyalty by "farming" them. I have a 3 x 5 card indexing system which allows me to send all 528 families I've helped a monthly mailer, a phone visit every 2 months, a visit in person every quarter, a gift at Christmas time, a gift of some flower or garden seeds in the spring, some bulbs in the fall, three cards from Client Follow Up out of Chicago for eight years, a pumpkin delivered to them on Halloween with a recipe, a calendar on January 1, and a New Year's letter thanking them for their business, referrals, and friendship, and outlining my goals for the coming year.

"Because of Tom's instructions on "How To", I have been able to do what I have done in my career and . . . I feel like this is only the BEGINNING."

Joan has been showered with prestigious awards and honors—all richly deserved. And this to someone whose start in real estate was, in her own words: "Four months dragged on with no direction, no instruction, and NO production."

What made the difference? The three D's: desire, direction, and doing. You have the direction now; you have the desire; but two out of three doesn't close clients. You have to be out there doing. The doors to everything you want are in your listing bank. Go knock on them. Keep on knocking. You can have everything you knock for.

10

LISTING TECHNIQUES YOU CAN
BUILD YOUR FORTUNE WITH

Do you remember taking your first listing?

I remember taking mine. Vividly. Since enthusiasm was the only thing going for me at the time, that had to be what brought me the listing. Enthusiasm came out wherever I went. When you're starting in this profession, what's on your mind most of the time? If you were like I was, real estate never leaves your thoughts for long.

Before you went out socially, did you stuff every pocket with business cards? I did. At the first party I went to after my license came, I tried to meet everybody. I was so excited. All those people—and none of them knew I was in real estate! I went around giving my card to everyone, and pretty soon I met a couple who showed a little interest.

"Oh, you're in real estate," the man siaid. "How're things going?"

"They're booming," I said. "Real estate is going magnificently. Tremendous. We've never had a market like this. I've been in the business a week now, and it's wonderful."

For a few seconds they just stood there blinking at me. Then we went on talking. After a few minutes I mumbled something about needing a refill and wandered over to the punchbowl. When I glanced back at them, they were whispering together.

A year later I realized what they'd been talking about after I walked away. It went like this:

Husband to wife: "Look, honey, you've been wanting to get rid of the house for a long time, but I wouldn't sell until we got our price. Maybe this guy can do it."

Wife to husband: "I was thinking it would be a shame to waste all that eagerness. And what've we got to lose?"

Before the evening ended, the husband walked over to me and said, "Tom, why don't you come by tomorrow night? I'd like you to take a look at our place and see what you can get for us."

My first listing appointment! I sailed out of that party with adrenaline pumping through my veins. Sleep was impossible. Was your first listing-eve filled with the same excitement, the same anticipation, the same dread that, before you have a chance to list it, their house would burn down?

I was still loaded with attitude when I went over to their home for the appointment. Since I was all enthusiasm and no knowledge, who arrived at the price?

The sellers.

Sure enough, two hours later I walked out with my first overpriced turkey. Did I know? Did I care? Not a chance. I decided then to take all the listings I could get. "Oh, you have a bungalow in Bermuda? I can handle it—gimme the listing." That's what you'll do when your horns are green.

And the morning after, when you took your first listing into the office, did you say, "Good morning, everyone" in a much louder voice than usual? And then did you make your announcement with a modest smile? "Well, I got my first listing."

There was a murmur of congratulations, wasn't there? I know what happened next. In the back of the office, Joe Negative got up from where he lives behind the donuts. Every office has one, and they all know an easy putdown when it's waved in front of them. Joe came over, looked at your listing, and said, "Just what I thought—it's overpriced. It'll never sell. If I wasn't already crying, I'd laugh."

When that happened to me, I wasn't as shocked as I should have been. No matter what Joe thought, I had a listing. I was sure the price thing could be worked out somehow.

Joe Negative gave me my first hint that price isn't a pussy cat, it's a grizzly bear. But the knowledge didn't really sink in for quite a while. It felt so good to have a listing. I wanted more. So I got out and hustled five more listings just like the first one. "I'm in business," I kept telling myself; "I'm really rolling now." But, with six overpriced turkeys, I didn't roll far.

An interesting phenomenon takes place when people put their home on the market. While you're writing up the listing, they're saying, "We're in no hurry. No rush at all. Don't sweat it—the main thing is, we want our price." For your own peace of mind, please remember that they're telling the truth when they say that. When they give you their overpriced-turkey listing, they really aren't in a hurry.

Then you put the sign up.

Short and to the point, isn't it? *For sale.* No ambiguity there. But even without seeing your sign in the yard, the emotional message strikes home a few hours after they've committed the sell-it decision to paper—and then everything changes. Within two weeks, they are different people.

Look at the psychology here. The emotional reason they bought the home in the first place was security. But they don't understand that. They think they bought the house for logical reasons, for tax benefits, appreciation, and such. So when they make what they think is a logical decision to sell, they don't realize they've chopped their security off at the shoe tops. But when they try to walk around on their ankles, it hurts. This makes them start looking for another home so they can feel secure again.

Then they get themselves in trouble. Right off they fall in love with a place they can't buy unless they get the full unrealistic price they've put on their old home.

Now they're in a hurry. Almost the morning after they approve the listing, it seems like everything turns upside down. Don't be surprised. Expect it.

When you have six overpriced turkeys, it's like they have a weekly meeting to coordinate their drive to push you out of real estate. One of them calls you at 6:30 in the morning to make sure you get up. Another calls you at lunch to make sure your digestive tract is in a knot. Another calls late at night to make sure you're showing their house tomorrow.

Slowly, painfully, I started to gain a little knowledge, especially about the importance of at-the-market pricing. As that happened, what dwindled a little bit? My enthusiasm. It shouldn't work that way—knowledge should increase enthusiasm. And it will if you study the right subject. Which is? How to avoid, overcome, and solve problems.

When you have overpriced listings, here's how it goes. The phone rings.

"Hello. Tom Hopkins here."

"Tom—? What are you doing? Where is everybody? You said you could sell the place. It hasn't been shown in four weeks!"

"You know, I think it might be a little high for the market."

"Well, how do you know until someone sees it?"

The man asked a good question, didn't he? By this time, you've figured out the answer: the agents all know his property is overpriced just by looking at the information in the book. But you don't want to say that or he'll ask another good question: "If the price was that much too high, why did you take the listing?"

If you already have several overpriced listings, you face the problem of deciding what to do about them. When the clients tell you to "get someone over here," you could pull a Blodgett. Like Fred the butcher in Chapter 4, you can start running your relatives through.

Please don't do that. And please don't burn up all your time, energy, and enthusiasm struggling desperately to appease angry sellers. You can't. And you won't make a dime trying. When the meat's spoiled, don't put it back in the freezer.

By causing you so much pain, lack of knowledge can overcome your desire to succeed. That often happens to us when we're new. We don't know how to take listings right, so we take them at any price and under any circumstances. Then, after the party's over, we wake up with a hangover we can't get rid of. Like many things, it's fun when we do it—the distress comes later. List in haste, repent at leisure.

You want to make sales when you're brand new in real estate. Sales are immediate money. When you were first hired, your broker or manager may have said, "Listing is the key to this business." Maybe so much was going through your mind you didn't catch the full impact of that statement or understand his explanation of it.

I have nothing to gain by encouraging you to become a professional lister except the knowledge that I've helped you achieve success. Do you know that the ones making the most money are the people who take the most listings? It's always the same. As I travel throughout Canada and the U.S. talking real estate, I often ask brokers, "Who made the most money in your office last year?"

The broker gives me a name.

"And who's your top lister?"

Nine times out of ten, the broker gives me the same name.

A piece of real estate that's listed right is as good as sold the night it's listed. It really is. When you know how to take good listings, you can figure out what your income will be a month in advance. For lots of my readers, I know that would be an exciting and welcome change. Why do I know that? Because I've been there, my friend.

So do yourself a favor. Trust me. The key to this business is the listing. Don't sell the key short. Put half your time and energy into listing and half into selling. There are many reasons. I've given you some of them before. When you have several realistically-priced listings, you control the marketplace. The company with the most listings has the most buyers. In every real estate office, all the selling agents are in reality working for the strongest listers in their service area.

Listers call their own shots. They don't have to sit in the office all day hoping a buyer will straggle in. Champions use their time making deposits in their listing bank when the buyers aren't out.

Maybe you've had a few bad moments thinking about how many people are flooding into this business. It's nothing new. Real estate has been attracting droves of new recruits for many years. There's a surefire way to eliminate this worry: join the group that welcomes more new people. Who do all those new people compete for?

Buyers.

And when they find one, who do they in essence bring that buyer to?

The agent with the listings.

Retsil Gnorts (read it backwards) is happy to have more people out there selling his listings. The more the merrier.

When the market takes another temporary dip as it regularly does and there aren't enough buyers to go around, who's out in the cold? Not Retsil. There are always some buyers in the market, and they still have to buy his or her listings. When the going gets tough, it's the buyers-only associate who finds himself looking for a time clock job to pay the rent.

Do you enjoy selling more than listing? If so, it's because you never learned how to list professionally. You'll know how to do that when you finish this book. Then I hope you'll tell yourself, "I'm going to change. I'm shooting for seven or eight listings a month. I'll collect twice as much off them as I'm earning now by selling exclusively, and I can still make a lot of sales.''

I've never told anyone to stop selling. In all industries, no money is made until someone sells something. That's certainly true of real estate. Your goal should be to list and sell with equal skill and success. The day you arrive at the pinnacle of power, prestige, and profit in this business is when you're regularly selling more than half of your own listings. By the way, that's tough to do if you only have one at a time. But when you're carrying a nicely rounded inventory of eight or more listings, it's amazing how often you can lead your buyers to them.

There are five potent reasons why you should sell your own listings:

1. Your inventory is not tied up by agents who will usually be average in performance. Average salespeople often fail to thoroughly follow-up all the way to closing, with the result that many sick but saveable transactions die.

2. Instead of installing the other agent's buyer client where your seller client used to live, you replace the client you've moved out with the client you've moved in.

3. Sometimes you'll spend more time pushing the selling agent to do his job than you would've spent working directly with the buyers, had they been your clients.

4. Having a reputation for selling your own listings is in itself a powerful listing tool.

5. You earn both ends of the brokerage.

During my last two years of listing and selling, I sold eighty-eight percent of my own listings. Only twelve out of a hundred were sold by other agents. It wasn't only for the reasons given above. I simply didn't have time for the problems that other salespeople created.

What am I saying? That it's easier to be a strong lister and a strong seller than it is to be either one alone. Yet so many salespeople want to concentrate on only one area. That's like a bird trying to fly on one wing. However, there's a point of tremendous importance here that you must fully understand, believe in, and live by if you're to become a Champion. When I talk about selling my own listings, I'm talking exclusively about positive activity, not negative activity. Go all out to sell your own listings; also go all out to encourage other agents to sell them too. If you're a member of the multiple, you must do both or you're cheating your sellers.* Never let it be said that your failure to cooperate with another agent cost your client a sale. It's always better to get the property sold, whether you sell your own listing or another agent sells it. It's always better to have another agent's buyer in your listing bank than a disgruntled owner whose house you didn't sell. In the nearly four years that the average buyer will live in your listing bank, you'll have ample opportunity to turn them into clients. If your commitment is long term and you continue to farm your listing bank vigorously for the next four years, that buyer will think of you when selling time comes. The agent who represented him in the purchase will be long gone and forgotten in ninety-five cases out of one hundred. So think and act positively all the time; the client's best interests are your best interests.

START BY BEING PREPARED

Please don't go beyond this point until the concepts of Chapters 3 and 4 are alive and well in your mind. There I showed you what happens when you miss your homework, when you show up for a listing appointment with empty hands and empty brains—the seller sets the price.

If you let that happen, there are two possible outcomes: when luck is with you, you'll get out there without taking the listing; when luck is against you, you'll list an overpriced turkey. Then you'll pay for your sloth and carelessness throughout the term of the listing.

Preparation is the lever that moves your work from slow futility to fast profit. You have to know the neighborhood—real estate values can change dramatically in just a few blocks, sometimes in just a few yards. You have to know your business—if you think the ways of the real estate industry are mysterious, they'll have difficulty accepting you as a real estate expert, won't they? You have to know your technique—many people hate to make decisions, and won't until someone comes along who's skilled at helping them do so. That's why

---

*If the client knows his listing is not going on the multiple, it's perfectly legitimate not to work with other agencies. The practice of operating as an exclusive agent has a long and honorable history.

my method concentrates on teaching you how to help people make decisions that are good for them.

So you need to have expertise in three areas: neighborhood knowledge, industry knowledge, and technique. Let's talk about a method that puts all three of those areas to work at once.

THE COMPARABLE MARKET ANALYSIS

In previous pages I've given you a brief glimpse of this essential listing tool; now we're going to cover the Comparable Market Analysis (sometimes we'll shorten that to CMA) technique in depth.

As I said before, you lose between 25 and 75 percent of your listing power unless you present a well-researched comparable market analysis during your listing performance. Putting it another way, suppose you've taken four listings at market price using the CMA technique. Without the CMA technique, you'd have taken no more than three of those listings at market price—more likely, only one.

I hope you'll think carefully about that statement. Any technique that increases your chances of taking a fast-selling listing by 300 percent is worth a considerable amount of effort, isn't it?

Why is this technique so essential? Can't you just tell them what the prices are?

People don't believe the figures coming out of the mouth of the silver-tongued devil known as a salesperson. But when they see those same figures written in black and white on a printed form, they do believe them.

You see, when you present the facts, you're quoting lower sales prices than the sellers have heard from other sources. And they want to believe those other sources that justify a higher price for their property. So when they look at your comparable market analysis what hits them?

Unpleasant facts.

First, your people see several comparable homes offered for less than they want for theirs. After discussing this with you, they begin to suspect that the price they had in mind is unrealistic.

As you draw their attention to the recent sales, they see what the home six doors up sold for a couple of months ago. That property, which has the same floor plan as theirs, never had a sign because it sold so fast—they didn't even know the people were leaving until she saw the moving van. Then they believed the first rumor that came around about the price the fast-sellers got. Now they're shocked and angry to discover that those people sold for $15,000 less than what they've decided should be their own rock bottom figure.

Yes, they're shocked to learn the truth. And they're angry—but not at you. They're mad at the jerks who gave their property away. You know the fast-sellers didn't do that. You know they were smart and realistic, and they sold for the maximum price with a minimum of fuss, bother, and expense—in other words, they sold at the market. But you don't argue the point; you let the facts do that.

The people you're trying to list see that Herman and Wilma Mildue actually sold for $148,000. That's another shock. They'd heard the ''about $190,000'' figure that Wilma tossed around in the bowling alley.

Then your sellers turn back to the houses currently for sale and notice that the Simpsons' home has been on the market for seven months. You discussed that point earlier but they didn't seem to catch it—their minds were on prices then. Now they give that time period some clear thought, knowing that a seven months' wait would spell disaster for them. When you lead them into a discussion of the expired listing—of why it happens and how disruptive it is for the home-owners involved—they begin to grasp your explanation of realistic value. They realize that you've brought a consistent price pattern to their attention with your carefully researched and well-thought-out comparable market analysis. Now that you've explained and re-explained the meaning to them of the CMA's three sections, they see the reality of the market-value concept. Suddenly, they know that the facts you're presenting are the hard truth they'll have to live with. And now, for the first time, you have the opportunity to list their home at a price that will permit the property to be sold.

Maybe you're still fighting the idea of using a CMA. Maybe you tried it and stopped. If you did that, you weren't using it right. Which probably means that you weren't writing a clear and complete comparable market analysis. ''I know what all the properties around here are worth'' is what some real estate agents growl when their manager urges them to use the CMA technique. But it's not important what you know—it's how smart you make the sellers feel that counts.

And you make them feel smart if, as a professional seeking to serve them, you have your facts in writing.

Most comparative* market analysis forms have spaces for five or six properties under each heading. Some salespeople don't fill them all out because they don't want to look up fifteen to eighteen properties. Some of them have said to me, "Look, Hopkins, I hate paperwork. I hate the detail. I just like to list."

I guess they think I love paperwork. I'll tell you a secret. I hated all the paperwork connected with real estate except the second kind. What's the second kind? The simple but never boring task of filling out the deposit slip that puts checks for brokerage fees in your bank account. I never minded that. I don't think you do either. But you can't do the second kind of paperwork until you've done the first kind, which is all the paperwork from the start to the closing of a transaction.

CMA's get easier as you go along. Beginning with my second year, I started filling out the top two sections mostly from memory because they were about my own sales and listings.

Keep your balance on research. Your first comparable market analysis—your first carefully researched and well-reasoned one, that is—might take you all day to complete. After that, you'll be doing them in much less time. There are too many other things that demand your attention to spend all your time researching.

Now that we've put our CMA together, we're going to do what the pro does: analyze the area. The average salesperson looks up the comparables and lets it go at that. He doesn't go see the properties. Don't tell me that gas is expensive. Lost fees are what's expensive. Again, being active and working in a specific service area saves you time. After a few months of alert and active work in that limited area, you'll know most of the properties that have sold or are on the market there, and you will have visited most of the expired listings. Are you beginning to see how it all fits together? If you've been farming your listing bank thoroughly, you'll have the whole CMA there in your head in a few months.

But you still write it down. You're still the silver-tongued devil, and they'll still believe the written data that you give them on the form far more than they'll believe or even remember what you say.

---

*Call it either *comparable* or *comparative;* the words have the same meaning.

If your listing appointment isn't in your farm, visit the area. Go see as many expired listings as you can find time for, because this is one of the most productive forms of canvassing. At the least, you'll get information to help you with your listing appointment; at the best, you'll get another listing appointment with the people whose listing has expired. A high percentage of those appointments will lead to listings. Never rely only on the research that you dig out of the records in your office. Unless you at least drive by every property on your CMA, you're knocking on the door to disaster when you arrive for your listing appointment. Will you agree that the condition of those fifteen properties will vary? Just one example will show you how failing to see properties will kill your claim to real estate expertise.

Let's say that you're working on the price question with Keith and Wanda Lloyd. You've gone smoothly through your listing presentation up to this point. Keith Lloyd has already let it out that he thinks their home, which is immaculate and has lots of extras, is worth $92,750. It's a popular floor plan in your service area, and you're familiar with the general layout.

Your research at the office turned up three other properties of the identical floor plan that are for sale within a few blocks of the Lloyd home. One of them, you notice, has been on the market for nearly a year, the other two for several months. All three properties are priced in the high eighties.

You don't find any recent sales of that model near the Lloyd home. One sold on their street a year ago for $92,000. But the same contractor built a number of them in another neighborhood about a mile away, and you find three recent sales there in the low eighties: $81,250, $82,500, and $83,950. Since you're pressed for time, you decide you've found all the information you need. "Obviously," you say to yourself, "that design is a drug on the market. Won't sell for more than $84,000 any more. But I'll pop an extra big one on top for bargaining, and go with $85,000 as the top figure I'll take the Lloyd listing at. Just to make sure, I'll drive by the three identical houses that are for sale over there."

However, since the road to the infernal regions is paved with good intentions, you don't make time for the drive-by, find yourself running late, and hit the Lloyds' door without doing any field checking on your office research. But you're not worried. You don't see how all three houses can be much different from the Lloyds' pile of bricks and sticks. So, at the proper time during your performance, you close for the listing at a price of $85,000.

The sellers stare at you in amazement. After a moment, Keith Lloyd says, "Have you been in those three houses you say are our competition?"

"Ah, no. I haven't actually been inside. But they're all in this neighborhood and—"

Mr. Lloyd breaks in with, "Have you even driven by any of them?"

"Well, I—"

"Obviously, you haven't," Keith Lloyd says. "For your information, house number one on your list is a hippie heaven. Must be twenty people living there—and it shows.

"House number two is a divorce situation. I guess they both just took off and let the place turn into a jungle. You can see the vandalism from the street.

"House number three is nice except that it backs up to the Interstate. I've met the people, and they know that highway noise is the reason their home hasn't sold.

"So now you walk in here—without even checking out those other properties—and tell us we'll never sell our house for more than $84,000. I'm not even going to mention the house up the street that sold for $92,000 last year. Frankly, I don't think you're the kind of real estate expert I want to do business with. Thanks for coming by and good night."

Things like that happen all the time to salespeople trying to earn a professional's income without bothering to do professional quality work. Why let it happen to you? It isn't that hard to do professional quality work.

Now let's talk about what properties you select to put on the comparable market analysis form. The purpose of the form is to concentrate the most important facts that bear on the price decision for the property you're trying to list in an easily understood format. What are the most important facts? Those that pertain to the properties that are most like the one you're trying to list. Most like in what way? In nearness, physical qualities, and time. The identical floor plan located on the same size lot a mile away may not be comparable at all: the second house may be downwind of a hog farm, reached only by a dirt road, and located in a different school district that's on the brink of bankruptcy.

In actual practice, you'll rarely have trouble knowing which properties to include after you've located all the facts. In case of doubt, it's quicker to use two forms and provide more facts to the sellers than it is to agonize over which ones to put on one form.

The properties you want on your CMA are those that the sellers will feel are comparable. You want them to rationalize: "If this property sold for that price, ours must be worth about the same."

Never underestimate the importance of location. In most cases, nearness is one of the most important aspects of comparability, and value differences between neighborhoods can be very difficult to get the sellers to agree on. However, when the two properties being compared are close enough to enjoy the same environment, adjustments can easily be made to reflect the value of a few hundred extra feet of floor space or a few extra amenities on one of the properties. Simply list all the items, place a value on each one, and total them up.

PACKING LISTING POWER INTO THE CMA

When you prepare a thorough CMA, you're almost certain to be presenting a lot of vital information the sellers have never had before. You'll be giving them data about properties they aren't familiar with, and also about properties they know but have only heard talk about. The longer they study your comparable market analysis, the more they'll realize that they're looking at the facts of record, not the fiction of rumor.

Here's what you should put on the comparable market analysis:

1. All active, comparable, nearby properties.

The CMA's for-sale section is your primary tool for showing what the competition is in their neighborhood today. When buyers wanting to live close-by can choose among comparable properties offered in the high seventies, sincere sellers recognize that they can't sell in the high eighties.

Include every sign they'd see walking their dog. The only nearby homes you can safely omit are those a stranger to the area would know aren't comparable to the subject property simply by glancing at them from the street.

What's nearby? Where you operate, what do people think is nearby? The answer to this question depends on whether you're selling ranches in Texas or condos in Connecticut.

2. All comparable properties that have sold within the last six months.

This part of the CMA puts the most reliable floor possible under the value of the subject property by showing what buyers—not looky-lews, not wishful thinkers, but real people spending real money—have been willing to pay for comparable property in the most recent past. The only action that establishes the market value of anything is an actual purchase. However, since there's no guarantee that another buyer who'll pay the same amount for the same thing will appear tomorrow, today's purchase becomes past history the moment it's made. All values change. On the London gold market, the price of the world's longest running measure of value changes daily, demonstrating that even for gold there's no guarantee that tomorrow's price will equal today's. Yet, though past sales are not a perfect base for setting present value, they are the only base we have to work from.

3. All comparable listings in the vicinity that have expired within the past six months.

The third section of the CMA puts a ceiling over the price that the subject property can command. This ceiling over value is as reliable as the floor put under value by section two's record of recent sales. In other words, expired listings tell you how much you can't get for the subject property. Except in highly unusual circumstances, the record tells it like it is. And when that story's told, it's the market speaking, not you. Make that clear. Don't let the sellers blame you for what the market says it won't do.

When there are no highly unusual circumstances and you can show that you've found comparable listings, people who are sincere will accept the market's ceiling. Insincere sellers won't.

You can't make money working with insincere sellers because they won't sell for any price a sincere buyer would pay or a lender would risk money on. That's an obvious point, but I'm amazed at how many agents ignore its sharpness and go on trying to make money where there's no money to be made.

Make a strong effort to find all the comparable listings that have expired. (Also, try not to take all of them from your own previous inventory.)

Research this information. If you're going for a listing appointment in your farm, you should have your own file of comparables that you can pull data from very quickly. It's worth setting that data up in a convenient way, isn't it, since you'll be using it over and over. If your listing appointment is outside your farm, you'll have other sources of information. Look up the cumulative report in your Multiple Listing Book.* Talk to your broker about what data is available in your office.

Many brokers use a service called Comps, Inc. to supply them with information about comparables. Other offices have their own files by tract and area for all sales and expired listings. Many brokers tell me they're discouraged about gathering this data, not because it's time-consuming and costly—which it is—but because they can't get their salespeople to take advantage of it. Your broker probably has all the tools he can't get you to use.

You may not be able to get inside all the comparable properties before your listing appointment—but you can drive by them all. Unless you do that, you're not prepared. You don't deserve the listing. Or perhaps you deserve what you're likely to get—an overpriced turkey.

Preparation plus attitude equals a transaction. In other words, if you have the right preparation and the right attitude, you'll take the listing right—meaning that you'll take it at market price. Whenever you do that, it has to sell. Otherwise, you didn't really list it at market price, did you?

There's another reason why you must drive the area before completing your research. Comparable files are usually set up by number of bedrooms, with all two-bedroom homes listed together, all three-bedroom homes together, and so on. Let's say that you're getting ready for a listing appointment with Ed and Louise Kellner at their

---

*Trademark of the National Association of Realtors.®

three-bedroom home outside your farm. You put all the three bedroom homes for sale in the neighborhood on your CMA, and swing past each of those houses on your way to the listing appointment. This gives you a nasty surprise: there are several properties for sale near the Kellner home that aren't on your CMA. From the street, you can't tell whether they have more than three bedrooms, which would explain why you didn't find them in your research. But there's no time left to check this out.

Later, at the Kellners, you reach the point in your listing presentation when you present the comparable market analysis. As you hand the form over to the Kellners, Ed pulls a piece of paper out of his shirt pocket and unfolds it. He has his own list of homes for sale to compare to yours. Right away, he's asking about three houses that aren't on your CMA.

"They've got to be four bedrooms, or I'd have them on the form," you say.

Staring at his list, Ed frowns. "I'm not sure they all are. Louise, didn't you say you've been in the house on Fig Street that's for sale?"

"That's right. And it's a lot like ours."

"Three bedrooms?"

"Definitely three bedrooms," Louise Kellner says.

Her husband leans back in his chair and says, "I'm sorry, but under the circumstances I don't see how we can make an intelligent price decision tonight."

A few minutes later, you find yourself in the street walking to your car. But you console yourself that all is not lost. You have another appointment with the Kellners for the following evening.

On checking the next morning, you discover why you didn't find the listing Louise Kellner spoke about: it's only a week old and won't show up in the multiple until the next book comes out. Had you driven the area early enough to have time to check new developments out, you would have known that the house on Fig has three bedrooms. While you're thinking about this, you get a call from another agent who says, "I'm afraid that I've got some bad news for you. You know the Kellners? Well, I met with them after you left, and they gave me the listing. Then they told me to give you a call and explain that there's no point in your going back over there tonight."

When I was new in the business, I had an ocean of attitude. I was enthusiastic. But I didn't know what I was doing, so I had no preparation. My wild enthusiasm brought me a few listings, but they were not the material from which transactions are made. Overpriced turkeys never are. An excess of enthusiastic attitude can't make up for a lack of preparation. If attitude is all you have, you won't get any transactions, just as I didn't get any transactions until I mixed a tasty blend of one part attitude and one part preparation.

The sad truth is that some people are all preparation and no attitude. They lose too. Some of the people in my office were professional appraisers. They had the expertise, but they radiated more negativity than any but the toughest of clients could handle. One by one they gave up trying to become high-earning real estate associates and went back to low-paying salaried jobs. No matter how our industry evolves, I promise you one thing: human nature won't change. People will always prefer to be around positive people. It's as certain as the law of physics on the flow of electricity—business will always flow to positive people and away from negative people.

Now let's visit Mr. Tweety. I've mentioned him before. He's the veteran by-owner. He hasn't been through my training, but he's had a lot of under-the-by-owner-sign training. He's heard everything a broker or salesperson can say, and he's perfected his performance.

Whenever you visit any seller, carry a clip board or a legal size pad in a binder. Put a blank CMA form on top.

When I visited a by-owner, you can be sure that I was dressed professionally. That's critical. Drive in there in your nice new car and show them you're successful. (If you don't have a nice new car, getting one should be high on your list of immediate goals.)

I knock on the door, back up, and do all the other fundamental things that we talked about in Chapter 8. Now I know that a doorknock doesn't make Mr. Tweety fearful or he wouldn't have a for-sale-by-owner sign stuck in his front lawn for eight years. But I whistle anyway just to keep in practice. When he answers the door, he instantly knows I'm a salesperson from the way I'm dressed and what I'm carrying. Clang go his defense barriers. He's instantly ready for battle. I begin with a smile.

"Good afternoon. My name is Tom Hopkins with Champions Unlimited. I'm sure you've been visited by other real estate salespeople trying to list your home.

"May I explain my reason for stopping. A family in the area has employed us to help them professionally market their home. To serve them better, I'm in the process of preparing a comparable market analysis of the area.'' Hold up your clipboard. It's important that Mr. Tweety sees the form.

"If you'll be kind enough to show me your home, in appreciation, I'll be happy to give you a copy of my findings. It should greatly aid you in substantiating your value to your prospects. May I step in?''

As with all the face-to-face techniques in this book, the power of the performance is in the words, the way you say them, the timing, and the coordination of movements, expressions, and gestures. That's why you practice the movements as you drill yourself on the phraseology; that's why you rehearse over and over until your entire performance is complete, casual, and effective.

Let's review the psychology of this technique with words that are more pointed than you'd ever use with a seller: "Mr. Tweety, I know you've had a bunch of us come by during the last eight years. I'm not here to list your house; I'm here because I'm working with someone who's sincere about selling. They are employing us to serve them better. I'm going to get some facts for them. Now, if you'll let me see this place, I'll give you a copy of those facts. If you're priced realistically, those facts will help you substantiate your value. If you're overpriced, they'll reveal some helpful truths to you. So you can't lose. May I step in?'' You'd never use those words to a seller because they're too blunt, but the Tweeties of the world will get the message that they can get something for nothing.

You're going to be delighted when one of them looks at you and at the CMA. His mind will be working fast: 'Maybe I can use his information to get more money for the place. What the heck? I'm not going to list it anyway. He's the first one who's said anything decent.'

So he says, "Come in." That's the first step—getting in. Now here's what you do once you're inside the home.

• Make lots of notes.
• Act like you don't want the listing. Avoid antagonizing him, of course, but remember that this isn't the time to start begging and fawning. (It never is.) The moment you beg for the listing with a veteran by-owner, you put yourself in the same class as everyone else, and they'll shoot you down every time. Watch this carefully because it's got to be done exactly as I'll now show you.

"Mr. Tweety, the paneling in the den here is very nice. Did you do that yourself, or was it professionally done?"

"I did it."

"Very, very nice. And the carpeting is upgraded too, isn't it?"

"Yeah. Laid it myself."

"Did you? Well, I want to make note of all these facts that you're giving me on my comparable market analysis. Let me ask you a couple of questions as we walk through."

The two of you have reached the patio. From there, you can see the landscaping in the rear yard. "I'll bet a lot of people who have seen the home have commented on how nice the patio is, haven't they?"

"Yeah, I did that too. I do everything."

"You know one of my problems? I can't do anything with my hands. I have to hire everything done. Luckily, you haven't had to do that. You've probably got yourself in a position here where you're going to make a pretty substantial profit on the place, aren't you?"

"Yeah, I should."

"Tell me, how long have you had the home on the market?"

"Eight years."

"I see."

Now I will walk through as I've done with Mr. Tweety, taking notes, asking questions, complimenting anything that I sincerely can, but not even mentioning listing his home. Watch now as just before I leave, I say, "I want to thank you again for showing me the home, and I wish you the very best of luck in selling it."

I've been getting to Mr. Tweety. I've complimented him and made copious notes so he knows I feel his home is important, but I haven't shown any interest in listing it. Remember, it's vital that you don't let any little hints slip out that you'd sure like to have the listing. So, after my farewell speech, he says:

"Wait a minute, hot shot. What can you get for this place?"

"Mr. Tweety, you were kind enough to let me come in your home to prepare a comparable market analysis for someone in the area. I don't feel that I'd be justified in discussing your home with you at this time. However, since you've asked, I'd be more than happy, when I bring my comparable market analysis back, to go over all the benefits we have. Now, I can't this evening—I have an appointment. Would tomorrow evening at say, six, be convenient—or should I wait until eight?"

"If you're such a pro, how come you don't know right now?"

"I could pick a figure out of thin air, but I'm sure that's not what you want. This is why I don't mind gathering the facts and analyzing my data. So, would tomorrow night be convenient, or would you rather wait until another night?"

"I'm a pretty busy guy, doing all the work around the house. I don't know if I want to be bothered."

"You wouldn't like to have a copy of this information that you asked for when you let me in?"

"Can you mail it to me?"

"Would you prefer that I mail it to you?"

"Yes."

"Fine. I can just drop a little note off to you, and you can look at the figures yourself and arrive at value. And when you're serious about getting market value, I hope you'll call a professional. Thank you again."

That exchange won't happen as often as you'll have them say, "Sure, you can drop it by." When you come back, what do you give Mr. Tweety? Your entire listing performance.

I'll tell you something about Mr. Tweety. I would not want to list his home. If the guy is treating me that way now, who needs the hassle?

I hope the day arrives soon when you can start selecting your sellers as much as they select you. If you're a brand new agent, you're willing to work with anybody you feel physically safe with. If you're a brand new brain surgeon, you'll operate on anybody. But after you've acquired the reputation of being one of the finest brain surgeons, you don't have to take somebody with a hangnail. When you've built a clientele in your real estate practice, you can't afford to waste your time, attitude, and enthusiasm on people who aren't cordial, who don't want to meet the other person halfway, who aren't sincere. One of the things you work for is the privilege of smiling broadly, and courteously referring Mr. and Mrs. Obnoxious to someone who needs the experience.

When I go over to Mr. Tweety's house, do you know what I know in advance of getting there? That I'm not going to get the listing. But I have the greatest opportunity to walk out afterwards and say, "I never see failure as failure but only as an opportunity to practice my techniques and perfect my performance." Because Mr.

Tweety would be tough; he would be mean; and those are the ones you learn from—don't you agree?

INSIDE ANOTHER HOME

Whenever you inspect a by-owner home because you're compiling a CMA for someone else, do these three things:

1. Make notes of the colors.
You want to be able to identify the house by its exterior colors. And you want to be able to discuss the interior too. Knowing the color of the carpet or floor covering is vital. If there's anything about the walls or ceiling, note that too.

2. Convert time on market to days.
Don't do that for Mr. Tweety. He's had his on the market for 2,920 days. If the by-owners says, "We put our sign up three months ago," write down 89 days. Champions work with precise figures. Be articulate. Speak in pointed numbers, not rounded ones. The more factual, accurate, and articulate you are, the more professional you are.

3. Try to get him to ask if you can sell the place.
You dress and act as professional as possible primarily in the hope that they'll say something like, "Hey, hot shot, do you think you can get my price?" "Can you sell the place?" "What do you think you can get for it?"
Then try for the appointment.
Whether or not you get an opportunity to do that, no matter how nasty, mean, and arrogant the by-owner was, send him a thank-you note for letting you see the home so that you could complete your comparable market analysis for your client. Don't make it a poison pen letter. And wouldn't that kind of by-owner be a lovely person to lay the by-owner first-aid kit on? Question-close him.
"Mr Tweety, you've been on the market eight years. Were you going to have the conveyance be the quit claim, bargain and sale, special, or general warranty deed?"
"Oh, you're not sure?" Then he sees that he doesn't know everything, and it gives you another chance to practice.

OTHER BROKERS' LISTINGS

Whenever you go into another office's listing, follow the code of ethics. Respect the other broker's agency as you'd want them to respect your agency at your listings.

We all primarily represent the sellers. I hope you'll never forget that. Our industry was built on the way we've represented sellers in the past, and it'll grow or wither depending on how well we represent sellers in the future. That's why I ask: If we abuse each other when we're talking to clients, how much confidence can the public have in us and our profession?

Sometimes you'll be sorely tempted to let the sellers know how much better off they'd be with you and your firm than with the one they listed with. But if you yield to that temptation—even with nothing more than a raised eyebrow at some strategic moment—you're not only being unethical and unprofessional, you're also being stupid. When you're in another agent's listing, keep your eyebrows straight and your thoughts pure. Let no criticism of the other firm, or praise of your own, escape your lips. Never forget that when you're there, you personify the entire profession. Anything you do that harms the other agent harms the entire profession, yourself included. Don't take this lightly. Unethical conduct, if allowed to feed on itself, can quickly take over in an area. Only you can stop that cancerous growth. If any of this unprofessional conduct is directed at you, don't respond by lowering yourself to that level. Both in the short run and over the long pull, the way to beat the unprofessionals is to be more professional yourself.

The rules and code of ethics vary from one realty board to another. Find out what they are in your area and follow them exactly. In many cities, you are forbidden by the rules and ethics of your local professional organization to drive over and inspect a property listed in the multiple unless you call the listing agent first and obtain his or her permission.

Let's assume that you've done that, and now you're at the door of Pathetic Realty's listing. Again, you're carrying a legal pad so that you can take plenty of notes. Here's the phraseology:

"Good afternoon, Mrs. Simpson. My name is Tom Hopkins with Champions Unlimited. I called and obtained permission from Pathetic

Realty to visit you. As you can see, I don't have a prospective buyer with me at this time.''

If you're not working for that firm, you have to let them know why you're there: "I would appreciate seeing your home so that when I am showing a buyer, I'll be aware of all the improvements you've made.''

Notice the exact words. Did I say that I am going to show their home? No. I said that *when* I'm showing a buyer, I'll be aware of all the improvements they've made.

Once inside the home, you say, "Mrs. Simpson, my purpose in stopping is two-fold. First, to familiarize myself with your property, and secondly, to prepare a comparable market survey for a client in the area who's thinking of having me professionally market his home. May I measure a few rooms and make a list of your improvements?''

If you're dressed professionally, if you use this phraseology with practiced confidence, if you gather information about her property like an expert, is she going to see a difference between your action and that of Fred Blodgett, the full time butcher and when-he-feels-like-it real estate person? This is the property that's been on the market for seven months. Nobody except Blodgett has shown it for 102 days, and Mrs. Simpson thinks there's always something strange about the people Fred brings through. Under these circumstances—and similar things happen far too often in most areas—do you suppose that Mr. and Mrs. Simpson are slightly unhappy they gave their listing to the butcher?

Now let's examine two common ways that sellers react to this situation. In both, Mrs. Simpson decides to come with me as I go through the home. I didn't ask her to, but she's a little curious.

"Mrs. Simpson, that paneling certainly enhances the living room. Did you and Mr. Simpson put that in, or was it professionally done?''

"I chose the wood, and my husband installed it.''

"A very tasteful choice, and your husband is a fine craftsman. The carpeting—it's one of the plushest weaves I've seen. It's new, isn't it?''

"Yes. We re-carpeted a year ago.''

"It gives your entire home an air of elegance.''

I walk through the house with her, trying to establish rapport, and making copious notes. I was professionally dressed and my manner was professional throughout the interview. Now, as I start to leave, what's very likely to take place? Remember that the lady has been waiting for action for seven months, and nothing's happened. Then I come in, open her eyes, and start to leave without including her in the bright world of professionalism I've just let her glimpse. Here's what I say as I'm leaving:

"Thank you again. I appreciate your showing me your home, and I wish you and Mr. Blodgett at Pathetic Realty the very best of luck in selling it, Mrs. Simpson."

"Mr. Hopkins, they're not calling—they're not showing our home. What is the problem?"

"Mrs. Simpson, I'd be happy to talk to you about your problem. However, ethically, while your home is listed, I can't. We at Champions Unlimited believe that our company is founded on ethics. So I hope you'll respect me for that."

I want you to realize what I did with that phraseology. Her home is listed with another firm; ethically I have no right to discuss her problem. Are you thinking, "But that part-timer isn't giving her any service." That doesn't alter the fact that the Simpsons entered into a written agreement with Pathetic Realty; it doesn't alter the fact that the ethics of our profession require—as they should—as they must—that you don't undermine another salesperson's agency. As long as it's listed, you can't discuss the price, the terms, the problems. Champions, don't do it.

And avoid any hint of smug arrogance when you talk about ethics or you'll offend more people than you impress. Say "I hope you'll respect me for that" with humility.

Do most people respect someone who is ethical? Yes, they do. Think about why this is important for a minute. If Mrs. Simpson sees that you're too ethical to take advantage of Fred Blodgett, she'll feel that you wouldn't try to take advantage of them either. And she also feels that, since you don't rely on dirty tricks for your success, you must have ability to be as successful as she's seen you are from the way you dress, the way you conduct yourself, and perhaps in the luxurious car you drive. Your refusal to be unethical, though disappointing to her momentarily, is the final touch that pulls it all together. When her listing with Blodgett the butcher at Pathetic Realty runs out, Mrs. Simpson is very likely to call you. Or, if you work expireds, perhaps you'll call her when you can ethically do so.

Here's the second direction that Mrs. Simpson might take as you're leaving. She might say, "Thanks for stopping by. They just turned my property over to Sally Thompson at Pathetic Realty. She works full time in real estate, and I hope she'll do better. I really like Sally, and I hope you'll call her when you have some buyers."

"So Sally seems to be giving you more service then?"

"Well, yes."

"I haven't met Sally yet. But I will, and when I do, I'm going to tell her you think she's doing a great job. And you're lucky to be doing business with a professional."

What I tried to show you in the above cases is that, if they knock their agent, you don't. But you do take note of their feelings and the fact that when their listing expires, they probably won't renew it with the same company. So if you show the Simpsons' home while you're showing your good listings—and demonstrate that home as I recommend in my selling seminar, tapes, and book—the odds are good that they'll call you when their current listing expires.

When she praised her agent, what did I do? I jumped on the bandwagon, didn't I? Since you're going to be a Champion, I'd like you to know that I, as president of Champions Unlimited, along with all our fine staff, have a basic desire. We all share that desire, which is a great goal. In fact, it's a dynamic and demanding purpose that runs deep and broad through our entire company. By providing quality training that's built on ethical integrity, sympathetic psychology, painstaking service, unflinching honesty, and genuine courtesy, our great goal is to have you, and all the other Champions who work at the same high level you do, earn all the fees in real estate. When that day comes, all the people who shouldn't have a license will have to get out of the business because they can't make any money.

All of us at Champions burn with this goal. I hope you'll make it yours too—nobody in real estate except ethical, honest, skillful, knowledgeable, devoted professionals. Out with the bums.

Out-perform them. Out-service them. Out-think them. But never knock the bums. A Champion never knocks anyone. That's for bushleaguers. Never knock the competition, no matter how richly they deserve it.

FIND A REO WHILE YOU'RE KNOCKING ON DOORS

Real estate orphans are people who are unhappy with the service their agent gave them when they bought their home. Do you know how many REO's are out there? Huge, uncountable numbers.

What does finding real estate orphans have to do with compiling a thorough CMA? Everything. One of the best times to find yourself a promising REO is while you're visiting all the recently sold houses that are comparable to the property you're trying to list. Unless you see them, you can't know how comparable those houses really are, can you?

Here's the Hopkins rule for REO families: When you find them, adopt them. Finding a real estate orphan is another bonus that you get for working up a professional-level comparable market analysis.

Come with me as I knock on the Sweeney family's door. I'm not going there at random. I have reason to believe from my office research that the house the Sweeneys bought and moved into three weeks ago is the closest comparable to the Watt home I'm trying to list. So I'm knocking on that door for two reasons: (1) to get vital information for my comparable market analysis for the Watts, (2) to find out if the Sweeneys are orphans. My approach is based on the probability that the Sweeneys are like most people who've recently moved into a new neighborhood: they don't know all their neighbors yet, and they'd like to meet the nice ones. I go through all the fundamentals at the door. When Mrs. Sweeney speaks to me, I turn to face her and smile.

"Good afternoon. My name is Tom Hopkins, with Champions Unlimited. I understand that you recently moved in, and I wanted to welcome you to our area."

As a real estate person, where is *our area?* Everywhere we service. Perhaps your service area is a five-mile radius around your office, but when you say with a warm smile, "I want to welcome you to our area," what does Mrs. Sweeney think?

"Maybe this man and his family live real close. I'll be nice to him."

"Mrs. Sweeney, I'm in the process of preparing a comparable market analysis for a family near here who are employing me to professionally market their home. I'd certainly appreciate seeing your home for comparative value purposes. Would you mind taking a moment to show it to me?''

Do you know that, when you approach them this way, a lot of new people will take the time to do that?

Once you're inside and have asked a few questions, make a few notes, dropped a few fresh compliments, and built a little rapport, here's what you ask to find out if they're orphans:

"I hope you were happy with the service rendered you by our industry." Avoid saying anything along the lines of "I hope your agent treated you right." You'll sound like the person they're mad at if you do. Never assume there's a problem. In fact, I used to talk myself into hoping there wasn't.

What are you in essence saying when you ask if they're satisfied with the service they received from our industry? The words really mean "Are you happy with the people who sold you your home?" But you wouldn't come right out and say that, would you? I thought not. However, Mrs. Sweeney gets the point, even though you've used the diplomatic wording.

She says, "You know, I'm surprised I even let you in. We've never had problems like this before. We got no service at all. The garbage disposal went out. They won't return our calls. Everything's different than they told us it would be."

Clearly, based on what Mrs. Sweeney blurted out, she's telling me that they are real estate orphans. Whenever I met someone unhappy with real estate people, I used what I call *putting the shoe on the other foot.* I'd smile and say, "So you were unhappy with these people. Obviously, they did not give you service."

They'll agree, won't they?

Then go on with, "If you were the president of a real estate company and a salesperson wasn't giving service to the clients, what would you do?"

What'll they say? Something like, "I'd fire them."

Smile and tell them, "I'm not sure, but I'll bet that's what happened." Move right on to positive things by saying, "I'd love to serve you over the next twenty years. As a specialist in this area, I could better serve you, couldn't I?"

Then I'd put their name and address on a card and mark it "orphan." That same day I'd send them a thank-you note for letting

188 How to Master the Art of Listing Real Estate

me see their home. Then their card would go in my general file. It's so easy. You can do the exact same thing, and it'll work for you just as it worked for me. Within a year of keeping in touch with them, they'll be your people. If they move away, they'll list with you. If they decide to stay in the area for many years, what'll they soon want? A larger home. Then you'll have both a buyer and a seller in the Sweeneys—two transactions from one set of orphans. Or they may decide to buy an investment property. Aren't these multiple possibilities exciting? They all flower on the same vine, the one called adopting orphans professionally.

In my opinion, when you find a family of real estate orphans, establish some initial rapport with them, and stay in touch for a year, you've earned their listing. When you've done that much, you've done more than ninety-five percent of the people who take listings will do, and that gives you ninety-five percent odds.

GATHERING DATA BEFORE CALCULATING VALUE

Use a legal pad of paper to collect facts on all the properties that will appear on your comparable market analysis form. Call that pad your data sheet. Fill up as many pages as possible with written data about the important elements of value each property has. The more useful written data you have, the more professional and competent you'll be about arriving at true market value. Here are the basic items that you note about each property that belongs on your comparable market analysis:

1. Names of people.
A pro knows every property that has a sign on it by the names of its owners.

2. Outside color
A pro also knows every property with a sign on it by its outside color. If you're working in an area where most houses are the same color, find a distinguishing feature about each house to associate it with.

3. Color of carpets.

A Champion tries to find out the color of carpeting—or the type of flooring if the house isn't carpeted—for every property that's comparable to the one he's trying to list. I'll show you why in a moment.

4. Price and terms.

Some sellers don't like to accept this truth, but the market for comparable properties is set by the best (for the buyer) combination of low price and good terms, without being influenced by the worst combination of high price and hard terms. An obvious point? Not to every seller. Many of them will try to tell you that value can be arrived at by some process of averaging the high priced with the low. Those same people would laugh at that idea when buying. The fact is, when comparable properties are offered at significantly different prices, the lowest-priced will always sell first and the highest-priced will be ignored. Of course, the properties must be truly comparable in location, terms, prestige, availability, condition, and amenities. When you see a sale that seems to go against that rule, you can be sure the buyer found an important element of value in the higher-priced property.

5. Time on the market.

This is an important consideration. The pro knows that if a property has been on the market longer than the average selling time, there must be a reason. The pro also knows that, although the reason usually boils down to some combination of unrealistic price and unfavorable terms in the existing market for what's being offered, other factors may be involved. The only way to find out is to see the property inside and out.

6. Urge to sell

When we're looking at other agents' listings, it's easy to overlook another vital factor: the motivation of the sellers. It varies widely—can change quickly—and is very emotional. Although it's often difficult to pin this factor down, probing for the reason and urgency behind their need to sell can give you valuable insights.

To many buyers, terms mean more than price. Many new agents fail to appreciate the crucial importance of terms until they acquire some experience. Young buyers often lack the cash for a large initial investment, but they frequently can qualify for a large monthly payment. Older buyers often have the cash for large initial investments, but they sometimes lack the income to carry large monthly investments. Many houses appeal to only one of these groups. If you're trying to list such a property, work hard to get the terms in line with the needs of the greatest possible number of buyers for that property. If the price is right but the terms are wrong, the listing won't sell.

You've been compiling a comparable market analysis for your listing appointment this evening with Gloria and Jack Watt. Let's review a fraction of the information you've gathered. (All terms are CNTCL—cash to new conventional loan.)

FOR SALE NOW

Simpson home: White exterior, beige carpeting. $97,500. 214 days on market. Weak motivation.

Tweety home: Blue exterior, green carpeting. $185,000. Eight years on market. No need to sell.

Bartlett home: Brown stucco, champagne carpeting. $159,500. 79 days on market. Motivation, weak.

Wenig home: Gray with rock trim, wheat carpeting. $154,000. 23 days on market. Strong motivation.

Moyer home: White with brick trim, camel carpets. $151,995. 7 days on market. Strong motivation. Offer pending.

SOLD PAST 12 MONTHS

Jackson home: Sold for $147,000 in 5 days. This house is six doors from the subject property.

Sanchez home: Sold for $149,750 in 31 days.

Mildue home: Sold for $148,000 in 168 days after being reduced from $165,000.

EXPIRED PAST 12 MONTHS

Ripple home: $169,000 reduced from $179,000. 180 days on market.
Gritz home: $162,500. 270 days on market.
Pomeroy home: $189,950. 90 days on market.

Most of the CMA's you'll compile won't give as clear a message as this one does because you usually won't be able to find as many comparables to work with as the example has. The more real comparables you have, the easier it is to see what the market is doing, and the more successful you'll be at convincing your sellers that you know what's realistic.

The message of the CMA you're taking to the Watts' house is that there's an active market for their property at just under $150,000, but the demand just isn't there for their floor plan at much above that price.

Now let's jump ahead to the situation you'll be working with when you are going over the comparable market analysis with the Watts. You know they were thinking about a price between $190,000 and $200,000. Mr. Watt is holding the form in his hand, and he looks down and sees the Jackson home sold for $147,000. That hits him hard. He thinks about it for a moment and then says, "What about the Tweety home?"

You say, "Oh, you mean the blue home on the corner?" Had Mr. Watt said, "What about the blue house on the corner?" you would have replied, "Oh, you mean the Tweety home." Cross-reference your CMA properties in your head so you can show that you know all the houses well. When you've made that point, smile and answer his question about Tweety's blue house with a question of your own:

"Have you been inside that property?"

They'll usually say no.

"As a professional, I stopped by today to inspect the property so I would be knowledgeable this evening. It's a nice home. They have green carpeting—" And you talk about the home for a moment or two, concluding with something like this: "The Tweetys are nice people. They've been trying to sell their home for about eight years now."

"Eight *years?*" Mr. Watt says.

"That's right." Give him a moment to think about it, and then go on presenting the truth about their property's market value to them. As you do so, frame your wording to constantly remind them that the knowledge you're passing on is fact, not opinion.

Then Mr. Watt says, "The property on Myrtle Street, is that the one with Pathetic Realty's sign on it?"

"Yes, it's white and has a picket fence all around it," you reply.

"Right," says Mr. Watt. "What's it like inside?"

"I visited Mrs. Simpson today," you say. "She was kind enough to show me through her home. It's a lovely place—they've lavished a great deal of thought and care on upgrading their home, just as you folks have. The carpeting is beige and very plush."

Mr. Watt is looking at the CMA form. "It says 214 days here—they've been trying to sell their house for more than six months?"

"You're right—for more than seven months. I think the reason why is shown by the comparable houses that did sell during that time. Of course, the Simpsons aren't my clients, so I can't ethically discuss their real estate problem with them."

"But you think they're priced too high?"

"Mr. and Mrs. Watt, I've never asked a client to make a price decision based on what I think, and I never will. That's why I spend so much time and effort on research—to discover what the market's verdict is. After I've done all the office and field work that's necessary to develop a clear picture of what the market is saying about a specific property, what I think is irrelevant. The market speaks for itself." Smile and then continue, "The market said 'No sale' to the Simpsons, but it said 'Sold' to six other families who offered comparable properties for less money. I've compiled those facts for you in the center section of the form."

Can you picture how devastating this knowledge is when it's used convincingly? Maybe you don't think you can use it convincingly. I hope you're worried about that instead of being too lazy to do the work. I can guarantee you this: if you'll thoroughly research your comparable market analysis—including visits to all properties on it—you'll be convincing because you'll know you're working with convincing facts.

What if they won't let you in the home at any of these doors? Just glance down and see what color the carpet is. Then look the property over carefully from the sidewalk, making copious notes as you do so. Do everything you properly can to be more prepared at the listing appointment than the sellers are.

INSPECTING THE PROPERTY

In the previous section we jumped ahead to the evening appointment. We'll do that again, but please remember that we're still preparing for that appointment. Let's talk about another important part of the preparation. You must inspect the subject property—the one you're trying to list—before your night meeting with the husband and wife.

If they both work, you won't be able to get inside the house during the day, but you'll always be able to drive over to it. Later in this chapter, we'll discuss the important afternoon meeting with one of the sellers—usually the wife. Whether or not you can get an afternoon appointment, do these four additional things when you visit the property during the day.

1. Find the messiest house on the street.

On almost every street, there's a home that's outstandingly messy on the outside. Take the Smedleys. They live four doors from the Watts and their home is a dump. The Smedleys have beat up old cars all over the front yard. One has flat tires and a bush growing where the engine used to be. What grass the oil spills haven't killed, the Smedleys never mow. And their front door has a hole that looks like it was made by somebody's head. The place is the eyesore of the neighborhood, and everyone knows the Smedleys don't care.

I used to look for them. Bear in mind that, even if the neighborhood eyesore isn't all that bad, it's still a very sore spot with your sellers. I always highlighted the messiest house on the street in my data sheet. Here's how the pro uses the eyesore during the listing presentation:

"Mr. and Mrs. Watt, I hope you realize that I in no way believe in knocking anyone. However, as your agent, I'm going to suggest that when people show your home, they bring them in off Baldwin Street instead of off Chamberlain. The reason is, there's a property four doors down the hill that I really believe takes away from the loveliness of your home.''

Do they know about that home? You can bet on it. Mrs. Watt says, ''You mean the Smedleys. Those creeps.''

Here again, you're pointing out another reason why you're worth your fee, and at the same time demonstrating your knowledge of their neighborhood and their situation.

2. Landscaping inspection.

On the legal size pad you're carrying to gather data about the subject property and the comparables—write a little story about the landscaping. I used to write something like this:

''Landscaping should be okay. However, might consider increasing the watering to green up the grass for better showing. Might consider pulling the three weeds on the south side of the home.''

What does that tell the Watts when I walk in after dark tonight with that information in my listing folder? That I've been there and done physical research. Do you see the power in this? I'm demonstrating competence, energy, and interest in serving them.

You see, when I walk in many times they're thinking, ''We have no intention of listing with anyone.'' But my efforts are obligating them to me emotionally in case they change their minds. Beyond that, I'm also giving them logical reasons for the emotional decision to list with me tonight by warmly demonstrating my expertise at the same time.

3. Paint condition.

This one works like magic. In your service area, how many homes do you think have been painted within the last five years—one out of three? If that's about right, the other two out of three homes—the ones that need repainting—are prime candidates for this technique. We're talking about average paint on average houses. An appraiser will agree that the home is suffering from deferred maintenance (lack of normal upkeep) if the house hasn't been repainted within the past five years. When your subject property is in this condition, use this technique. But don't use it when the paint looks bright from a distance and is just peeling and falling off a little here and there because this technique won't work unless the house really needs repainting. The old paint job must be faded and rough and somewhat weathered away. Perhaps the wood underneath is cracking.

The average seller whose home is in this condition knows the house needs repainting. Often they're thinking, "I'm saving by not having to paint the place—I'll put that money into our new home."

When the house you want to list needs repainting, scrape off a small amount of stucco or wood trim with a pen knife and put the paint chips in an envelope. Don't carve, just scrape. And do your scraping on the side of the house where it won't be noticed. Put the envelope of paint chips in your listing folder.

When you bring the envelope out that evening, here's what you *don't* say: "Mr. and Mrs. Watt, I've got to tell you that your home has to be painted before it'll sell for value." Do they like that? No. Will they paint the house because I told them to? No. Am I further from getting a market-price listing? Yes. My psychology was wrong. A Champion turns the need for repainting into a listing tool with this phraseology:

"Mr. and Mrs. Watt, the buyer will probably want to repaint within the next year to put the home in top market condition, don't you agree?"

If the sellers do agree, they are also agreeing that their home is not in top market condition. That's an important agreement.to get, isn't it, because your listing performance succeeds only if you can get them down to within bargaining distance of market value.

Here's how you handle the paint chips envelope. You'll be sitting in front of them during your listing presentation. Look at your listing folder and say, "I came by today and inspected the home." Pick up the envelope now. "The landscaping should be fine. You might consider pulling that little patch of weeds on the south side. The paint condition, though . . . " Rip open the envelope and pour the contents in the middle of the table. Don't have a huge mound—enough chips to cover a half-dollar will do fine. As you talk, move these chips around with your finger. "Mr. and Mrs. Watt, the buyer will probably want to repaint the home during the next year to put it in top market condition, don't you agree?"

"Well, yes, I suppose they might," Mr. Watt says.

"How long has it been since the exterior was painted?" you ask.

"Five years."

"I took some shavings here just in case you thought it would be a wise decision to paint the exterior. I could get some bids. If we matched the color as closely as possible, you could save some money. We could probably repaint the exterior for $1,500 to $1,800.

"On the other hand, you may want to wait and just let the buyer do the painting, and we could reflect that cost in the total investment that we arrive at."

Do you see the strategy here? I offered the service of getting bids and helping them decide on getting the painting done. However, if they don't want to do that, we can reflect the paint condition in the asking price that we agree on.

Perhaps you're sitting there thinking, "They won't come down $1,800 just for that."

Only very highly motivated sellers will right away. But your attention to the paint condition detail is just one more lever to move the pricing decision of most sellers closer to market value.

By the way, when you present an offer that's a little below their asking price because they started above market, guess what you pour out on their kitchen table again?

The paint scrapings in the envelope.

4. Roof Condition

I'm not a roofer, but I can tell whether a roof will last through the closing. I'm sure you can too. Here's the dissertation I'd love for you to write about the roof:

"Roof should be okay. However, if government financing used, may require roof certification."

Did I say that it must have a roof certification before the home can qualify for government-insured financing? No. I said it *may* require it. Imagine the scene as I discuss their roof with both the Watts that evening. From time to time during my listing presentation, I've flipped over a page of my legal pad. I have it out where they can see it at all times. Things like the dissertation above are written legibly. Here's how you handle this aspect like a pro:

"Mr. and Mrs. Watt, when I was by today, I inspected the roof and it should be okay. However, if government financing were to be used, they may require a roof certification."

"What's that?"

"Let me explain. Both the Federal Housing Administration and the Veteran's Administration, the FHA and the VA, guarantee or insure home loans. Our best buyers may be people who can't or won't make the purchase unless they can obtain the favorable terms of government backed loans. For that to happen, the buyers must qualify as good credit risks. Your home must also qualify as a good credit risk, because it's the property that secures the loan. In order for a property to qualify, the appraisers must give it a certificate of reasonable value. Unless that document is in the file, the sale won't go through.

"In their appraisal processes, both the FHA and the VA pay close attention to a roof that's over five years old. Before issuing the certificate of reasonable value, they may require that a certified contractor inspect the roof and give them what's called a roof certification. Basically, it means that the expert says the roof is in good shape.

"However, today we have many sources of conventional home financing. So we may not be using a government-insured loan. On the other hand, the new graduated payment FHA 245 program is becoming very popular. You may want to consider that program. Of course, as your agent I'll do my very best with the buyer or the buyer's agent to secure the type of financing that will save you as much money as possible.*

"I guess what I'm really trying to say, Mr. and Mrs. Watt, is that when you do business with me, I won't let there be any surprises."

SURPRISE IS A LISTING WORD

The entire speech given above has two important goals. The first is to set up your discussion of the fact that home financing is complex, and you know your way around in it—you have a complete understanding of the intricacies of FHA, VA, conventional, and creative financing. The sellers probably have never heard of a certificate of reasonable value before. Now, if they've had any thought

---

*In Canada refer to Canadian government insured and participation types of financing.

of trying to sell themselves, they're beginning to realize just how involved real estate transactions really are.

The second reason for your roof performance is to set up the last sentence in the speech: "I guess what I'm really trying to say, Mr. and Mrs. Watt, is that when you do business with me, I won't let there be any surprises."

What is the one thing that everyone marketing a property is afraid of?

Surprise.

When you're moving far away, when you're squeezing to buy the next house and pay for the move, when you're committed to any of the things that people selling houses commit themselves to, what happens when you get hit with a new surprise?

At the very least, you're anxious. You worry about the unexpected—and usually still unknown—costs and inconveniences of the latest surprise. And there's always the fear that the new problem will bring your entire move to a halt.

"We have to get a termite inspection."
Surprise.
"There's dry rot around the shower."
Surprise.
"The appraisal came in low."
Surprise.
"The VA is insisting on gutter downspouts."
Surprise.
"We have to paint the wood trim to pass certification."
Surprise.
"The buyer didn't qualify."
Surprise.
"The second buyer is trying to back out."
Surprise
"The $50 deposit isn't binding them."
Surprise.

I hope you see the psychology behind me saying, "I guess what I'm trying to say is that, when you do business with me, I won't let there be any surprises." Every surprise costs them pain and money. So tell them that you won't let any surprises slip up on them.

Another reason for your afternoon visit is to decide whether giving the roof performance is the best launching for the financing and surprise discussions. If you decide it's not, devise another way to put these techniques in action for you this evening. They're too important to miss out on just because the house is new or government financing isn't available.

ROLL YOUR OWN BOILERPLATE

Professionals use it to help them do a better job in less time. What is boilerplate? It's written material that can be used over and over. Attorneys put boilerplate paragraphs in wills, agreements, and court documents; doctors hand boilerplate diets and instructions to patients; architects write specifications in boilerplate format today so they won't have to work up the same specifications tomorrow for a similar job.

Nearer to what you're doing, the top people in commercial leasing and industrial site location use boilerplate to give their clients a large amount of information about a community's climate, population, facilities, and resources.

You must do the same. Gather information about your service area. Then write a story that highlights the local parks, schools, shopping, bus service, church locations, freeway or turnpike access, weather, cultural and economic opportunities, and any other features that contribute to the good life there.

The usefulness of boilerplate to inform possible buyers about your service area is obvious; its usefulness with sellers isn't. Let me explain how it will help you take listings.

People usually believe that they bought in a good part of town. If they try to go by-owner, they'll push the area hard to out-of-town prospects. Sellers know that buyers have to buy the area or it's no sale on the house, so they want to know that you'll promote the neighborhood enthusiastically and effectively. That's why you have the boilerplate in your listing presentation manual—it lets you quickly convince the sellers that you're an outstanding expert on, and booster of, the community they're leaving and you're staying in.

By the way, won't you sound more convincing when you tell buyers that your service area is the greatest place in the world to live than would someone who's leaving? You might want to make this point to a few sellers.

Put your boilerplate together in sections; each section covers only one subject. Let's say you start with churches. Your local paper runs a special page on church services every weekend; you can type up a complete list of church locations from that page and have your first section done in a few minutes. Its heading is OUR LOCAL CHURCHES.

At the bottom of every page of boilerplate, type this line: "Compiled by _____." Keep the boilerplate originals in a folder and run copies as you need them.

A moment's thought will tell you where to get information on each category. Parks? Visit the city or county recreation department and get copies of their handouts. You'll probably be able to make up a beautiful piece of boilerplate just by cutting out and pasting up the printed material that's available free from the school superintendent's office, the chamber of commerce, and the city hall.

Write your boilerplate about all the benefits and amenities of the area that you'll tell buyers about, and then make a list of the disadvantages, the detriments, the problems that the neighborhood has. The sellers may be leaving, but you're staying—and you want to make clients of the buyers, not enemies. You want them to know the disadvantages before they make their decision. And some of those disadvantages may need to be reflected in the market value of the property.

Let's list a few of the possible disadvantages:

1. Known flood or earthquake danger.
2. Built on landfill, with danger of settling.
3. Located on, or behind, a busy street.
4. Tributary streets leading to the main highway are badly congested during rush hours.
5. Industrial or aircraft noise.
6. Downwind from the garbage dump, hog farm, pulp mill, or nuclear generating plant.
7. No sewers.
8. The elementary school is located on the other side of a major highway.

There are many other possibilities, and not every disadvantage is important to every buyer. Here's a good test. Does the seller want to conceal a particular disadvantage? If so, the buyer must be told about that disadvantage. How important the disadvantage is to a given buyer is for that buyer to decide. It's your obligation to represent the seller to the fullest extent possible *without injuring the buyer*. In other words, as a real estate professional who is or soon will be a Champion, you're building a career based on honesty, service, and knowledge. You can't do that without being fair to buyers.

Many sellers fail to grasp what a dangerous position they put themselves in if they conceal problems from a buyer. The next-to-worst thing that can happen occurs when the buyer discovers the concealed problem just before settlement and backs out at the last minute. The worst hits later, when a problem discovered after the closing winds up in court, and both the agent and seller have to pay damages. Think before concealing. Honesty is the best policy because it charges the lowest premiums.

Tell the buyers of any disadvantage or problem that isn't obvious. They can see for themselves that there are no sidewalks, but they may never suspect that the basement floods until the rains come.

LISTING IN TWO STEPS

A professional lister always tries to do it in two steps. Many Champions have told me that they get the listing thirty percent of the time using one step, and their average goes up to seventy percent when they do both steps. These figures parallel my own listing experience.

Step one is an afternoon appointment with the wife; step two is the actual listing presentation to both wife and husband that usually takes place in the evening. I talk about meeting with the wife in the afternoon, but sometimes it's the husband who's at home during the day while the wife is out pursuing her career.

Since half a couple can't list without the other spouse's approval, why do I want to see one of them in the home during the day?

To learn how to take the listing.

Why blunder in there tonight and try to guess how to win the listing, when you can walk in this afternoon and find out exactly how to do it? That's what the pro does. Let's pick up the phraseology after you've made the evening appointment. This all occurs during your morning phone conversation with Gloria Watt.

"Mrs. Watt, I'd like to stop by for a few minutes this afternoon if that's at all possible. You see, it'll help me do a better job this evening when Mr. Watt is there if I can see the home first. I have a considerable amount of research to do before this evening, and the more I know about your home, the more accurate and valuable my research will be to you and Jack. Would one o'clock this afternoon be convenient, or should I make it around two?"

Be sure that you explain, as I did, why you want to see their home before night. Otherwise she may think you're just snooping around trying to find out if they're talking to any other agents. The Watts live in your listing bank, and Gloria called you when Jack came home and said, "They made it official today. We're transferred and promoted. So we have to sell this place. Got any ideas who we should talk to?"

Gloria says, "I'd like to check with this one man who's been around three or four times. I told you about him."

"The guy who gave us the pumpkin?"

"That's right, honey. He's really nice."

"Okay, call him up. See if he can get over here tomorrow night. As soon as you set a time with him, I have a couple of other real estate people I want to check with. Let's see what the best of them can get for us."

What's Jack out to do? He wants to learn everything you know so that he doesn't need you anymore. Does that sound familiar? It does if you've been in the business for long. Your job is to know so much that Jack soon realizes he doesn't have time to learn all you know—so he does need you.

When you go over to the Watts' home at two this afternoon, be professional. Go through all the fundamental steps just as you've done every other time you've knocked on that door. And be on time. You're there not only to learn how to take the listing, you're also there to demonstrate expertise and reliability so that you'll have the wife on your side tonight. Being late won't help.

As you walk through the door (notice that I'm suggesting you address her by surname at this point) use this phraseology:

"Mrs. Watt, it would be a great help to me, and enable me to do a more professional job this evening, if you'd be kind enough to show me all the things you've enjoyed in your home."

You have your legal pad with you, of course. And you'll make lots of notes, won't you? These notes are invaluable. Sometimes I knew exactly how to work with a couple before I was half way through step one, but more often it wasn't until I'd taken my notes back to the office and worked over them that it dawned on me how to best handle the upcoming listing appointment.

The next three techniques will be a tremendous help in getting set for that appointment.

1. Taking the measurements.

Jack Watt made it clear to Gloria that he's going to try to sell their home himself. He asked her to have you come by and he called the other real estate people because he wants to get all the free information he can. That's standard. The pro expects it. Now, walking through the home in the afternoon with Gloria Watt, you have a hundred-foot cloth measuring tape inside your legal binder where she can't see it. The end of the tape is sticking out so you can easily pull it out.

"Mrs. Watt, the paneling gives this room a very cozy feeling. It looks like it was professionally done—or did you do that yourselves?"

"We had a contractor put it in."

"Very nice."

Have you noticed that I ask about the paneling in every mythical house we visit? I do that for good reasons. The question is designed to let you compliment their taste without sounding insincere. Also, since it's an alternate of choice, the question is an effective way to get her talking on safe subjects. You can use a similar question about a skylight, the French doors, whatever. Please don't lock onto paneling. I don't want you to feel like saying, "Don't you have any paneling in this place? I can't get started without it."

"The carpeting looks like it's very upgraded. Am I right in assuming that?"

"You're right."

Look for an off-sized room, a family room or a den, that the homeowner probably doesn't know the dimensions of. You walk into the den. "Oh, this is a nice large room, Mrs. Watt. Do you know its exact size?"

"I'm not sure."

As if you're looking at the room to gauge its size, turn your back and pull out the end of the tape. Then warmly smile and say, "I'd like to check. Would you help me measure it, please?"

"Oh. I'm not sure we're going to sell." She's beginning to realize that you're taking her call seriously—that you're a professional who means business.

"I understand that, Mrs. Watt. Your husband would want a professional job this evening wouldn't he?"

"Yes."

"I don't mind the extra effort. May we?"

She can't say no when you're so nice, and when you want to work harder to serve them better. So you measure the room and note down the dimensions. Then start rolling the tape up and say:

"Mrs. Watt, the longer I'm in real estate, the more I find that people really demand accuracy from the professionals who represent them. This why I measure everything to the inch, because, I'm sure you'll agree, accuracy today is important, isn't it?"

"Yes, it is." What else can she say? "Oh, no, we like to work with sloppy, careless people."

Now she's agreed that accuracy is important, and by implication, that you are an accurate professional. What you do now depends on how she reacts to measuring the first room. If she isn't comfortable helping you do it, stop after the first room. But if she's going along with you, measure every room in the house.

2. Warming your listing chances at the water heater.

You don't have to know anything about plumbing to use this powerful special technique. All you need to learn is the phraseology and two words, galvanic corrosion. A number of processes go under that name but we're interested only in one: the corrosion that takes place when two different metals are in contact around the hot water heater. The most common situation involves copper pipes connected to a galvanized steel water heater. Unless the two metals are insulated from each other, an amazing thing takes place: a type of electricity literally rots the galvanized steel out. That's a quick and simple definition of galvanic corrosion. If you'd feel stronger with a little more jargon to throw around, galvanic corrosion is the migration of ions from a base metal such as iron or steel to a noble metal such as copper. The migration is caused by an electrical current created by their contact. This electrochemical process is enormously speeded up by the presence of sodium, that is, salt. As you know, our drinking water contains minute amounts of salt. So everything necessary for galvanic corrosion to rot out the steel is present if copper is part of the system. Then the only thing holding off galvanic corrosion is the insulator between the two different metals. Usually, the copper pipes are hooked on about an inch from the water heater. The first thing to wear out from electrolytic attack is the insulation, and some builders use very inexpensive couplings. Of course, when the pipes rot out, unpleasant consequences follow for the homeowner.

Maybe you're not interested in plumbing school. But you are interested in becoming a strong lister. Let me show you how to put this little bit of knowledge to work. At an opportune moment, use this phraseology:

"Mrs. Watt, would you mind showing me your water heater?"

"The hot water heater—?" The odds are good that she's hardly given it a thought since they moved in.

"Yes. I'd like to check three things: the gallonage, the recovery rate, and the condition of the pipes. And that's the best place to look. Would you mind?"

"No." Usually she's puzzled by this move of yours. Gloria Watt doesn't know whether she should be annoyed or impressed, but she's beginning to suspect that you're a very thorough and knowledgeable pro.

You walk down the hall with her and she shows you where the water heater is. I used to get down so I could check the gallonage and recovery rate on the label, and also check for corrosion. I'd make my notes and then look carefully at the pipes. While I was doing that, the homeowner would be watching closely. Then (unless I'd discovered a water heater that was about to blow) I'd say,

"Well, it looks fine. What I was really checking for is a thing we in the industry call galvanic corrosion."

Now, you have to explain what that is. Give her the quick definition of it above. See how simple that was? I don't care if you don't understand it—of course, it's much better if you do—this is a terrific opportunity to demonstrate knowledge.

Did you notice that I slid one other little item into my water heater technique? I mentioned recovery rate. Lots of people might expect a real estate expert to know the gallonage of a water heater just by looking at it. But you can't tell the recovery capacity without looking at the label. What is recovery capacity? Let's compare two 50-gallon water heaters. The recovery capacity for Brand A is 20-gallons an hour, and for Brand B it's 40-gallons an hour. This means that Brand B heats water twice as fast as Brand A does, which can be very important to a family that uses lots of hot water in a short period of time.

3. Cooling your listing problem with their air conditioner.

Again, we demonstrate knowledge through a practiced technique. For this one, ask the tonnage of their air conditioning, convert that into British Termal Units, and give it back to them. It's really very simple. Here's how I do it. As I walk down the hall with the wife on the afternoon scouting trip, I noticed on the thermostat whether they have refrigerated air. The Watts do. So I say,

"Mrs. Watt, I notice that you have refrigerated air conditioning. Do you know the tonnage of the unit?"

Of course, if it's nice and cool inside and 105 degrees outside, that's another clue. In that case, you'd say something like,

"It's delightful to come into this refrigerated air on a day like this. You must have the right-sized unit. Do you know its tonnage?"

"Three tons."

"Oh, then you have 36,000 British Thermal Units. That should be more than sufficient, based on the square footage. Excellent."

There are 12,000 British Thermal Units per ton. A pro never talks in terms of tonnage—it's British Thermal Units, or BTU's, all the way. Many people have heard of BTU's, but they don't know what they are. A British Thermal Unit is equal to one degree of Fahrenheit in a pound of water. Let's say you have one pound of water boiling at 212 degrees. Take away 180 BTU's from that pound of water and you'll have a pound of soft ice. Pump another 32 BTU's out. That pound of ice now is solidly frozen at zero degrees Fahrenheit. Put 105

British Thermal Units back in the pound of ice and you'll have a pound of water ready for your hot tub. Simple, isn't it? Each ton of air conditioning represents the capacity to remove 12,000 British Thermal Units of heat in an hour. When they mention tons, give them British Thermal Units.

I took a listing from a by-owner one day just because of this BTU technique. If you get one more listing a year because you read this book, it'll be worth it, don't you agree? If you'll practice, drill, and rehearse all the techniques in this book, and then put them to use the way I tell you to, you'll get five more listings a month. Maybe ten. But let me tell you about my BTU listing. We had a pet by-owner in the office. A pet by-owner is the one who hates real estate people. I'm sure that your service area has one. Ours lived on Ahart Street. His attitude toward real estate agents was best described by one word: vicious. So, naturally, we sent all our new people over to see him as sort of an initiation. It was kind of fun—for the old-timers, that is.

One day I heard about a really enthusiastic young man who was joining our firm. We'll call him Steve because that's not his name. He was about twenty-two at the time. I was working diligently at my desk—writing thank-you notes or something—when young Steve walked up and said, "Are you Tom Hopkins?"

I agreed that I was.

"I heard about you all through the training. You're supposed to be the best in the company."

"Thank you. I sure work hard."

Steve said, "I hear you specialize in by-owners."

"Yes, they're my favorites. I get about eight of them a month."

Steve said, "Well, I want you to know that I'm going to work by-owners, and you're going to have some competition."

I smiled and said, "You know, the water's just great. Jump on in."

All the guys in the office had heard him. One of them, an old pro named Bob, spoke up. "Steve, you want to work by-owners? I just heard about a new one. Come on over here and have a seat."

They talked at Bob's desk for a moment. Then Steve jumped up and ran for his car, calling out, "Thanks a lot, Bob," over his shoulder as he went.

Bob watched him go and then grinned at the rest of us. "I sent him over to see the animal," he said.

When Steve came back an hour later, his face was flushed. He looked tired. We were all pretending we weren't waiting for him. After a minute, he said, "Don't even go near that new by-owner on Ahart Street. The man should be locked up—he's crazy."

Everybody burst out laughing, and Steve stood there for a moment wondering why. Then it dawned on him that he'd been had. He wasn't too happy about it. So he marched up to my desk and said, "Hopkins, you're supposed to be so great—you couldn't even list that one."

Everybody in the office heard the challenge, and that put my pride on the line. Trying to get out of it without losing face, I said, "I'll bet you $100 I can list that by-owner in three weeks." That'll shut him up, I thought.

No way. Steve didn't hesitate a second. "You're on."

"Oh, great," I said. I felt so stupid about getting myself committed to listing the animal that I hardly heard the whole office roaring with laughter at how the joke had been turned on me. When you're the top producer, they love to get you in a corner to see what you'll do—which is fine. Challenges are wonderful training; they make you rise far above your ordinary level.

Then Steve made a mistake. Never give a pro information after you've bet against him. Steve did. "Tom, you shouldn't have taken the bet. That guy isn't playing with a full deck. Before he threw me off his lawn, all he talked about was his dumb air conditioning. Can you believe it? The nut has a pair of five-ton units on that little foruteen-hundred-foot box he lives in."

I didn't want to lose any time—never a good idea when you've put yourself in a jam—so I took the information and drove over to Ahart Street. A couple of blocks from the house, I pulled to the curb and spent ten minutes psyching myself up. Then I drove in his driveway.

The by-owner saw me pull in. That same instant he knew I was in real estate from my car and the way I was dressed. The vibes of viciousness hit me before I got out of the car. But I expected that. I went right into my approach:

"Good afternoon. My name is Tom Hopkins. I stopped by because your sign is in my service area. If I have someone in the car that I can't serve, and if they like the outside of your home, could I just send them over here?"

He had a snarly, sarcastic way of talking. "Why would you do that?"

I said, "Well, I know if I sent you a qualified purchaser, you probably wouldn't mind sending back anyone who didn't buy your home, would you?"

He still felt like snarling. "I wouldn't pay one of you people a commission for anything."

I said, "Now, hold on. Your home is in my service area." I paused for a second and looked at him. "If you sell it yourself, there would be no commission." I waited another instant. "Besides, I came by for another reason. I heard something today that I could not believe." I lowered my voice and said slowly, "Do you, in fact, have two 5-ton air conditioning units on this home?"

The man swelled up with pride and the snarl vanished. "I sure do."

I waved my arms and said, "Sir, based on your having one hundred and twenty thousand British Thermal Units, I'd like to inform you that you've got the greatest cooling capacity of any structure in this city."

He said, "Why don't you step in and look at the rest of the place?"

Two and a half weeks later I took that listing. Without getting inside, I never could have. And I would never have seen the inside of that home if I hadn't expressed appreciation for what the owner thought was important. To that man, being able to take his home down to twelve degrees was critical!

All these little things are important. You may be wondering if you can make them work for you. You can. Make yourself practice them. When you've done one once with·a seller, that technique is yours from then on. It becomes a permanent part of your performance.

THE MAIN REASON YOU'RE THERE

That's what we're going to discuss now. The main reason for your step one meeting during the day is to find the answer to this question: How can I list these people?

You'll get the answer to that question if you'll ask the right leading questions in an unthreatening way. This means that your manner and tone are casual as you do so. And you put a lot of spacer material between the leading questions—meaning that you don't keep pounding in to get the vital information zap, zap, zap. Instead, you talk on safe subjects for a while, slip in a leading question, and go back to talking easy stuff for another few minutes. Then, as though it just occurred to you, ask another leading question.

As you go through the house with her, keep looking for things to compliment, for things to talk about, for things you have in common. Be sure that you don't give away that you're using technique. She can't know that you're there to ask specific questions; she can't know that you even know what you're going to ask her. If you're a new Champion, until you've memorized this material and used it repeatedly with sellers, write these questions where you can hide them in your legal pad. Then you can check what questions you should ask when she's not looking. Here are the leading questions:

1. Past selling experience.

If they've sold seventeen homes themselves in the past ten years, it's a fair bet that they aren't listing with anyone now. So you casually ask, "Have you folks sold another home before?"

2. Past problems.

This one can put the listing right in your hand. If I know what problems they've had with real estate sales and agents in the past, I can figure out how to show them in my performance this evening that they won't have those problems with me. So, after you've discussed the previous sales they've made, you ask: "Did you have any difficulties?" You'd probably add, "—with the house you sold in Minneapolis?" or "—with any of the three homes you sold before you moved here?"

3. Need to sell.

When you're taking a listing, the most powerful tool in the world is knowing why they need to sell. And by that I mean knowing the real reason, not what you might guess. Here's how you ask this question, and notice how well it'll fit in after you've complimented something they've done to the house:

"You've done a nice job on the home. After all this work, why would you ever consider moving?"

By setting this question up right and then asking it sympathetically, I usually got the results I wanted: the owner usually told me the real reason they were selling. Had I come right out with a blunt, "Why are you selling your place?" she might not tell me that they've been transferred to another part of the country. Instead, she might say, "Oh, we both want a bigger home, but we don't have to sell—and maybe we won't."

4. Their value.

What are they thinking about price? I want to know before I go in for the big showdown tonight. Don't rush into this one. You'll often find that the normal flow of conversation will give you a beautiful opening for it. But don't wait until she's starting to fidget either, because it's one of the most important questions you're there to find the answer to. You should ask it in these exact words:

"To do a better job this evening, Mrs. Watt, do you have an approximate idea of what you would like for the home?"

Practice saying this with the attitude that whatever she says has no bearing on your chances of getting an at-market listing tonight. You must keep a poker face here. Let's say you know the home is worth about $75,000, and she looks you right in the eye and says, "We want $90,000." If you choke up—or break out laughing—you're finished. Show no emotion no matter what she says about price.

5. Her likes.

Ask her the things she likes about the home. I used to say, "Gloria, pretend that I'm a buyer. What are the things you like most about this house that you think I'll like best too?"

Many of the things she'll mention will be features her husband likes also. By finding them out, you can make sure that you let the husband know you appreciate those things this evening.

6. Loan documents

If she's been nice and warm and helpful, go with this question; if she hasn't been, pass it up because you can hurt yourself with it.

Ask for their loan or mortgage number. If she gets the tin box out to find it, try to get all the papers to her house. Now, if the lady has been suspicious and uptight, you'd be in trouble trying to do that. But if she's friendly and unworried, you can jump a big step forward by taking the papers after giving her a receipt for them. Then bring them back promptly for your evening appointment.

"I'd like to try to ascertain information about your loan for this evening. Now, it would help me do that if I could get the mortgage number. Most people have all the papers to the house in one box. Do you have a place like that?"

If she says, "Oh, no, all the papers are in a safe deposit box at the bank," tell her, "I'll try my best without them." But she may say, "Oh yes, we have a box with all the papers in it; I'll go get it." When she brings the box, if there's a good feeling going between us, I'll say, "You know what I'd love to do? If I could get the legal description off the deed, get the lot size off the title insurance policy, check the insurance papers, confirm the loan balance, I'll certainly be more knowledgeable for your husband this evening. Why don't I give you a receipt on my card and just take the papers. I'll bring them back tonight."

Now the odds are good that she won't let you have them. But if she doesn't give you the papers, what'll she let you have to buy you off from taking them?

All the information from those papers.

Unless she's relaxed about letting you have them, say something like, "Gloria, I think you're a little uptight about my taking the papers. Just give me a moment to look at the covenants, conditions, and restrictions, and at the title insurance policy, and let me copy off the information. That's all I need."

She'll almost always give you the go-ahead to do that. But sometimes she'll say, "Take the box. You can bring it back tonight." If that happens, I guarantee they won't list with anyone else before you return.

7. Tonight's table.

Early in my career I discovered that it's very difficult to take a listing while you're all sitting in easy chairs in their living room. The mood is all wrong. When you speak some truth that doesn't delight the husband, he'll exchange looks with the wife. She doesn't know what the look means except that it's not a yes-let's-go-ahead-tonight kind of look. They can give signals while you're writing, and before you know it, they're out of control. If that happens, suddenly they have to sleep on it; they have to think about it; they have to talk to their real estate advisor friend.

You want them sitting across from you at the table—either the kitchen or the dining room table. The kitchen table is best because it's usually cozier and more intimate. And there's a subtle shift of authority toward the woman when you and the husband are in her kitchen. That helps if she's the one you've met several times, she's the one who called you, and you impressed her with your expertise in step one.

If you're not controlling them, they'll try to control you. So set it up with the wife to have your meeting at the kitchen table if possible, at the dining room table if not. Toward the end of your step one interview in the afternoon, do this by saying,

"Gloria, tonight I'll be presenting the results of my research to you and your husband. I don't know what conclusion it will point to yet, but I'm confident both of you will want to give it careful consideration. To help you do that, and to keep us all from getting lost shuffling papers around, I'd like to ask for your help on one small but very important thing."

"What's that?"

"Could we meet at the kitchen table instead of in the living room? I know it doesn't sound like it's worth mentioning, but if I'm running back and forth with papers, I can't do a professional job for you and your husband."

She'll rarely turn you down when you sincerely ask for her help with those words.

"Okay, sure," Gloria says.

Rope it down tight with, "I'd really appreciate your having the table ready for our meeting with Jack, Gloria."

As you're leaving, confirm the time of your appointment this evening. Unless you remind her, she may forget. Here's how I'd make it seem very real. When I was ready to leave, I'd look at my watch and say, "Well, it's after three already—which means I have less than five hours to finish my research and get back here for our eight o'clock appointment this evening. Thank you so much, Gloria. I'll see you and Jack at eight o'clock sharp. Goodbye.''

PREPARATION BACK AT THE OFFICE

Please, before you do anything else, get ready for your evening appointment. This is particularly important when you're new in the business or new to using Champion technique. Don't get sidetracked by any of the other things you could be doing so that you run out of time and have to rush this final and most important phase of your listing-taking routine. Once you're listing in high volume, your confidence, reputation, and great knowledge will carry you through with less preparation for each performance. But in the beginning, go overboard on preparation. It helps enormously to work to a plan. Mine follows:

1. START YOUR PSYCHE-UP

The first move on this vital process is to set up an assumptive listing folder. You're not going there tonight to chit chat, you're going there to take the listing. So start your psyching up process as soon as you get back to the office. Write their name and address on the assumptive listing folder. You've done your field and office research on comparables; now you're in the final stages of taking the listing. So you start assuming that you're going to take the listing because that puts positive forces to work in your mind. I'm not saying you should tell yourself, "It's in the bag. I'm going to walk in there tonight and sign 'em up in a hurry. No sweat." What I'm urging you to dwell on is almost the opposite:

"By the time I get there tonight, I'll be the best prepared agent in the world to handle their listing. They're going to give it to me because I'll eliminate every doubt that the wisest thing they can do is to let me serve them. I've paid the price to own this one. I'm going to go in there tonight and give my greatest performance ever."

Here's what should be in the assumptive listing folder you'll carry with you tonight:

A. A Listing form.

Please, try never to go out on a listing presentation without the form. I've done it. I've been busy and have forgotten to take a listing form with me. Suddenly I'm at the point where I want to start writing on the form—and I don't have one. Maybe you can excuse yourself, go to their bathroom, climb out the window, race back to the office, find a form, and get back before they decide you're not the expert they want to work with—but I never could. Put a listing form in the assumptive listing folder. And put a dozen extras in the trunk of your car, sealed in an envelope so they'll stay clean.

B. A comparable analysis form.

C. A sellers' proceeds form.

D. A picture of their home. Take one when you're there on your afternoon appointment or drive-by.

2. DEVELOP YOUR DATA

At this point you have a lot of rough notes and maybe some ideas about how to work with these people. Now study the data and develop your plan for taking that specific listing. Start with the listing form. Fill in the following information:

A. Lot size.

I'd call the title company and say, "I've got a legal description here. I'd like the lot size." When they gave me that information, I'd put it on the form.

B. Legal description.

Do you realize that most of them don't know that their home is Lot 76 of Tract 9876 of the Happy Homes Subdivision?

C. Taxes.

Most people don't know what their annual property tax is now. In many areas it's included in their monthly investment and they've lost track of the amount. If you call the tax assessor's office with the parcel number and legal description, they'll give you the annual taxes. Put that information on the form—it's impressive.

D. Room sizes.

If she wouldn't let you measure, don't guess. Never guess at any fact in real estate or you'll learn the hard way that guessing will cost you big money. Be accurate to a fault. Do you know that there are one or two listings in the multiple book in your community that are not accurate? At least. And it's not your board's fault—they have to rely on the accuracy of the individual agent. Unfortunately, some agents—the temporary people in this business—are careless.

Be accurate. A Champion never signs his name to anything unless he can swear it's accurate. I hope you'll agree with me, and let no listing go in the book unless the taxes, legal description, loan balance, room sizes, and all the other factual information are accurate.

E. Write a description of the home.

Do you know that the remarks are one of the most critical parts of the listing? If you enjoyed good rapport with the wife in the step one meeting, you'll usually be able to write a set of remarks that'll help you get the listing. Keep in mind what's important to them. And don't write three hundred words when there's only room in the book for fifty. When I wasn't sure about what remarks they'd want, I wrote a trial version on a separate piece of paper.

3. SIT BACK AND THINK

Most agents don't do this, and it's one of the most important phases of preparing for a successful listing presentation. The more listings you take, the quicker you'll see the way to go when you sit back and think—but even when I reached the eighteen listings a month stage, I found that I still needed to take a few minutes to quietly reflect and review the information I'd obtained. It always helped me to do it systematically, step by step.

A. How long in the property?

Have they lived there five years, or only six months? In the first case, they've probably built up a considerable equity. In the second case, their net proceeds from an at-the-market sale may give them less cash than they put into the home. The pro thinks this through and adjusts his strategy accordingly.

B. What did they pay?

Talk to your broker or manager and find out the sources your office uses to find out what people paid for property. Different methods are used in different areas. This information usually is a matter of public record. If so, you can get it.

C. Think about their employment or income situation.

If the husband is the family's only breadwinner, what's happening with his job? Does the wife have a business career? Review what you've learned and you'll understand more about what emotions are dictating the logic of their decisions. Then you'll know more about how to influence those decisions, won't you?

D. Why are they selling?

A pro always wants to know why they're selling. Have they been transferred? Has he lost his job? Are they planning to finance a business venture with their home equity?

E. The urgency.

Probably no other factor is more important to know than this one. What is the real urgency behind the sale? Are they about to lose the home through foreclosure, or are they eager to move on to the new job he or she has been promoted to? Maybe they'll never tell you the real reason, and you'll never know it unless you figure it out for yourself. Reflect on everything you've learned and been told. Does it all fit together?

F. Will I enjoy working with these people?

Granted, maybe you've only met the wife, but you can get a good feel as to the kind of people they are from that. I had a philosophy. If she gave me a lot of runaround and a lot of hassle, I'd still give my entire performance that evening, but I wouldn't be upset if I didn't get it. Maybe they just weren't my kind of people. It happens all the time.

4. ARRIVE AT VALUE

This is another thing that most agents don't do. My job now is to establish the actual price that this home is worth in today's market. Here's how we do it:

A. How well do the comparables really compare?

How close in value are the homes on your list of comparables? Are they in the same neighborhood so that all the off-site factors are the same? Are they similar in age, condition, size, construction, number of bedrooms, amenities and landscaping?

Did Mrs. Watt let you know that she doesn't care for Mrs. Mildue? Then if you come in tonight and tell her that the Mildue home is just like hers, you've created a problem for yourself, haven't you?

B. Is the home sharp, average, or poor?

Because of the emotional appeal of a beautifully maintained home, you can increase the value if it's sharp. If the home is in average condition, you have to bring it in at close to market value or it won't sell. If the home has been poorly maintained, you must work the price down below the normal market value before it'll excite a buyer.

C. What will it take to get this home sold?

This is another thing a pro always asks himself. In today's market, given all the comparable properties that are on the market, the number of buyers coming in, the financing situation on that particular property, what must be done to make the property sell? Maybe they have to change their crimson and blue color scheme. Maybe the house is too packed with furniture.

What can you do to interest other agents in the area in showing this property to their buyers? Unless you ask yourself these questions—and find good answers to them—I don't know why they should list with you.

D. How do I tell the sellers?

Think about and rehearse how you'll tell them the things you'll have to get across if you're going to take an at-market listing. Let me slip a fact about real estate to you. Very few homeowners are planning to sell a beautiful property for less than market price; most are planning to sell a less than beautiful property for far more than market value. The crux of your job is to inject reality into their thinking. Doing that effectively takes planning. You can't just go in there and say, "Mr. and Mrs. Smedley, I'd like to be honest. You'd like that too, wouldn't you?"

"Oh, yes."

"Well, your home is a pigsty."

Don't attack the people, attack the problem. Think about the best way to motivate them to do what has to be done to increase the emotional appeal their house will have to a buyer. Then practice saying that in the best way.

By the way, I'd let someone else have the pleasure of listing families like the one I've called Smedley in this chapter. As a Champion, you can afford to avoid the aggravation.

E. If the property is overimproved, depreciate the improvements.

The appraiser for the lender will depreciate overimprovements in arriving at value. Before you go in, list the appraisal value of the overimprovements in this manner:

	ESTIMATED COST OF OVERIMPROVEMENTS	ESTIMATED LENDER'S APPRAISAL VALUE
Swimming Pool	$10,000	$3,000
Patio	$ 2,000	$ 500
Carpet	$20 per yard, 1800 sq. ft. 200 yards $4,000	$2 per yard $400

When you present the facts in this manner, it isn't you who's quoting bad news, it's the professional appraiser.

F. What is the demand?

There are some areas where every broker in the city is panting for listings. If you have an opportunity to give your performance for such a listing, you might have to compete with a bidding situation to begin with, but there's a top market value in that area too. Get it at market value if at all possible because you and your office need that inventory.

What if the property is in an area where the demand is average, low, or even nonexistent? Don't let some other agent, one who hasn't done his homework, pull you into a bidding competition in such areas. What you never need is an over-priced turkey where there's little or no demand.

G. Set your maximum price.

Very few agents go through any of these procedures, which is why the Champions who do them all make so much money. Every one of these things gives you an extra edge of money-making ability. Setting a maximum price that you'll take a listing at *before you go in for the appointment* is one of the greatest tools I know of. First of all, if you'll stick to your top price through thick or thin—and if you know you will—that knowledge makes you work harder to get the listing at your maximum price or less. Secondly, it will eliminate the enormous loss of time, money, energy, and enthusiasm that every overpriced turkey you list costs you.

The maximum amount at which you'll take the listing must be a written commitment that you make with yourself when you're alone studying the facts of record. Tell yourself, "I'm going for that listing at $155,000. I know they're thinking $190,000, but if they list with someone at $190,000, they're the ones who'll lose because it'll never sell for that. I'm going in there tonight and use every technique I've learned from Tom, and I'm getting it at $155,000!''

H. Prepare and rehearse your final game plan.

As you go over everything the wife said and all the data you've collected, plan your listing presentation in detail. Now you know what points are important—plan how you'll emphasize those points. And now you know some things you shouldn't say, don't you? Plan how you'll give them the facts they have to understand before they can arrive at an intelligent decision. Work out exactly what you need to say, and rehearse how you'll say it. When you've done that, there's only one more item in your afternoon preparation for an effective listing performance that evening.

I. Schedule your final psyche-up time.

One common mistake I hope you'll avoid: don't fail to respect yourself as a real estate expert, a pro, a Champion. If you want those titles, you won't go skidding in breathlessly for a listing appointment after a mad dash from some other activity. You'll allow yourself time to get there without hurry—after you've psyched yourself up for at least ten minutes.

Please don't omit the final psyche-up. This is one of the greatest moneymaking edges that the big winner has. If you read the sports pages at all, what theme is repeated over and over? The loser wasn't mentally prepared. It's the same in the real estate business. But psyche-up doesn't happen automatically. You have to make time and solitude for it. Psyche-up has to have a regular place in your schedule—it must be an honored part of your I'm-going-to-take-a-listing ritual.

THE FINAL PSYCHE-UP

You'll be a little bit psyched-up anyway because of all the research, preparation, and review that you've done, but don't steam yourself up hours before the appointment or you'll be emotionally worn out by the time you get there. Hold off on the psyche-up until just before you get in your car to go over to see them.

If you've never deliberately psyched yourself up before, doing it may seem a little weird. You may be a little uncomfortable the first few times you practice this technique. Remember that psyche-up doesn't go well unless you really get into it. Please believe me—if you can learn how to psyche yourself up, you'll multiply your performance in every area of your life that you put this method to work in. Throughout my career, it's been unthinkable not to psyche-up to meet a challenge if I could possibly do so. My ability to do that was one of my greatest listing and selling strengths—and it's helped beyond measure in everything I've accomplished since.

It goes best if you have a routine for psyching-up. After you've done it a few dozen times, you'll perfect your own system and be able to use it for anything on short notice. Let me suggest a program for listing appointment psyche-up.

1. Run quickly through all the papers you've written preparing for this listing. Tell yourself that nobody else has done that much, that you deserve the listing.

2. Stare at the top-price commitment you've made to yourself for listing that property, and repeat how much they need to sell, and how they won't be able to sell, unless they list with you at that market price.

3. Close your eyes. Then picture yourself taking the listing. Look through your own eyes as you do so. See the clients as you say and do

what must be said and done before you'll get the listing. And feel your pleasure at writing another listing at market value.

4. Write down the reasons why they will list with you. Write the reasons out every time.

"Gloria and Jack Watt will list with me because I know more about their property than any other agent in the world.

"Gloria and Jack will list with me because I specialize in their area.

"Gloria and Jack will list with me because I'm honest and ethical.

"Gloria and Jack will list with me because my company gives great service—" Spell out the reasons why your company gives exceptional benefits to its clients.

"Gloria and Jack will list with me because I'm the hardest-working agent in town."

If you can't come up with at least a dozen reasons why Gloria and Jack should list with you, maybe they shouldn't. Any great salesman will tell you that it's a hundred times easier to sell something you believe in—and if you don't believe in yourself, how can you sell yourself? That's what listing is, selling yourself, your knowledge, and your skills. Make sure you have something worthwhile to sell.

5. Use body language in your psyche-up. Maybe you want to sit at a desk and silently psyche-up. Maybe you'll do it better walking around—waving your arms—shouting. Do whatever works for you, but get the adrenaline pounding.

6. Write out a series of psyche-up slogans that you go over and over before every listing appointment. *I will take their listing at market value. I will have my sign in their yard. I will get a key to their property.* I WILL WIN.
WHY?

Because I Have Faith, Courage, and Enthusiasm.

11

CREATING A HIGH-SCORING LISTING PRESENTATION

We've done all the preparation and all the work. Now it's time to put it all together—now it's time to go over there and take the listing.

You can control your own attitude, can't you? You can think positive thoughts; you can keep negative thinking out of your mind; you can psyche-up. But what's the attitude of the husband when you arrive after you've spent some time inspecting the house with the wife earlier in the day? Based on your practiced performance, she's somewhat impressed with you, isn't she? And she's told her husband that you're hot stuff.

"He measured the whole house, and he even inspected the water heater. He told me we've got 36,000 BTU's and not one bit of galvanic corrosion. Honey, I think he's our man."

Is that good or bad? At first, it's bad. The husband doesn't want you there for your reason; he wants you there for his reason—to check prices and get all the information he can from you to help him sell it himself. So the more his wife brags about how great the agent she found is, the more he's thinking, "Maybe she's sold, but I'm not. I'll show this agent what's what in a hurry."

Then you drive up. He looks out of the window as you walk up to their door. You're radiating enthusiasm, confidence, and energy.

What does the husband see? A fee of several thousand dollars strolling up his driveway.

Your first goal is to prove you're worth it.

What is he feeling? Fear. He's afraid of losing money. He's afraid of being lied to, taken advantage of, made to feel stupid. He's afraid you'll tie up the home and then do nothing. He's afraid of committing himself, of giving up his options, of putting his family's destiny in a stranger's hands.

All these fears are subconscious. He doesn't stand there saying them all to himself. He doesn't have to—he's feeling them. So the first step toward proving that you're worth your fee is to start breaking down his fears. In other words, you must gain his liking and trust. Most new salespeople realize that this is what they should do—but they go about it in the wrong way by being too accomodating. They let the prospects take control of the interview—in fact, they force them to. Keep this in mind: unless you control the interview, they control it, and the person in control is the only one who can win.

HOW TO TAKE CONTROL

The process is quite simple. You work to a plan that keeps you one jump ahead of them throughout the evening, a plan that allows you to guide the entire meeting from one reasonable step to another until you take the listing. However, unless you do this with confidence and subtle firmness, they'll fight you. You can't win while they're fighting you. But after you've practiced, drilled, and rehearsed your plan based on this book's principles and phraseology, you'll be working your plan so smoothly and nicely that they'll never think of fighting you. Here's how to raise the curtain on Act One of a successful listing play:

1. Be a pro all the way.

Dress professionally. Go through Chapter 8's fundamental steps at their door, and introduce yourself with warmth and enthusiasm when you meet the husband. Let him know that you've taken the appointment seriously enough to be on time by saying these words: "We had an appointment at 7:00." (Look at your watch.) "It's right at 7 o'clock now." Another professional touch is to hand your card to the husband when you enter the home.

2. Refer to the wife formally in the beginning.

Start off calling her Mrs. Watt, not Gloria. Do this even if you were on a first name basis with her that afternoon. Let the husband know you respect the fact that you're in his castle; show him plenty of deference so he won't feel obliged to defend his authority and position. Whether you're a woman or a man, this is vital. A husband can think two women are ganging up on him and resent that as much as he'd resent a strange man's familiar manner toward his wife.

3. Boost his ego.

It's crucial at this point to make him feel that he's the key element in the listing process so he won't fight the idea of working with this person (you) that his wife brought in. Here's what you say to accomplish that:

"I saw the home earlier today with Mrs. Watt. However, to establish the highest possible market value, I think it's important that you show me all the improvements you've made, and express your feelings regarding the home."

4. Keep him on his feet.

You're in trouble unless you tour the house right now. Why? Because if you sit down in the living room, you'll talk money. Never sit down and start negotiating money a few seconds after meeting someone—that's the fast track to failure. Slow the process down. Give yourself time to learn a little bit about him; give him time to get over feeling that you're a stranger.

5. Clinch the best possible negotiating arena.

You worked with the wife this afternoon about having your meeting at the kitchen table, but you can lose what you've gained during the first few minutes of your evening appointment. Avoid that by taking the first opportunity to confirm where you'll meet and negotiate. As soon as you're near the kitchen, say this: "May I put my briefcase down?" Then head for the kitchen, set your briefcase on or by the table, and go on with the tour. When that's over with, you'll all naturally come back to where you want to be—at the kitchen table.

6. Build rapport as you tour the home with the husband.

Keep looking for common denominators. Ask friendly questions.

Talk about his interests. Discuss his employment—but approach this carefully and with empathy; maybe they're selling because he's out of work.

7. Slant your vocabulary toward him.

Top-flight salespeople speak many different levels of English. You can too—all it takes is a flexible attitude and an open ear. You don't have to use phony accents, but you can talk a little more downhome with a carpenter, a bit more uptown with an attorney.

8. Praise the wife's housekeeping—if you sincerely can.

You're also complimenting him when you compliment her, aren't you?

9. Stay away from price until it's time.

You haven't made your presentation yet—your carefully researched comparable market analysis is still in your briefcase—so it's disaster city to talk money now. But they'll try. You're walking down the hall with the sellers and the husband says, "You were by today—what do you think we can get for this place?"

"Mr. Watt, I haven't finished compiling my data—I'll know in just a moment."

"You're the professional—can't you just give me some idea?"

If you do, you'll be galloping off on a fullblown price discussion standing there in the hall, out of reach of your CMA. Be nice—but firm. "Mr. Watt, I could pick a figure out of thin air, but I'd rather rely on facts. Please—may we wait until we get to the table?"

"Well, I don't want to waste a lot of time tonight, so how about coming up with a ballpark figure?"

I used to smile and say, "Mr. Watt, I consider myself as professional as any doctor. If you were sick, would you want your doctor to diagnose what's killing you after one quick look?"

I can't overemphasize the necessity of avoiding price until you've prepared the way. The sellers often hit hard. "Oh, come on—tell us what it's worth. We're all adults here." The pressure for talking price too soon can get very heavy.

If you crack under that pressure, you're gone. Nine times out of ten, the sellers want more than your top figure. Pop that figure out now and who's talking?

Not the marketplace. Not the professional appraisers. Not the lenders. Not the research authority. Just you.

And who are you?

The husband doesn't know—the two of you met just minutes ago. Talking price before getting the weight of your research and your presentation behind you is like trying to pour concrete without cement. So, until the tour with the husband is over and you've reached the proper moment in Act Two of the listing play, you must hold off all discussion of price.

Act Two takes place at the kitchen table. This is when successful agents put their visual aid books to work—a technique that's second only to the CMA in listing effectiveness. I'll tell you about it in the next section, but before I do that, let me ask you a question. Since the visual aid book and the comparable market analysis are easily the two most effective listing methods known, why not use both?

CREATING LISTING POWER WITH A VISUAL AID BOOK

Many companies spend thousands of dollars developing visual aid books because their new salespeople need all the help they can get. Yet when management looks at results, they find that most of the people using the expensive new visual aids aren't beginners, they're veteran agents with long records of superior performance. It's easy to get the top producers to use a fine new visual aid; they know that prospects need more than an agent's face to look at, more than an agent's voice to learn from. Heavy hitters are quick to see the value of a graphic presentation that'll allow them to deliver more information and develop more credibility in less time. The light tappers, on the other hand, aren't interested in anything that'll organize their activity. These people won't be in the business long because they never acquire the professional tools and skills of the trade they've chosen. They plan to be free spirits and make lots of money playing it by ear. What they don't understand is that success doesn't come in their model.

The finest script for Act Two of your listing performance is a visual aid book that you've personalized. If your company supplies one, start with that. If not, develop your own. Either way, a little effort creates a visual aid book you'll soon realize is worth far more than its weight in gold to you.

Build this pricelss listing tool in a flip chart or three-ring binder that holds the standard 8½ x 11 inch paper. Get a stand-up model. They come in both styles: *flip chart* with the long edge of the paper on the bottom, *binder* with the long edge of the paper on the side. Use plastic sheet protectors—the non-glare type is best.

Between the time when Gloria Watt called you this morning and now, as you're sitting down with both of them at their kitchen table, you've been in control, haven't you? They aren't fighting you because you've been so reasonable, professional, and confident—and also because you've been so very nice. Without realizing it, the Watts have fallen into the habit of letting you take the lead because you're leading them where they want to go. At the kitchen table you must maintain that control or they'll sleep on it instead of giving you the listing.

The tour with the husband gave you a last chance to confirm or change the conclusions you reached during your afternoon think session. You've asked yourself these ABC questions:

(A) Are they sincere about selling?

Whether or not they're realistic about price at this moment, do they feel they have to sell before they can do what they want to?

Unless the answer to this question is a firm yes, what you're doing there is practicing your technique and perfecting your performance. That's wonderful—really. Full dress rehearsals are hard to come by, so don't waste one. Give it all you've got. Just don't be disappointed when you walk out without the listing.

(B) Have they already decided to use professional help in marketing their home?

It's a serious mistake to see a by-owner hiding inside every seller's shirt. And it's an even more serious mistake to spend any of their short attention span talking sellers out of something they've already decided not to do.

If you believe the answers to (A) and (B) are both yes, you can concentrate on the big one:

(C) Why should these sellers list with me instead of with some other agent?

Answering that question so convincingly that they'll give you the listing is the sole purpose of the visual aid book. It won't get you the listing at market price—your professional technique with the comparable market analysis form does that. But first you have to sell them on your expertise, energy, and honesty. How can you do that without bragging, which so often turns people off? Somehow these two blunt questions must be satisfactorily answered or you won't get many listings:

Who are you?
What have you done?

The visual aid book can give the right answers for you in a powerful, graphic way that minimizes the bragging hazard. But if you're new to real estate, the plain truth is simple: you haven't done much yet. Are you wondering how the two blunt questions can be answered honestly without destroying yourself?

Don't worry. Here's a list of twelve convincing items for your book that you can start gathering on your first day in the business:

1. Certificates you've earned at the professional seminars you've attended.

While you wait for your license to come in the mail, go to seminars and learn all you can about how to earn a professional's income with that license. Put all your attendance certificates (or a typed list of the seminars you've gone to) in your visual aid book. Then open every presentation—from the *very first one*—by pointing to the evidence of your professional training and saying, "A reputation for professionalism is important, isn't it?"

2. A crisp, 8 x 10 inch color photograph of your office, with the entire sales force standing in front of it.

Suggested phraseology: "I'm proud to be associated with this strong team of professionals because, collectively, our office has over _____ years of experience* at serving, with honesty and integrity, the real estate needs of this community. The point I want to make is this: when you employ me as your professional representative, you're also employing all the benefits that only a dedicated and proven local organization can provide: instant name recognition, a vast

---

*To get this figure for your office, simply add up the number of years each of the agents there has worked in local real estate.

amount of community goodwill, a reputation for professionalism and integrity, and the assurance that we'll be doing business here when you or the buyers want us a week—or ten years—from now.''

3. A photo of the president of your company.

Early in my career, I put one in my book. I was very proud of our company's president and, in bragging about his accomplishments, I built up the whole company—and basked in the reflected glory without sounding like I was bragging about myself.

4. Plenty of boilerplate.

In the last chapter you learned how to develop this material quickly. Put your name on every page so they'll know you created the boilerplate yourself. If you have the professional tools—and if you use them with confidence and skill—they'll never suspect you're new and inexperienced.

5. Cartoons, graphs, pictures.

Be alert for arguments that'll strike with more impact—and cause less backlash—when you show instead of tell. Keep it simple. One idea to a page. If they don't get the messgage instantly, it's too complicated. One of the most effective pages in my book was a cartoon showing a nine-foot Frankenstein peering down at a tiny woman and her two small children. The three of them clung together as they stared up at the monster with expressions of panic on their faces. Frankenstein had ripped up their by-owner sign and was holding it over them like a club. Under the cartoon I wrote this caption, ''Do you really know who'll come into your home?''

A cartoon puts ideas like this across better than a thousand words. Say half that much about frightening things and they'll be wondering about you. If cartooning isn't one of your talents, find a picture of Frankenstein and write the caption under it—that's all you really need.

6. Photograph of your office's for sale sign in front of a home with your name rider on it.

Here's what you say: ''There's something about the colors and size of our company's sign that sure does the trick. Buyers are always calling to ask us about the properties we have our signs on. A sign that generates lots of calls is a great help, isn't it?

7. Photo of a happy family shaking your hand under a sold sign on the front lawn of a house.

The people can be any family—even your own friends or relatives—because you're not going to say you moved these people. Here's what you do say: "It would be convenient to move as a family, wouldn't it?" Then you flip right along to the next page of your visual aid book, which is a:

8. Photo of a moving van.

Call up one of the major moving companies and they'll be happy to send you this picture for your book. The phraseology is, "Lots of people aren't fortunate enough to sell within their time limits. Don't you agree that double moves are expensive?"

Do you see how the visual aid book is used to start the yeses coming? Keep that yes momentum going right through to the approval of the listing agreement.

9. Typed list of all the transactions your office has had in the past month, year, or three years.

Select whatever period gives you an impressive looking document. All you need for each transaction is the property address, the sale amount, and the sale date.

10. A map of your service area.

Don't stretch this out to the furtherest limits you'd go under any circumstances—what you want here is the compact area you're planning to cover thoroughly. Use these words:

"As a specialist in this area, I could serve you better, couldn't I?"

11. Map of your listing bank.

Leave this page out of your book whenever you go outside your farm to make a listing presentation. But when you're working in it, pass over item 10 and go directly to this map. "As a specialist on these five hundred homes, I could serve you better, couldn't I?"

12. A copy of the ad you placed in a local paper when you joined your firm.

You didn't know you were going to do that until this minute, did you? Don't say anything in the ad that isn't true, but don't tell the world that you're brand-new either.

If you're stalled until your license arrives, use the time to put your visual aid book together. Then you'll have a book full of commitment-provers and credibility-builders ready for your first listing appointment. That book will give your confidence and capability a tremendous boost right when you need it most—at the beginning.

Keep adding to that book. Here are three more powerful graphic pages that you can add as you work through your first weeks in the business.

13. A color photo of you promoting a listing at your local realty board meeting.

Show up a little early with a commercial photographer. Dress professionally, of course. Just before the meeting begins, while everyone is still getting seated, jump up on the stage and act like you're pushing a listing hard. Practice your gestures and intense expressions beforehand, and tell the photographer exactly what you want: a dramatic photo of you in action before an audience. Give the photographer a few moments to shoot several pictures so you can pick the best print among several.

Here's what I wrote under my best print: "I will expose your property to the top salespeople in the multiple."

This picture with the above caption was very effective for me. It's another thing I created very early in my career when it would do me the most good. And good it did. I noticed that people were interested and impressed—and their mood started tipping my way—when they saw that picture. Get this photo—I don't know of anything that'll show your energy, boldness, and professional talent more powerfully. And it's so easily done.

14. Photos of your first transactions.

In the foreground, beside your office's sign with your name rider on it, you and the sellers are exchanging big grins and a handshake. At first, when you need all the help you can get, spend a little to get a lot of emotional impact: have a commercial photographer give you prints that'll fill the page the way your book is turned. When you have five or six of these large I-did-it pictures, you've reached the point of diminishing returns. Switch to small snapshots or instant prints—a friend can take them for you—and start putting four happily-moved families on a page.

15. Photo of you getting an award for being your office's top lister or top seller of the month.

The award might even be for taking the largest listing written east of Broadway and north of Jefferson between 2 and 3 a.m. on Friday the 13th. If you've earned one but your office doesn't give awards, buy your own—any trophy shop can supply a plaque made to your specifications. Then have someone hand it to you while a commercial photographer records the event.

Now you know how to put a visual aid book together that'll have graphic impact and emotional selling power. Arrange your book carefully. A professional presentation—one that inspires confidence and makes people want to list with you—moves quickly and smoothly from point to point without backtracking or leaving anything important out. Assemble your book. Then role play in front of a mirror with it. Practice, drill, and rehearse your words, gestures, and movements. Keep in mind that your phraseology, and the techniques you use to showcase the book, are as important as its contents.

FOUR EASY WAYS TO POLISH YOUR PERFORMANCE WITH THE VISUAL AID BOOK

1. Sit across from the husband and wife.

Place yourself where you can see both of them at the same time. Avoid any seating arrangement that'll make you swing your head from side to side to look them both in the eyes because that situation robs you of control.

2. Look at the page you're talking about.

Their eyes will follow yours. When you look at them they'll look back at you; when you look at the page, they'll look at it too.

3. Hold their interest with variety.

Change the pace constantly. After a cartoon or two, show them a graph. Follow the graph with a map, and then turn to a few pages of text (boilerplate) that you flip through quickly before switching to a photo. Never drone on and on—tell them something, ask a question, and tell them something else. To grip their attention, keep challenging them with fresh ideas and new formats.

4. Use tie-downs.

Look back through the fifteen items and you'll find lots of *tie-downs*: "As a specialist in this area, I could better serve you, *couldn't I?*" "*Don't you agree* that double moves are expensive?" "A reputation for professionalism is important, *isn't it?*" As you develop phraseology for your visual aid book, be sure to work in tie-downs so you'll get agreement on the most important points.

AFTER THE TOUR

Let's continue with our evening meeting. You had your visual aid book organized and your technique with it rehearsed before Gloria called you this morning. Now, after touring the house with Jack, you're just sitting down at the kitchen table across from them. Here's how to begin your listing presentation:

"Mr. and Mrs. Watt, many people feel that all real estate companies and salespeople are the same. Before making a decision on a company or its representative, I think it's important that you are aware of what the company will do for you. I'm very proud of my firm, and I'd like to show you the benefits we have to offer."

Don't wait for their permission—launch right into your listing presentation. Keep it moving. One of the advantages of a well-organized visual aid book—one that's not cluttered with material you don't need or use—is that they can see how much of it is left. If you're moving through it quickly, they're more likely to sit still and pay attention since they can see it's not going to take all night or be boring.

The final part of your presentation introduces the comparable market analysis. Lead into it with:

(If you're new)

"Mr. and Mrs. Watt, I'd like to begin by thanking you for allowing me to be here tonight. In appreciation, I've taken a color photo of your home.'' (Hand it to them.) "It came out rather nicely, didn't it?'' Then go on with:

"Most of my work today consisted of formulating this comparative market analysis. One of the basic factors that determines whether a property will sell is the establishment of a fair market value price. As you can see, this form shows the properties that have been sold in the area, the properties for sale now, and the properties that did not sell during their exposure to the marketplace. Let's go over the form together.''

(If you're a practiced veteran)

"Mr. and Mrs. Watt, I spent most of today researching data and compiling a comparative market analysis on your property. Would you take a moment and verify my accuracy on these details?'' (Hand them the partially-filled-out listing form that you worked on at the office.)

Jack Watt will probably say, ''We haven't decided to list with anyone yet.''

Smile. "Oh, I'm certainly aware of that, but I'm also confident that when you see the benefits we have to offer and the service I'll give you, you'll agree that (*your company's name*) is the firm you'll wish to have represent you.''

Champions get their listing form on the table at this point. Then they pick up the previous phraseology from the second sentence: "One of the basic factors that determines whether . . . Let's go over the form together.''

Hand each of them a copy of your comparable market analysis, and retain one for yourself. Having two copies of the CMA for them is critical; you need response from both the wife and the husband. If one of them doesn't get a copy, that person is going to feel slighted and will probably start fighting you.

As they look at the form, watch their expressions. Remember Wilma Mildue? Gloria, who used to bowl with her, thinks Wilma is a shrew. But after the Mildues's house sold, Jack talked Gloria into calling her. Now Gloria tells you, "I spoke to the owners of this one, and they said they got a lot more for it than you show here.''

Expect to be challenged every time you present a CMA. When it happens, a pro smiles warmly, and calmly says,

"We find this happens quite often. People who have had their home on the market, when asked by a neighbor what they sold it for, often reply with, 'We got what we wanted.' The inquisitor, knowing what they were asking, assumes they received much more than they actually did. It's a *common problem,* but I can assure you that *these figures are facts of record.*"

Emphasize the words given above in italics. You've just called their friends—or at least their informants—liars. But you've done it in a pleasant, professional manner. That is, you've brought the facts of record to their attention that they need to know before they can make an intelligent decision.

Gloria Watt is a little upset that Wilma lied to her, so she says: "Our home is nicer than these places. Well, I haven't seen them all, but our place is certainly lots nicer than Wilma's."

Always agree. Do not fall on the floor roaring with laughter. Here's the proven response to the often-heard "Our home is nicer" statement:

"Indeed it is. Your home is one of the nicest in the area. Quality improvements and pride of ownership are so important in selling a home.

"However, it's a proven fact that the improvements primarily enhance the property's ability to sell faster, and don't always increase the value in proportion to the costs of those improvements."

Isn't that smooth and effective? And it's so true.

Then Jack Watt says, in the same tone he'd use to tell you where to jump, "We wouldn't sell our home for these prices."

'Hotdog,' you should think when you hear that. Why? Because they are telling you that they do know what they would sell it for. Establishing that figure is one of your preliminary goals, isn't it?

This next phraseology is important. Please practice until you can say it slowly, sincerely, and word for word:

"Well, based on that statement, you obviously have some idea of what you'd want. What do you feel the price should be?"

No matter how much smooth empathy you put into asking that question, you'll often get an answer like this from Jack: "You're the professional—you tell us."

When anyone says that to you, what have they done? By calling you a professional they've complimented you, haven't they. So thank them, repeat what they've decided about you, and then tie it all down: "Thank you." Smile. "And a reputation for professionalism is important, isn't it?"

Practice these things. Role play them. Gear yourself up until you're just waiting for them to give you the stimulus so you can come right back with a minor close.

Charge right into the rest of your rehearsed speech for smoothly fielding his fly at overpricing:

"The sales price of a property is flexible, depending upon the terms and the length of exposure to the market. You would like to move in the next *(quote the period you know is their need-to-move time)*, wouldn't you?"

The words are important, your tone and manner is even more so. If you ask that question in a smart-alecky way, you can destroy yourself with it, just as you can by misusing any other technique. Your manner has to express a sincere concern for helping them accomplish their objectives as you say, "You would like to move within the next sixty days, wouldn't you?"

Jack Watt says yes, so you move into your next planned step:

"Well, I think it's important that we keep as close to market value as possible—so do you have some idea of what you would want?"

He's studied your CMA and can't punch any holes in it—you've got the proof. So now Jack knows that he isn't going to get what he wants, which is $190,000 for a house that should go on the market in the low $150's if it's going to sell as quickly as they need it to sell. This means they have gut wrenching problems to wrestle with. Jack may not be prepared to admit in front of Gloria that they're not going to get as much money as he'd told her they would based on the garbage information we saw him collect in Chapter 4. And Gloria may be in shock because she's afraid that, if they have to sell in the low 150's, they won't be able to buy the house they want. In most listing situations, you'll have some version of these emotional problems to contend with. Often there'll be another difficulty: your sellers have bought a house they can't qualify for unless they sell theirs at an impossibly high price. Here are some questions you should be asking yourself at this point:

How heavily are they committed, emotionally and financially, to their unrealistic price?

Can they adjust to realistic pricing?

If they can adjust, how long will it take them to get realistic?

Even at the risk of alienating them, should I go all out to list them at market price tonight?

Or should I take the listing high, with the understanding that we'll bring the price down to a realistic level in an agreed time if we don't get action at their price?

Or should I give them a few hours to adjust to reality, and schedule another meeting tomorrow night with both of them?

You'll usually have to answer these questions in the heat of the listing interview—but you'll make better decisions if you've given them thorough analysis during your afternoon think session.

The ball is still in the Watts' court: "—so do you have some idea of what you would want?

After some sparring between Gloria and Jack, it's evident that Mr. Watt is the one who'll answer the question. By now, Jack has acquired a grudging respect for you, and he doesn't want to appear stupid. So, after grinding his teeth, after looking again at the line on your CMA showing the Bartlett home on the market for 79 days at $159,500, after making some agonizing reappraisals of their financial situation, Mr. Watt says, "Well, we wanted a whole lot more, but I guess our rock bottom figure would be about $165,000, wouldn't it, honey?" He's closer, but he's still not realistic.

Gloria swallows hard and says, "Well, that's all right with me."

But it isn't all right with you. At that price you know their house won't sell fast enough to let them move in two months—no way.

But you don't look shocked. Your expression shows puzzlement, nothing more. No amusement. No anger. No struggle to keep from saying something sarcastic—just puzzlement. Learn to say these words with sympathy:

"Mr. and Mrs. Watt, maybe I missed something in the property." This has to be said very warmly—and with great empathy—or they'll blow you out of the water. "Could you take a moment and tell me why you feel that way?"

When you say that, you must sound like you've made a mistake. Now it's their turn—let them pour it on:
"Okay, Tom, I'll tell you why. This is the finest location in the state. We have mercury switches, awnings on every window, and the paint is guaranteed to outlast the house. Our ceiling has fourteen inches of insulation, every bush in the yard is individually drip-irrigated, and we've installed an industrial-grade can crusher for the trash."
Don't interrupt—listen to the whole story. And pay attention. When it's your turn, you'll need to come back, strongly, smoothly, and professionally. To do that, use:

THE FOUR TURNAROUND PHRASES

Practice the four phrases that follow. They are among the most powerful short combinations of words that you can put to work in selling. The system is simple and devastatingly effective. First agree with them—then state your own contrary point.

"I understand how you feel; however—"
"Your point is certainly valid, although—"
"Looking at it from your view, that's true, but—"
"I can certainly see your point, except—"

You warmly agree—then you disagree with friendly warmth. First you make sure that the person you're persuading knows that you heard what he or she just said. If you fail to do this, that person won't be persuaded at all by your argument, he'll just be thinking about making his points all over again the first chance he gets.

HANDLING THE "WE CAN RENT IT" BALLOON

"We can always rent—we don't really have to sell now."
If they say that, have they ever been a landlord before? Nine

times out of ten, they haven't, or they'd never do it again with a single family residence. The entire reason for this objection often is simply to slow things down, in which case you can ignore it. At other times, it'll become their justification for taking no action tonight unless you get this objection out of the way. Do that with a similar situation close:

"It's certainly true that owning rentals has been a good investment for many people. However, it's definitely a fact that very few tenants take the pride in the property that the owner does."

Is that true? You bet it is.

"By holding the property for two or three years, any appreciation could be offset by what we call deferred maintenance—necessary repairs. Have you ever rented or managed a home before?"

They'll usually say they haven't.

"It can be a rude awakening."

I tell my seminar students to say this: "Recently I spent three days with a broker who had been in real estate for fourteen years. He decided to rent the home he was leaving." (I did when I moved from California to Arizona. Renting that house was the biggest mistake of my life.)

"This broker thought he had carefully selected his tenants, but he soon found out he was working with professional renters. After six months of not collecting rent and eviction attempts, he finally got his property back. Refurbishing it to its former condition cost him two thousand dollars, and he was out the cost of carrying the property all that time too."

Since you haven't spent the three days with me, you won't want to say it just that way. Perhaps your manager, or someone else you know, has had a similar experience. They're not rare. Ask around and you'll hear some sad but true stories about problems with renters in single family residences. Research this point and be ready for his objection with a similar situation close that's effective and true. The point you want to convey is this: if experienced brokers can't protect themselves against rip-off renters, what chance do amateur landlords have, especially if they have moved far away from their rental?

WORKING THE PRICE DOWN TO MARKET

On many listings you'll need all your skill and knowledge to cajole the price into bargaining distance of market value. It's a hard, thankless task—which is why so few agents do it. As a result, an enormous number of overpriced listings are written every year. These listings hurt everyone. Least hurt are the agents who won't take them—they'll get a second chance when the wishful thinking expires. More hurt are the agents who win the bidding contests and write the overpriced listings—their only reward will be expense and trouble. But the real hurt falls on the owners—instead of moving when it's convenient, they wind up selling when they're emotionally—and sometimes financially—desperate.

So, as you work at getting a price that's near market, bear in mind that you're doing it primarily for the sellers' benefit. All you have to lose is a few hours work—you can list another home in a fraction of the time you'd waste trying to sell a $150,000 value for $165,000—or even more. Work hard at helping the owners see where their best interests are—in getting a selling price, not a sale-killing price. Yes, it's often hard to do this, but it is the very essence of listing. If you aspire to be a Champion lister, realize that your finest professional moments will come when, based on thorough research, you persuade a reluctant seller to accept reality and list at market price. Your situation is the same as a coach: if he's tough during training, he may not be popular—until the team wins. Then they'll carry him off the field on their shoulders. Your rewards also come only after success. Overpriced listings start with smiles and end in bitterness.

Use this three-step program to set yourself up for closing on market price:

1. Go over all your estimated seller's proceeds form and explain all the costs. Your purpose is to find out what they must net after the sale, what their net walkaway cash needs are. Many people aren't interested in what you sell the place for as long as they get that specific amount of cash out of it.

2. Mentally compute how far off you are.
"Mr. and Mrs. Watt, forgetting price for a moment, if I were to write you a check right now, how much would you want for your property after all the charges, including the mortgage, are paid?"
"We couldn't take less than $60,000."
"We definitely need that much," Gloria Watt says. When you hear that, it almost always means they've already spent that much, mentally if not actually. So they're not going to find it easy to look at

price logically (no one ever does) because a lower price doesn't just come through to them as an abstract reduction of a number. It hits them as the loss of their vacation to Mexico, the postponement of buying their new furniture, and no new stereo.

Sometimes "We definitely need that much" means another broker has verbally "guaranteed" them that price. What value do verbal guarantees have? Try to deposit one in your bank account and you'll find out.

Do you have a problem with math? I did, so I learned some quick mental formulas for arriving at approximate net figures. Do you realize that almost all real estate decisions are made on the basis of rough figures? When the choice is being made, quick and roughly accurate figures work; slow, penny-perfect figures don't. (As with most rules, there are exceptions to this one. Don't hesitate to pull out the calculator and work everything out to the last cent if they make it plain that quick estimates make them uncomfortable.)

But if quick estimates make *you* uncomfortable, you need to study this section and change your thinking because you've been losing control of too many situations right here. Most people can only be held at the point of decision for a very short time—let them dangle and they'll fall off. Learn to be as quick with approximate figures as you are with your practiced words—it's the only way you can stay in control and lead them to the decision you want them to make.

Let's work the example out. The Watts need to net $60,000, and you know their mortgage balance is $82,046.79—$80,000 for fast figures—making the total $140,000. Add closing costs. For quick estimates, I used ten percent. Not only was it close enough, it's wonderfully easy to figure—just drop a zero. You've got to keep it simple or the tension and pressure will mess you up.

In this case, by dropping a zero off the payoff total of $140,000, I get $14,000. Add the two sums together and we have $154,000. But I'm not done yet, because I left $2,000 out when I rounded their $82,046.79 mortgage to $80,000. Add that back for a grand total of $156,000—a price that's within bargaining distance of market value. Hurrah, I'm working on a live situation—the Watts don't need to sell for $165,000.

You can make quick estimates like that in your head, can't you? Drill yourself on it. Practice until you can come up with the total price as quick as you, or the friend you're practicing with, can come up with hypothetical mortgage and walkaway figures. A pro can do this very quickly without touching a calculator or pencil. But sometimes you can hurt yourself here by being too slick. Guard against having them suspect that you know what they're thinking; it worries some people and makes others feel stupid—and they'll start fighting you. Keep ahead of them when you can see inside their heads. Here's how:

3. Use a legal pad for your price calculations, but don't let them see the figures. If they don't seem them—and if you keep nodding reassuringly as you work—they'll think you've agreed to their value.

CLOSE FOR THE PRICE

Never forget for an instant that an overpriced listing is nothing but a dead weight that'll pull you down—you don't want it. So keep focusing on your goal. Your goal for the price was $154,950 and your top figure is $159,995—but only with the understanding that the price will be reconsidered after thirty days.

But they're thinking in terms of starting at $165,000 on the theory that they'll probably have to come down. Watch these words carefully—they work beautifully:

"Mr. and Mrs. Watt, I'm trying my best to put myself in your shoes this evening. Many salespeople are mainly concerned with taking listings, and will tell the sellers anything they want to hear. I don't think this is fair, because your main concern is selling the property, isn't it?" (Don't pause—you must jump on the next sentence.) "That's why I spent all day preparing facts to substantiate fair market value. I've seen salespeople take a listing at any price and then, six months later, the property is still sitting there. The advantage of first time exposure is gone. In many instances, the sellers even receive less than they would have, had they started at a realistic figure."

If you're a veteran in this business, you know that the above statement is true. Over the last few years, you've known lots of sellers who've listened to incompetent salespeople—and the incompetent can outbid you every time, can't they? But nobody has ever figured out a way to convert those incompetent bids into spendable money.

Use an alternate of choice to arrive at value. They're feeling hurt to get down to $165,000, and you know the market is $150,000. If I was sitting across from Gloria and Jack Watt tonight, do you think I could take their listing for a swift-selling $149,995?

No way. Jack and Gloria built their hopes and opinions on a bigger pile of garbage than I could shovel away in one night. I'm talking facts and logic; they're feeling emotions. At $165,000, they see exciting goodies in their future that they can't afford at market price. Of course, $165,000 is a mirage—the money just isn't there. But hope dies hard.

Though you can't write it for $150,000 tonight, you can bring the listing in for less than $165,000 if you can assure them—and back up your assurances with facts—that they're above market at anything over $150,000. Here's the next step:

"Based on the facts, Mr. and Mrs. Watt, I feel we should start between $152,500 and $157,500."

Why do I use two figures? I feel certain that I'm not going to get it at $150,000. An important point to remember here is that if they had not been so far off in their thinking, I would have set my range a thousand or two under market. Suppose I'm working with clients who want $85,000 for a house with a market value of $75,000. I'd probably suggest this:

"Based on the facts, Mr. and Mrs. Johnson, I feel we should start at a figure between $72,500 and $77,500."

In this case, I'd love to have the first figure in the Multiple Listing Book start with a seven. If I have to go as high as $85,000, I'd only do it if they gave me the listing for six months, and agreed to reconsider the price after thirty days.

With the Watts, I want the second figure to be a five because I know that putting it in the $160,000-up class will kill the action. Bear in mind that my research was thorough, and truly comparable properties are available for less than $155,000. To the objective observer, there's nothing about the Watt house that would excite buyers to pay $10,000 to $15,000 more for it than for the others, or that would induce a lender to finance a purchase at the higher price. When you're working with custom homes that vary greatly in amenities, construction, size, view, and so on, also bear in mind that you can't work this close because the properties on your CMA won't be this closely comparable.

OPERATING ON THE PRICE WITH THE DOM (Days On Market) STUDY

Listing their home for sale is a highly emotional experience for most people—more emotional than many of them realize. After they list, it takes time before they sort out their new priorities and pressures, before they realize what doesn't matter anymore, before they see logical things through their emotional screens.

Earlier we talked about how often people are in no hurry to sell the night they list, and tell you that nothing is important to them except getting their price. Then, with the listing decision behind them, they go out, find their future, and in a few days change completely. Now they want their old home sold fast. Now they're more involved in where they're going than in where they've been.

Welcome this change. It means they've broken the bonds that kept their emotions chained to their old home. This break has to happen before anyone can have a happy move.

You see, they were suffering from decision overload the night they listed with you. All their options were open before you arrived. Look at all the decisions they had to make then: whether to list with you or not, at what price and terms, for how long, what to take and what to leave, what to fix and what to forget—and what to tell and what to hide from you. And all these things are solidly connected with their lives. In the old slang phrase, listing hits them where they live. So they're very emotional when they list, and emotional people aren't famous for making logical decisions without objective guidance. In my experience, sellers rarely suspect how they'll look at things just two weeks after listing. When I'd had a year's success in this business, I knew more about what my sellers would soon be thinking about their listing than they did.

In Chapter 3, we introduced the DOM study. When they're weighing the question of price, use this report to pile more counters on the side of reality. Here's how:

"Mr. and Mrs. Watt, this is a Days On Market Study that covers all nearby sales in our price category for the past (month, six months, year—whatever you have). I wanted you both to see this information because it tells us a lot about the relationship between market price and speed of selling. I know that speed isn't as important to you as

price, but it's at least possible that your attitude on this will
change—or that the situation will change—making the timing a crucial
rather than a minor consideration for you.''
        Again, you have copies for both of them.
        ''Notice the home at 2020 Country Club Drive. It's very
comparable to yours except that the grounds are huge and they front
on the golf course pond. This property came on the market more than
a year ago at $199,995 and, after several reductions, it finally sold last
month for $163,000. It was on the market for 391 days.
        ''Compare that to 220 Concord, where there's a pool and only
three bedrooms. So it's not comparable to yours—but what's
interesting is that it went on the market at $157,500, and sold just
three days later at $156,500.''
        Do you see how you work with the DOM study? Without saying
so, you're telling them that for less money than they're asking, people
can buy a home that offers more in location or amenities. And at the
same time, you're making vivid points about how overpricing will take
them over their time limit.
        This method doesn't take the place of the comparable market
analysis; it simply gives you more persuasive power—and often all
you need is just a little bit more power to take the listing. The days on
market study has a great advantage—you make it up in advance using
low-priority time. It's not something that has to be created during the
last few hours before a listing presentation. And you can use your
DOM study over and over.
        So put a shell in the other chamber and fire both barrels at them.

LISTING THE HOUSE BY ITS BARBECUE

        Lots of people are strange about decisions—they'll never come
right out with a big one. With these people, if you force them to say
yes or no, they'll always say no. So you don't put them in that
position. Many times I've spent half an hour discussing what personal
property they're going to leave. They had never said they were going
to list with me, but after that half-hour, they approved the listing.
Never force them to make a big decision—just work with them on lots
of little decisions. ''Do you want to leave the fireplace
equipment?—the barbecue?—the draperies?''
        Discuss the pros and cons of these little items with great

interest—and put every decision they make on the listing form. The moment you put your pen to the listing form at their kitchen table, you're halfway to writing a good listing.

After you've covered all the personal property and led them through all those decisions with friendly interest, what do you do? It's simple. "Have we covered everything? Fine." Turn the form around, drop your pen on it, shove the form under their noses, lean back, smile, and say,

"Well, Mr. and Mrs. Watt, with your approval here, I can start getting you happily moved."

Now, to read the form, what must they do? Pick up the pen. Mr. Watt does that, looks at the form, and sees the time you've put on it.

"This is a listing for six months," he says, bristling a little.

Do you see the psychology here? Instead of talking about whether or not you're going to get the listing, they're talking about how long they're going to give it to you for. Sometimes the way to get the listing yes is to let them say no to the length of time you've put down.

Here's your answer to Jack Watt: "We could go longer, of course. However, I feel this will be enough time." You don't know if it's too long or too short, do you? When you say that, they'll probably come back with, "Oh, no, we'd never tie our home up that long."

If you go in there committed to getting a 180 day listing, you may have to settle for 90 days—if you shoot for 90 in the beginning, you'll often get knocked back to 30. Today, you must get longer listings.

HOW TO TURN DOWN A TURKEY

If you have to turn the listing down because they won't budge from a price that's so high it only spells trouble, you'll be glad you did after you do. I always referred an overpriced listing to another broker. When it goes into a listing auction like that, you don't want the property tied up for six months. Don't let the loser who wiggles his ears last have it that long. He gets it for thirty days only—the market may catch up to the price if he has it for 180 days. See Item 28 in the phraseology at the end of this chapter.

SET THE SELLERS UP FOR FUTURE EVENTS

Once you have the listing approved, it's time to brief them on what to expect in the selling process. Cover these points with your new clients before you leave:

1. Prepare them for the property preview by the agents from your office. The phraseology is given at the end of this chapter as Item 23.

2. Instruct them how to turn their house on: Lights bright, draperies open, stereo low. Explain why they should go through a cleanup, freshen up, turn-on routine whenever the house is to be shown.

3. Cover yourself on the damage that incompetent agents will do so they won't blame you. There are salespeople in almost every office who never think about the clients or their profession's reputation. They don't care whether they call a seller or not before showing the property—they'd just as soon knock on the door without warning.

Please do yourself and the entire profession a big favor—always call first. Sometimes, after you've called, you end up not being able to show it for reasons beyond your control. Do the profession and yourself another big favor and call back to apologize. So many sellers are left sitting there waiting for you to show up after they've charged around getting the place ready—and then they never see anybody or hear another word. Some of the "salespeople" in this business are only good at training the public to hate us.

Explain to your sellers that you can't control everyone in the industry but, if they'll make a note of everyone who shows the property or calls, you'll follow-up. Then if the clients have any complaints, you can call the agent responsible and with great politeness ask that person to please help upgrade the profession's image.

4. Tell the sellers not to approve anything about the listing or the sale that doesn't come through you. I always asked them to make sure they notified me, before doing anything about it, if they were asked to

approve anything. You should be advised of everything relating to the sale of that property. Sometimes an amendment can be sent to them directly without your knowledge. That document may not be to your sellers' advantage, but you can't protect them if you don't know about it. That's your main job: to protect them. You're their agent, their representative. Let them know that they can rely on you.

5. Have them take out any personal property that is not staying if buyers would expect it to stay. I've lost sales because of a chandelier; I've lost sales because of a throw rug; I've lost sales because of fireplace equipment. You see, a lot of buyers get to the point where they think that if they lose the chandelier, they've lost a good buy; the sellers get emotional and stand on principle—or whatever they call it—and a $200,000 sale goes down the drain over a $500 chandelier. See Item 22 in the phraseology.

6. Set them up for a low offer.

Make sure they understand that the price of property is set by the most willing sellers getting together with the most willing buyers. In other words, it's set by the market. You don't set it. And remind them that you're obliged to present all offers. See Item 27 of the phraseology.

7. Prepare them for a fast offer.

If they don't expect one and aren't mentally prepared to handle it, they'll hate you instead of being happy if one comes in. Suppose that after two hours of negotiating with Steve and Millie Renaski, during which time you maintained that the market price is $75,000, you finally list it at $87,500 with the understanding that they'll reconsider the price after thirty days if there's no action.

When you post the listing in your office, another agent says it's just what his buyers are looking for—and tomorrow night you have an offer for $85,000. What will Steve and Millie Renaski think? That you were trying to give their home away for $75,000 and beat them out of ten big ones. That is, they'll think that unless you set them up. The words to make them happy with fast offers are Item 24 of the phraseology at the end of this chapter.

TWELVE TRICKS OF THE TOP PRODUCER

Actually, I'm going to give you thirteen, and the extra one is as important as anything in this book. Here it is: *don't depend on memory for doing details.* You've put yourself on the fast track to Championship status and the big money, which means that you'll soon have more business than you can handle unless you're highly organized. Even in the beginning, you don't need to waste time cleaning up the big mess that forgetting to handle a small detail will cause.

I'll give you many helpful forms in Chapter 14; we'll cover time-planning in Chapter 13; but take time now to create a checklist for all the after-I-take-a-listing details. This checklist will get you off to a fast, professional start at marketing your new listing. Run off some copies of your checklist, staple one inside each of your listing folders, and mark off each item as you complete it. Ask your broker about Items 4 through 7; procedures vary from office to office.

1. Get your broker's approval of the listing.

2. Send a thank-you note to your new clients. Do this immediately. It reassures them when things happen right away. This note should be handwritten—you'll find the wording in Chapter 14.

3. Send the "Guess what your neighbors just did" card to at least the ten homes across the street from your new listing and the five homes on each side of it. (Get the sellers permission, of course.) The wording for this "New on the market" card is also given in chapter 14.

4. Get your listing in to the multiple office immediately for the hot sheet and MLS book.

5. Arrange for the sign and install the lockbox.

6. Put your listing in your office's up-desk inventory book.

7. Set up your office's file of the listing.

8. Schedule your follow-up with the client.

9. Develop your marketing plan for the listing and put it into high gear.

10. Call the sellers at least once every week. Unless you keep in close touch with them, little problems will become bigger than you can cure before you know you have any.

11. See the sellers in person at least once every month.

12. Reduce the price and extend the listing until it sells.

PHRASEOLOGY FOR THE LISTING PRESENTATION

The words that I recommend you memorize for your listing presentation are given below in *italics like this:*

1. When meeting Mr. Seller for the first time:
"Good evening, Mr. _____. My name is _____. (Enter the home.) Before we review my findings and research regarding the property, would you mind showing me your home? I saw it today with Mrs. _____; however to establish the highest possible market value, I think it's important that you show me all the improvements and express your feelings regarding the home."

2. To establish the arena:
"May I put my briefcase down?" (Head for the kitchen table.)

3. As you open your visual aid book at the kitchen table:
"Before we begin, Mr. and Mrs. _____, many people feel all real estate companies and salespeople are the same. Before making a decision on a company or its representative, I think it's important that you are aware of what the company will do for you. I am very proud of my firm and I would like to show you the benefits we have to offer."

4. Going over your findings:
"Mr. _____, I spent most of today researching data and compiling a comparative market analysis on your property. Would you take a moment and verify my accuracy on these details?" (Hand them the partially filled in listing.)

5. Your answer to, "We haven't decided to list with anyone yet." (Smile.) *"Oh, I'm certainly aware of that, but I'm also confident that when you see the benefits we have to offer and the service I'll give you, you'll agree that _____ is the firm you'll wish to have represent you."*

6. Presenting the comparable market analysis:

"Mr. and Mrs. _____, most of my work today consisted of formulating this comparative market analysis. One of the basic factors that determines whether a property will sell is the establishment of a fair market value price. As you can see, this form shows the properties that have been sold in the area, the properties for sale now, and the properties that did not sell during their exposure to the market place. Let's go over the form together." (Hand a copy to each of them.)

7. Your answer to "We know this home and the owner said it sold for more."

"We find this happens quite often. People who have had their home on the market, when asked by a neighbor what they sold it for, often reply with, 'We got what we wanted.' The inquisitor, knowing what they were asking, assumes they received much more. It's a common problem, but I can assure you these figures are facts of record."

8. "Our home is nicer than these."

"Indeed, it is one of the nicest homes in the area. Quality improvements and pride of ownership are so important in selling a home. However, the improvements primarily enhance the property's ability to sell faster, but don't always increase the market value in proportion to the cost of the improvements."

9. "We wouldn't sell our home for these prices."

"Well, based on that statement, you obviously have an idea of what we should sell the property for." (Smile.) *"What do you feel the price should be?"*

10. Your answer to "What do you think it's worth? You're the professional."

"Thank you. A reputation for professionalism is important, isn't it? The sales price of a property is flexible, depending upon the terms and the length of exposure to the market. You would like to move in the next (state length of time applicable), *wouldn't you?"*

11. Your response when they say yes to 10:

"Well, I think it's important that we keep as close to market value as possible, so do you have some idea of what you would want?"

12. Your response when the client names an overmarket price: (Act concerned, not smart-alecky. Look puzzled.) *"Mr. and Mrs. _____, maybe I missed something in the property. Could you take a moment and tell me why you feel that way?"*

13. Hear them out, then agree with them before making a point of your own. Always begin with a phrase similar to one of the lucky seven below.

A. *"I understand how you feel, but we should also consider—"*
B. *"Your point is certainly valid, although—"*
C. *"Looking at it from your view, that's true, but—"*
D. *"There's no question about it, your comments make sense. However—"*
E. *"I can certainly see the truth in that, except—"*
F. *"I agree with what you're saying, and I'd like to take that reasoning a bit further. In this case—"*
G. *"Beyond a doubt, that's true. Still—"*

14. To focus the discussion on their cash needs instead of price: *"Mr. and Mrs. _____, forgetting price for the moment, if I were to write you a check right now, how much would you want for your property after all charges including the mortgage are paid?"*

15. Closing for the price.
"Mr. and Mrs. _____, I'm trying my best to put myself in your shoes this evening. Many real estate salespeople are mainly concerned with taking listings and will tell a client whatever he wants to hear. I don't feel this is fair because your main concern is selling the home, isn't it? This is why I spent all day preparing facts to substantiate a fair market value. I've seen salespeople take a listing at any price. Then six months later, the home is still sitting there and the advantages of first-time exposure are gone. In some instances the sellers finally receive less than they might have, had they started at a realistic market value."
Alternate of choice when the seller wants more than market price.
"Based on the facts, I feel we should start at somewhere between $(slightly below market) and $(somewhat above market).

16. Seller says, "We can always rent; we don't have to sell."
Your phraseology: *"That certainly is true. Renting a home is a*

good investment. However, it is definitely a fact that very few tenants
take the pride in a home that an owner does. By holding the property
for two or three years, it's very possible that any appreciation in value
could be offset by deferred maintenance and necessary repairs. Have
you ever rented or managed a home before?''

Seller says no.

"It can be a rude awakening. The other day I was talking to a
broker who had been in real estate for ten years and decided to rent
his home. He thought he had qualified people, but was sad to find out
that they were what we call 'professional tenants.' Well, six months
later, after receiving no rent and going through eviction proceedings,
he got his home back. He said it took almost $2,000 to repair and
refurbish the home. This is the type of thing that worries me; doesn't
it bother you?''

17. To answer the objection, "We don't want to give out a
key."

"Fine. It's not mandatory that we have a key. Mrs. _____,
are you home most of the time?''

Seller: "Yes."

"When do you go shopping?''

Seller: "Monday morning."

"It would be a shame to have a qualified buyer unable to see
your home on a Monday morning, don't you agree?''

18. "We don't want a sign."

"We don't require a sign on a property. However, about 45% of
our buyer activity comes from calls regarding properties with our sign
on them. We are interested in full exposure, aren't we?''

Seller: "We don't want the neighbors to know."

"We have had other people who felt the same way. Interestingly
enough, we have found that with the home being shown and with real
estate cars and salespeople coming through the property, most
neighbors are aware of what's happening. We have found such
benefits from having signs on a property that, as your representative, I
really suggest we consider having one; don't you agree?''

19. "Will you advertise the property?''

"The decision regarding what properties to advertise is somewhat
left up to management. The advertising department has proven that the

only reason a property should be advertised is to make the phone ring. Based on most callers trying for a bargain, we have had great results in advertising a property priced below market value or lacking improvements, and then, after buyers see that home, a home like yours literally sells itself. But let's wait and see what management feels upon inspection of the property.''

20. Minor closing questions:

A. *"Mrs. _____, would you want us to call for an appointment before showing the home or just stop by?''* (Write answer on listing form.)

B. *"Mr. _____, which do you feel would better suit your plans, a 30 or 60 day possession date and close of escrow?''* (Write answer on listing form.)

C. *"Let's see, what are you going to leave in your home?''* (Name personal property) (Write answer on listing form.)

D. *"Mrs. _____, Tuesday morning is our preview of new property day. Would you have the home just as nice as it is today, so I can impress the other salespeople when they see it?''*

21. Going for the approval:

Turn the listing around, hand the pen to one of them, or put it on the listing form. *"Well, Mr. and Mrs. _____, if you'll put your approval right here* (point), *I'll go to work getting you happily moved.''*

OR

"Mr. _____, your name goes right here (point) just like you'd endorse a check. You can be assured I'll do my best to get you happily moved as soon as possible.''

The phraseology that follows is used after the listing is approved.

22. Critical instruction about personal property:

"Mr. and Mrs. _____ since you've definitely decided against leaving the (name the personal property involved), *let me suggest something that could head off a big problem. The* (chandeliers

or whatever) *enhance your home so much that anyone making an offer will probably fall in love with them. Then we all have a problem. I've lost sales over a throw rug. Please, let's not have that kind of problem here—we won't if you'll put those beautiful things in storage. It would be a shame to lose a sale over one of them, wouldn't it?"*

23. Set the sellers up for the preview:
"Mrs. _____, I will be bringing the salespeople by on _____ to preview your home. This is a very important day! If the salespeople are impressed with your property, they will be much more apt to show it to their prospects. The more showings we receive, the greater our chances are for a sale. So, let's have the home looking its very best by _____, O.K.? A few suggestions I might make are _____." (Lights on, stereo playing softly, sweet rolls in the oven, etc.)

24. Set the sellers up for a fast offer:
"I think it's important that you realize that most of our sales staff are working with about 5 prospects at all times. They may have a buyer waiting for this type of property, so maybe we'll be lucky enough to obtain a deposit in the next few days. That would be great, wouldn't it?"

25. Set them up for showings without a warning call:
"As we discussed earlier, Mr. and Mrs. _____, we will stipulate that each salesperson call for an appointment to show the home. However, sometimes after showing a buyer another home in the area, a salesperson may think of your home, and in the excitement of telling the buyer about it, forget to stop by a phone and call. If this happens, please understand. If you are too inconvenienced at the time, ask them to return; but, if it's possible, let them see your home, for they may be good, qualified buyers and purchase it that day."

26. Set it up so that you can protect them: (Use first names here if possible) *"My job is to represent your interests. Because of this, I'd appreciate your not signing a contract unless I approve it. If a salesperson or broker wants to present an offer to you, please make sure I'm notified, so I can protect our position."*

27. Set them up for a low offer:

"Finally, I think it's important that we realize that buyers establish value by what they actually pay for property. We're of course, shooting for (price). However, if a lower price is offered, we will carefully go over it to see if it's feasible and, at that point, discuss the plan of action to take. Thank you again for your confidence in listing your home with me. I'll do my very best to justify your trust. Good night."

28. When you're turning a listing down because you've determined that it can't be obtained on a reasonable basis:

"Mr. and Mrs. _____, I sincerely am interested in representing you and marketing your home. In good conscience, though, I can't honestly put a sign on the property and list it at a price that is too out of line with the market. Maybe I've missed something and I might possibly be wrong. Many real estate firms will take a listing just for the sake of putting up a sign and hoping the property will sell. I can't do that. May I suggest that you feel out the market and give the listing to another firm, at your price, for 30 days and see what happens?"

PART THREE

CONTROLLING YOUR EMOTIONS AND ORGANIZING YOUR SKILLS

12
HOW TO USE REJECTION TO DEFEAT FAILURE AND CREATE A WINNING ATTITUDE

A Champion, when asked how real estate is, will enthusiastically say, "It's unbelievable." That covers it either way, doesn't it? We have a number of goals at Tom Hopkins Champions Unlimited. Two of the most important are to teach real estate people how to develop and keep a good attitude, and to sell them on the practical benefits of working for their clients with total professionalism and total honesty.

Your goal in reading this book is to learn how to make more money. I hate to disappoint you, but you're not learning how, you're reading how. The only way to learn how to make more money from these pages is to master the material and then use it. This means that you practice the techniques, drill yourself on them, and rehearse every pause, gesture, and word. Then you go out, find people, and put your new knowledge to work.

HOW TO CHANGE OVERNIGHT

Some people are amazing. They spend between seventeen and seventy years cutting the grooves deeper on their personalities, and then they expect a seminar or a book to change them overnight. Let's talk for a moment about what's possible here.

First, I can't change you. Only one person can. Guess who. That's right—it's entirely up to you.

Second, you can decide at any time to master these techniques and use them to become more successful. In this sense you can change overnight—and you're really a different person the instant you commit yourself wholly to this goal.

However, your quick decision won't make any large and lasting impression on your life unless you follow your new ways of success—and avoid your old less-than-great habits—for twenty-one consecutive days. That isn't long. Give your new money tree time enough to take root.

But don't forget that you were born to be happy. If you're not happy except for a short time after some sudden jolt, it's because of the decisions you've made or left unmade during your life. Please don't blame any long term unhappiness that you might have on someone else. Happiness is internal; it can't be external. Now that you're seriously considering changing your life—and you are or you wouldn't be looking at this page—please resolve to be happy. If you're ready to accept the challenge of change and start becoming the person you're dreaming of being, do it. If you're not ready, don't; stay the same as you are now. Either way, be happy. And, if you decide to change, give every new habit twenty-one days to take hold. Otherwise, reading this book is a waste of time.

A PROBLEM WITH NEWNESS

When I started out in real estate, it went great until they asked me a question. Then I had a problem. Not only was I ignorant of the answer, often I didn't even understand the question. But this was only on the surface—what really counted against me was having no idea that people were asking the same questions over and over, and every one of them was an opportunity, not a trap.

The Champion thinks of questions as stimuli, and knows that for every stimulus there is a correct response.

Imagine touching something that's very hot. You'll certainly get a stimulus and instantly make the correct response. When you have professional real estate skills, your response to a stimulus question will be as sure and almost as fast as jerking your hand away from a hot rock. These rapid professional responses are the trained reflexes we talked about in Chapter 5.

To be successful, you don't have to react instantaneously—you'll have two or three seconds to do that in most cases. With some people, the pace is even slower. But don't bank on it. The true pro can respond with the correct words very quickly when he's with fast-thinking clients.

Every transaction is different in detail—but it's amazing how the same things keep coming up over and over. Let's mention a few:

"We have a friend in the business."

"The last company we listed with charged a lower commission."

"We want to sleep on it."

"We don't want a sign."

Since you're going to hear these things over and over, and since every one of them can cost you the listing if you don't make the correct response, doesn't it make sense to learn the words that'll eliminate their friend, convince them you're worth your higher fee, show them why they shouldn't sleep on it, and demonstrate why they should have a sign?

Unless you hear the stimulus, pause for a brief moment to find the correct response, and then deliver that response convincingly, you're not a pro. And if you're not a pro, you aren't going to earn a pro's income. So identify all the stimuli that you're going to get over and over. Then practice, drill, and rehearse the most effective responses until you'll come up with the right one, swiftly and sincerely, every time.

After you've done that, all you need to put your knowledge to work, and to start taking listings with it, is to overcome your fear of rejection. You can have all the responses down pat, but they won't make you any money if you're hiding behind the donuts in the office.

Go out and knock on doors. Aha. I'm reading your mind. You don't want to.

Why not?

We're all tempted to blow smoke here. Doorknocking isn't ,my style. I don't like to disturb people. And so on. But the truth is, if we don't want to knock on doors, we're simply afraid of rejection just like everybody else is. That's a solvable problem.

HOW TO PUSH THE FEAR OF REJECTION OUT OF YOUR WAY

You won't put much effort into beating this problem unless you admit to yourself that it's a big barrier to your future earnings. Please face up to this fact.

Sometimes the fear of rejection stops you from doing things like canvassing by phone and ringing doorbells, doesn't it? Or, if this fear doesn't actually stop you, it's always there, ready to help you find reasons for starting late, quitting early, and wasting time between calls, isn't it?

How can you overcome this fear?

By selling yourself on the realities that'll make you a success, instead of on the realities that'll reinforce your fear. Let me explain.

There are many ways to look at how you're paid for taking a listing that sells. Let's talk about the two ways that relate to how you earned the fee.

We'll begin by assuming that you make $1,000 on the average listing after the split and after deducting the cost of any little fires you pay to put out instead of letting them burn the transaction down. Let's also say that you usually give your listing presentation in two hours.

One way to look at your listing activity is to say to yourself: "I make $500 an hour when I'm writing listings, but not one red cent the rest of the time."

Or you can say, "I've learned that knocking on ten doors turns up one listing appointment, and from ten listing appointments I'm sure to get one listing that'll sell. This means that I knock on 100 doors and hear 99 noes to earn $1,000—so every *no* has to be worth $10 to me."

Which of those two ideas do you want to dwell on? Both propositions have an equal amount of truth in them. But the first drives out all feeling of accomplishment at taking the rejections and makes it much harder to continue taking them long enough to be successful.

The second idea lifts you up and makes it easy to keep on going. Jot down your daily progress:

Date	Noes Received	Earnings
6/3	14	$140
6/4	15	$150

Talking to friends, relatives, and neighbors doesn't go on the tally—that's gravy. And only genuine homeowners count. But if you'll use the techniques in this book with enthusiasm and confidence as you work with the husband or wife at 100 homes, I guarantee you'll write one saleable listing.

Actually, I believe you'll do better. In many parts of this continent, more than one listing opportunity will be found behind every ten doors. Also, when you've acquired professional skill with these techniques, you may regularly convert half of those opportunities into listings that'll sell. If your average fee is $1,000, this means that every no is worth $30, $50, or even $70 to you. And if your average take-home per listing sold is $2,000 (in many areas it's more) that doubles the value each no has for you. At these prices, can you afford to let a single precious *no* get away from you?

For three years, I knocked on twenty to thirty doors a day. So I've made lots of money collecting my noes and forgetting the rejection so I could keep on moving. Nothing has changed. You can start tomorrow and do exactly the same thing I did a few years ago. Isn't it great that you'll get paid for accepting rejection? Watch how it works.

Knock, knock. "Good morning, ma'am. Tom Hopkins from Champions Unlimited. I stopped by this morning—"

The lady breaks in and says, "You're in real estate. I've had eight of you people come by since we moved in. Don't ever knock on my door again." Slam.

So you say to the closed door, "Well, thank you for the $10 ($50?—$150?)." Then you head for the next door, the rejection vanishing like a drop of water sizzling on a hot pan.

That door slam is about the worst it ever gets, and how bad was that? It's really a very easy way to make money, and the more you do it, the easier it gets.

THE CUBE OF TWENTY PUTS $8,000 A MONTH IN YOUR POCKET

The sweetest part of my system for making rejection pay is that you decide how much you want to make door knocking—and then you go out and get that money. Put your own numbers into this speech, and then say it to yourself every morning as soon as you get up:

"Every *no* I get is worth $20 to me, and I make $8,000 a month door knocking for them. Since I also makes lots of sales, I can only give parts of twenty days a month to pounding the pavement. This means I've got to get twenty noes on each of those twenty days."

To make this work, use the figures that apply to you. Numbers you know aren't true won't push you along the sidewalk and up to the next door. In the above example, the agent may be working with an average earnings per listing sold of $1,000, but she knows from experience that she'll convert half her listing appointments into saleable listings. Or she's getting one saleable listing per ten appointments, and one appointment per ten doors knocked on, but her average take-home is $2,000 per listing sold.

CHANGE YOUR ATTITUDE TOWARD FAILURE

Getting you to do that is another of my major goals. I work with some people who don't have much of a problem here. They jump on these ideas, charge out, make lots of money—and then go into a slump. Why? Because they've stopped doing what caused them to make money. They'll stay in their slump until they go back to the fundamentals, until they return to doing what they get paid for—accepting failure and rejection without letting it stop them.

The key to success is handling failure.

You don't learn how to do that naturally. Like playing the ukelele, handling rejection well is an acquired skill. Some of your emotions tell you to sulk or swear when you're rejected, and then avoid any situations in the future that're likely to put you in line to feel the pain of rejection again. Other emotions tell you to get more out of life for yourself and your loved ones. Concentrate on what you have to gain, and learn how to change your attitude toward rejection.

Begin right now. First, write this phrase: "I never see failure as failure—" Five mottoes beginning with that phrase are given below. Memorize them. Then, when you need their help to take the edge off a rejection's pain so you can keep moving forward, they'll come quickly to mind.

When you're rejected, you've failed to achieve what you wanted, which means that rejection is a common form of failure. Now let's go on to five more ways to change your attitude toward failure and rejection.

1. I never see failure as failure but only as a learning experience.

Every sale that falls out is a learning experience; every problem you have is a learning experience. Don't get down when you have a learning experience, get even. Learn all there is to learn from that failure—then put it behind you and get on with your plans for your future.

2. I never see failure as failure but only as the negative feedback I need to change course in my direction.

Outside a restaurant with a lively bar, I once saw a gentleman, who'd had too much to drink, try to unlock his car with the wrong key. No matter how many times he tried, the wrong key still didn't work. After I'd talked him into taking a taxi home, it occurred to me that sometimes we all keep trying to make the wrong key unlock the door, keep using techniques that don't work in our listing and selling endeavors, keep putting the wrong solution to the problem long after we've tried it and failed.

But when have we failed? I've just told you to knock on a hundred doors and wade through a hundred rejections to get one listing that'll sell; now I'm telling you to change course when you get negative feedback.

Do both. It takes some stick-to-it stamina to keep knocking on the hundred doors that'll provide your first listing fee. And, while you're doing it, you'll have plenty of learning experiences, plenty of chances to change course in your direction to make your technique more effective.

Don't use negative feedback to change course from working to hiding. Some agents check in at the office early on a morning, eat some donuts, and head out—to drive around avoiding by-owner signs. They stay away from their listing banks because people find them there. They just cruise, listening to the stereo, until the earliest hour they can go home. That's not the change of course I had in mind.

Make sure that every change you make in your methods is toward more efficiency, more effectiveness, more honesty, more professional conduct—and more money.

3. I never see failure as failure but only as the opportunity to develop my sense of humor.

The whole secret is to laugh sooner. Without conscious effort, your worst blunder will eventually strike you as being funny. The longer you wait to laugh, the more that failure will hold you back. So make a determined effort to laugh sooner, and learn the trick of telling a good story on yourself. The greater the embarrassment or the confusion, the funnier it'll be when you tell it to others. Laugh sooner—there's no better way to take the fangs out of failure.

4. I never see failure as failure but only as an opportunity to practice my techniques and perfect my performance.

You'll get lots of opportunities for practice in the beginning. This is as it should be—you need the practice more now than you will later.

5. I never see failure as failure but only as the game I must play to win.

Play the percentages. The greatest hitters strike out a lot—you have to be willing to play the game if you're going to win the pennant. Real estate is a game. Life is a game. Both have their rules; luck plays a small part; but the winners play ball. They play hard, fast, and often.

There are people in your office who never get a complaint call. They never have a sale fall out—the one they made last year was solid from opening to closing. Play the numbers game—the agents who contact the most people make the most money.

THE CREED OF THE CHAMPION

Before I give it to you, let me quote from a letter Jeanne Arnew of San Jose sent to a member of our team: ''I have had over 30 transactions in the past seven months since receiving my license, and I attribute 80% of my success in real estate to Tom Hopkins. Not only his techniques, but the attitude he instills in you—that makes you believe in yourself.''

That's what the creed is all about. It's the central core of the Tom Hopkins Champions Unlimited philosophy. This is what we all live by. I hope you'll learn it word for word because if you'll live by this creed, it'll give a solid-fueled boost to your earnings and put the rest of your life on a higher plane.

I am not judged by the number of times I fail but by the number of times I succeed, and the number of times I succeed is in direct proportion to the number of times I can fail and keep on trying.

What counts isn't how many transactions fall out, how many doors slam, how many things don't work out, how many people go back on their word. What counts is how many times you pick yourself up, shrug, and keep on trying to make things go together. Maybe you have financial problems. I was flat broke when I started in real estate. If you've got one nice suit of clothes, you're that much ahead of me when I started. My first broker's training program went like this: ''Hang in there.'' I know about the problems, the obstacles, and the troubles of getting started in real estate because I did it the hard way

But the problems are temporary if you take control of your thoughts and develop the right attitude. Do that and you'll soon see all your troubles fall off the scale. Only one thing counts after a few weeks of concentrated effort: your ability to brush the obstacles aside and keep on trying, learning, and perfecting your performance until you pile success on top of success and reach the highest levels you aspire to.

13

GETTING A FIRM GRIP ON THE SLIPPERY MINUTES

It's easy to procrastinate in real estate, easy to spend the whole day actively doing nothing. That is, it's easy until a month is gone and you have nothing to show for it except bills.

Do you have organizing and time planning problems? If you do, you're fortunate—great salespeople aren't naturally organized. They're not detail lovers. What they want is to get out there, meet the people, and sell or list the house—curses on the paperwork.

But you're paid for doing what you don't want to do whether it's paperwork or prospecting. Both of those things can overwhelm you unless you've learned how to pull effective action out of the raw material of life. And what is that raw material? Nothing but a lot of slippery minutes strung together. That's all any of us have to work with—bunches of fast-fading and easily-misplaced minutes. So, to be successful, we have to find ways to gain firm traction on life's slippery highway. If I can get you to plan your time and organize your action, you'll get so much time-traction that the results—in terms of more money in your pocket—will amaze you.

Being organized allows you to cope with problems efficiently. I often say that the real estate business—when worked professionally— is a gold mine. It's also a problem mine. If you ignore the problems in real estate, will they go away? Or will they grow from little creatures into huge monsters? You know and I know that untended problems in real estate don't fade—they flourish. When we try to hide from them, they grow so big they eat us alive when they catch us, which usually happens about fourteen hours before the transaction is scheduled to close—but won't unless the problem is solved.

THE THREE BASICS OF TIME SAVING FOR SUCCESS

Is there a professional way to handle problems in real estate? There certainly is. A four letter word—*fast*—sums up the essence of professional problem handling. Lost time is the worst enemy that successful solutions have. When problems arise—and in real estate they will as surely as corn grows in Iowa—your clients must be made aware that you have done everything a skilled and professional agent has the power to do toward solving the difficulty. They also must be made aware that you acted promptly. In other words, they need to know that their problems are with their problems, not with your sloth, ignorance, and carelessness. They won't know that unless you get back to them fast, and take other action, if any is required, equally fast.

But solutions won't always be within your power, will they? As long as you do your job quickly, and keep them informed, that's all right. Sometimes the best advice you can give your clients is that they should let the other party sweat for a few days. This too is all right—if your advice aims at results you believe are in your clients' best interests.

The first basic of time saving is: *Do it now if it can be done now—especially if it's unpleasant.*

Otherwise, all the fear, guilt, and evasion that'll fester in the shade of the problem you're trying to avoid will make you waste far more time and money later than it would take to cope with it now.

Hand a loser several phone messages and what'll he do? First, he'll groan and suffer about the ones he was afraid he'd get—then he'll call the easiest one in the pile. And the problem calls? He'll leave them until tomorrow, next week—or never. Hand a Champion some phone messages and he'll call the toughest one first—and if there's a problem, he'll get it on the road to a solution before he'll make his easy calls. As usual, the Champion arranges things so that he can finish on an up note and walk away feeling like the winner he or she is.

Doing it now if it can be done now, especially if it's unpleasant doesn't just apply to problem solving. This concept should be your guide to everything you know you should do in business—and maybe in your private life as well. But we're constantly faced with situations where more than one thing must be done right now—which of them gets our attention first?

The average salesperson says to himself, "Okay, I can't do everything at once, so I'll set priorities. First I'll work on the item that'll make me the most money because that's my reason for being in business. Then, when that's out of the way, I'll go out prospecting."

Champions have a completely different priority: they get the hard things and their activity goals achieved first—then they jump on the things they're looking forward to doing. Why? Because Champions know that what's hard and what makes the most money are usually the same things in the long run. They know that every time they handle a hard task today instead of avoiding it, they raise their prestige, increase their self-respect, and make their tomorrows easier, happier, and more profitable.

The second principle of time saving and success is: *Take time every day to think.*

People don't realize they are deliberately shutting their brains off by keeping them filled with trivia all through their waking hours. By the way, it's not thinking when all you do is review your prejudices, reinforce your fears, and excuse your evasions. Take time every day to look clearly and openly at who you are, where you're going, and how you're going to get there.

The third principle of time saving for success is short and sweet: *Be organized.*

Think of all the things you *can't* do if you ignore this principle.

1. You can't make much money unless you're organized.

In real estate, it takes a large volume to create a large income—and details left unattended can break more transactions than the fastest tongue can open.

2. You can't make efficient use of your time unless you're organized.

A large volume of real estate transactions comes only from a large volume of meaningful contacts with people—and this is something that only a time-efficient agent can achieve.

3. You can't build a referral business unless you're organized.

Maybe you think they'll only remember that you finally sold their turkey. No such luck—if you failed to give them service, they won't remember anything except the calls you didn't return, the promises you didn't keep, and the frustrations they felt. Sure they'll give you a referral—when fish start singing.

4. You can't enjoy any time off unless you're organized.

As any veteran of the business can tell you, it takes effort and organization before a real estate person who is successful can take time off. Some people do well in this business for a short time and then burn out because they never figure out how to take time off. After my first three years, I was headed for Burnout Island. Oh, I'd never missed having Christmas Day off, but the rest of the time I worked. Then it suddenly got to be too much. I started taking one day off a week, but I was worried at first that I'd lose a tremendous amount, that it would take me all week to straighten out the problems, that I couldn't make it work. Imagine multiplying your annual days off by fifty—I think I had reason to worry a little. So I prepared for it thoroughly. Preparation is half the battle for time off in real estate; the other half is being determined to let nothing, and I mean nothing, stand in the way of your time off. Over the course of six months in this business, you'll make more money on a six day week than you will on a seven—unless you're as fanatic as I was during the first three years of my real estate career.

My Wednesdays-off plan worked beautifully—the crowds were small wherever we took the kids during the week, our family had fun together, and I went back on Thursday mornings feeling refreshed, enthusiastic, and ready for another hard-driving week.

The key is preparing your people. I told everyone, "Here are three phone numbers: my office, my home, and the phone in my car. Except on Wednesdays, you can reach me 24 hours a day at one of these numbers. Wednesday is my day off, and I'm not available then, but at any other time, you can always get me on the phone right away. If something that can't wait overnight comes up, John Smart at my office will take good care of you—but, every day of the week except Wednesday, I'm just a quick call away."

The test of whether you can stay away from Burnout Island comes when an agent catches you right before your day off and says he has a hot offer on one of your listings. The only moneymaking answer a Champion can give is, "That's wonderful. I'm delighted to hear that. Call John Smart at my office and he'll take care of everything. I'm off until Thursday morning."

"But—"

"John will take good care of you. And thanks for calling. Goodnight." But this is only for Champions—when you're new in the business you can't do that; you have to kiss your day off goodbye and go fee-hunting instead.

If you're a budding Champion, here's a valuable tip: when you're able to give top priority to the taking of one day off a week, don't stay home the night before. If you're going to be late, head of out of town directly from your last appointment, and meet your family a few miles down the road. Otherwise, somebody will catch you before you can get away the next morning and dump a little something on you.

That little something will probably be a problem, but it might be a possible opportunity. Either way, when you have that item taken care of, all chance of getting a quality day off will be lost. It's so easy to let this happen over and over—and it doesn't take long to destroy your family's faith in the whole idea. When that happens, so much anxiety will hang over your days off that most of the benefit will be cut out of them.

After your first six successful months in this business, nothing will do more to insure that your success will continue than locking into one day off a week. After being on this schedule of having assured time off for a month, very few calls will come in for you on your days away because everyone knows you're not there. That's how it worked for me.

Select your day off with care; then stick to it—switching around kills the system. I recommend having your day off printed on your business cards: "Available 24 hours every day except Wednesdays, call—"

PROFESSIONAL PEOPLE FILES THAT WORK HARD FOR YOU

The average salesperson has a filing system known as the rubber band. When I was in management, the people who weren't making any money would come into my office for a consultation on how I could help them boost their incomes.

"Do you have many prospects?" I'd ask.

"Oh, yea, sure—look at this pile."

"When did you last take the rubber band off?"

"Well, it's been a while."

You see, this kind of salesman is afraid to call the prospects on his dog-eared old cards; he knows all those people have bought from or listed with another office—and he doesn't want to hear it. How grim real estate is when you operate like that. If the rubber band is the mainstay of your present filing system, hustle down to the nearest stationery store and buy a few inexpensive items that'll allow you to set up a battery of organized professional files in a few minutes. Here's the list of supplies you'll need: some 3 x 5 cards, four sets of A-Z file guides, five file boxes, and a few file folders. The low-cost cardboard lift-top boxes for 3 x 5 inch cards work fine.

With this simple system, you'll have your files organized in no time at all. After that, they'll give you ten dollars' worth of results for every quarter's worth of time you put into them.

Files for Sellers.

Two of the file boxes are for your sellers. The first, which you may want to label S-1, is for your listing presentation leads. This is where you file a card about the nice couple you made a listing presentation to last night. They said, "Well, if that's the way the market is, we'll probably wait until next year."

If you believe them and don't keep in touch, a couple of weeks from now you'll drive by their home and get a rapid rush of rejection when you see another broker's for sale sign planted in their front lawn. Then you'll ask yourself, What happened? We can speculate endlessly about that—but one certainty will always remain: you didn't stay in touch. The whole idea behind this part of your professional file is that when people have been thinking about moving, the emotions bonding them to their home get frayed. Then these people start seeing all sorts of reasons why they can and should go somewhere else. In other words, they start itching to move. The Champion makes sure he's there to scratch that itch. If you're going to be a Champion, you'll go through your S-1 file every other day, and you'll find reasons to call anybody you've presented to who's still itching to move.

The second box, which you might label S-2, has a front and a back section. In the front your warm canvassing leads are filed A-Z. Some people call them cold canvassing leads, but if you know exactly what to say, those leads are nice and warm. Go through this list every other day looking for people who might be getting hot on the idea of listing. Call anyone whose current thinking about real estate you aren't sure of.

In the back section of S-2 are your by-owner leads. These are filed by phone number.

By phone number? Why?

If they change their ad, that's the only thing they can't change. Many by-owners, after getting lots of calls from real estate people, decide it would be fun to fool a few of them. Here's what happens when an agent, who thinks he's found a new by-owner, phones:

"Good morning, ma'am. This is Milton Sparrowskull with Pathetic Realty. I saw your advertisement in the paper and—"

"Milt—you've been by here three times already—we changed the ad." In essence, she's saying, "Ha ha, dummy—you flunked our intelligence test. I guess you're not such a hot shot after all."

That's why a Champion watches the ads by phone number, and calls on any change. But the Champion uses a much different approach:

"Hi, Mary—Tom Hopkins—I like it. Your new ad ought to bring in a lot more calls. Tell Ed I think it looks good."

Mary gets the message: *You didn't fool me*. But you don't want to say that—you don't have to. This technique opens up a lot of interesting situations. Sometimes they'll ask, "How did you know?" I'd say, "Mary, as your agent-to-be, it's my job to know."

Call them on any change. If the ad isn't there anymore, that's a change. Here's the phraseology:

"Hi, Mary—this is Tom Hopkins—I just wanted to call and congratulate you."

"What for?"

"Why, for selling your home. I noticed that you pulled your ad out of the paper."

"We didn't sell it—when the ad ran out again we decided not to put it back in right away because—well, you know, it's expensive, and—"

Now you're really set to move in on them. Isn't that exciting?

General File

The third box holds your general file. Put a card in there about each of your past buyers and sellers. Then create a file card for everyone you know or have done business with—your hairstylist, gas pumper, drill instructor in boot camp—your dog's vet, your acquaintances from all the organizations you've ever worked with or belonged to—people you've met socially, school friends, all your business associates—everybody has to live somewhere.

If you want more speed and convenience, use a Rolodex for your general file. Keep your general file, (card box or Rolodex) near your phone—when anyone calls, instantly refer to their file card, see what the involvement was, and impress them with how much detail you "remember." Everybody knows you can't put everything about everyone in your brain—but each person still wants you to remember everything about them. They feel warm toward you when you do, and rejected when you don't.

Holding onto details and keeping them handy so you can retrieve them quickly is what they make paper for. Use your brains for things paper can't do.

When Jim Jones calls for the first time in two years, what does the average salesperson do? He goes crazy trying to remember who under sweet heaven is Jim Jones?—and winds up giving away the fact that he can't recall much of anything about this former client. So Jim Jones feels put down and, many times, the referral or repeat business he called up about will wind up with someone who'll treat him as though he were important.

The pro reaches for the J's the moment he hears that Jim Jones is calling. In an instant he has the right card in his hand and is saying, "Jim, it's nice of you to call. How's Diane? And How's Suzie and little Jimmie? Are you still over at Builders United? Oh, are you? Great. Things are going well, I hope. Fine. You know, if I'm not mistaken, you're originally from Owensboro, Kentucky, aren't you? I had some people in from Kentucky a couple of weeks ago and I was thinking of calling you. What can I do for you, Jim?"

Is that different? Yes. Is that professional? Yes. Does that pay big returns on the small efforts it requires? Yes.

In one convenient place, your general file holds the addresses of all the people you might want to reach by mail, and the phone numbers of all the people you might need to call for any purpose. Once you've started your general file, a member of your family, or a part time helper, can help you complete it. Then, whenever you're ready to make a mailing to your list, your helper can take over all the details of getting the newsletter or announcement into the mail. This list, as you'll discover as soon as you start to use it, will soon be of great value to you.

Files for Buyers.

The last two of your five file boxes are for buyers. Use one box for hot buyers and another for cold buyers.

FLICK THROUGH THE FILES DAY

Now you have four files for people who are currently active in real estate—two files for sellers and two for buyers. Go through all four of these files every other day. Ask yourself these questions:

What are they thinking about real estate today? Are these people about to change from warm to hot? What can I ask them or tell them to justify my dialing their number right now?

Since an essential part of the follow-up that creates your income is done with these calls, take long enough with each card to bring the person to mind. Think about their situation for an instant—then act on your hunch. Keep on doing that for three weeks and you'll discover that you're developing a sixth sense for the hottest opportunities in your file. Every time you call any of your prospects, jot the date on the back of their card so, the next time you look at that card, you'll know how long it's been since you've worked with that person on the phone.

Buyers are odd, sellers are even. To smooth out your work load, call buyer prospects on odd days, seller prospects on even days. Of course, you'll call the hot buyers and hot sellers you're working with whenever you have a way to move them closer to a transaction.

FOLDERS FOR THE ACTION-ORIENTED DESK

Champions think of their desks as places where business is done and money is made, not as the stronghold where they trade discouraging words with other losers and hide out from reality. When Champions are at their desks, they are working—and they're ready for whatever may come.

Have everything at your desk that you need to make money, and nothing else. Keep this in balance—you need pictures of your family to glance at from time to time to draw strength and purpose from; you need whatever favorite items make the place yours. But you don't need clutter, confusion, and a drawer full of last year's hot sheets. Keep your desk clean, but have what you need. In your file drawer you should have—

1. Expired listings.

Label a folder *Expired Listings* to hold copies of your expired listings and all important documents relating to those expirations. You must have this information handy in your desk so you can react quickly when these former clients call you about becoming active again.

Put a card on these sellers in your S-1 file. Because they're itching to move, you want to make sure to keep in close touch with these people.

Maybe you're thinking right now, "I'm not going to have any expired listings." Good luck. I believe that the greatest lister in the world will, after a few years in this business, have had many listings that expired. Most people can accept that their home didn't sell and not blame you if you kept them informed, showed them that you cared, and exposed their property well. What they hate is when you don't give them service and they never hear from you. That's why you call your sellers and follow-up with them regularly.

The market changes constantly. You can write a listing tomorrow that, three weeks ago, would have been gone in 72 hours—but there's been a ripple in the market and that beast just sits there. The veterans of this business all have war stories about listings they've had that should've sold and didn't. If you've done your job, the clients can't get mad at you when the listing expires, but they feel bad—the world doesn't like their home. That heavy rejection makes a lot of people say, "We'll just wait then." What they're really saying is, "You don't like our home, world? Then we aren't going to let you see it anymore."

But they're still itching to move. In sixty to ninety days, that house will be back on the market; if you haven't kept in touch, it'll show up on someone else's inventory and you lose. So let them see your smiling face and hear your sweet voice—scratch, scratch, scratch on that constant itch of theirs.

2. Closed sales.

Please keep a folder in your desk that has information on all your closed sales. If your broker wants the original documents to stay in the office's main file, run copies of the important ones for your desk.

With this data at your fingertips, you can immediately start talking knowledgeably when any of the people who've bought a house from you call, wanting to sell. You'll probably have more information about their property within reach than they can locate without a lot of effort—which is the position a professional likes to be in. But don't roll all your facts out over the phone—get right over there and talk face-to-face to them before another agent moves in on you.

3. Income tax and business receipts.

This is another vital file that should be kept handy in your desk and added to regularly. Almost everything you spend money for in the business end of real estate is deductible—if you can prove that you spent the money. The best way to keep good tax records—that is, the method that takes the least time and has the least risk of missing deductions—is to make a permanent record of your expenses the same day you spend the money. Get in this habit—it'll save you a lot of time and money every April.

PLANNING/APPOINTMENT BOOK

Keeping a little box in your car to pop receipts in is handy, but don't overlook having some form of diary—the IRS requires this for any entertainment expenses you're planning to deduct. Your appointment book can serve this purpose.

Most Champions keep an appointment book within reach throughout their business hours; they simply have too much going on to function efficiently without a convenient, take-along record of their appointments and of the details they must follow up on each day.

You can find a variety of daily diary/appointment books in stationery stores; other good ones are advertised in business magazines. Try to find one that you are comfortable with. A good diary/appointment book will have the following standard features: lines for appointments broken down at least in ½ hour increments, space for listing your priorities or goals for the day, as well as room for a Things to Do type of list. Your diary/appointment book should also have calendars showing the full month as well a breakdown for each week of the month. Many of them will also have sections for names, addresses and phone numbers; mileage and other business expenses.

The most important aspect of the diary/appointment book is that you must rely on it every day. It should always be with you. Find one that doesn't tell you to give up and go home at five or six o'clock. By not having space organized for evening appointments, that's what most of them do. Since the best listing appointments usually take place at night, why set yourself up to feel bad every time you write one in your book? Get one with spaces you'll feel good about filling.

THE STRENGTH OF THE STANDARD WEEK

In most jobs, we have to be in a certain place doing certain things for certain hours of the week. The boss does the time planning for us—all we have to do is punch in, keep breathing as we do the job, and then go home.

People who come to this business from a job that involves a company-imposed work week are often bewildered by the average real estate office's free atmosphere. Without someone telling them what to do, they're lost—they just don't get anything done that'll make money.

The Champion is the same—he'd be lost without someone telling him what to do. But there is one important difference: the Champion fills that vacuum by being effective at telling himself what to do—and generally he demands more of himself than he'd give any boss.

He—or she—sets life goals, and then breaks those goals down to ten-year goals, five-year goals, and finally to yearly, monthly, and daily goals. Then the Champion translates those money and accomplishment goals into the action that will achieve them.

This is done very simply: by scheduling enough daily activity to reach the desired result in the desired time. In other words, you schedule a successful life the same way a factory schedules its production.

You don't have to spend a great deal of time at setting goals. As you get more into this technique, you'll find that you do most of it at odd moments over a period of time. If you reduce your odd-moment thinking to paper, it's goal setting; if you don't, it's daydreaming. Begin by jotting some general ideas down on paper, and then add details and refine your thinking about what you want from life as you go along. How much time does it take to decide you want to double your income—or multiply it by a factor of ten? How long does it take to decide you want a new luxury automobile?

Yet so few people will do this on paper. Even fewer will make a regular habit of thinking with determination and realism about what they really want beyond getting through another day. Please accept the importance of managing your life instead of drifting through it. Map out your course on paper, set your goals a bit higher than you think you can achieve right now, and soon you'll be achieving far greater things.

Companies would get into trouble fast if they tried to operate without schedules. So will you. If you force yourself to operate without a working routine, every day, perhaps every hour, you'll find yourself debating what the best course of action is right now. So what will you usually do? Whatever seems like a good idea at the moment. All too often, that will be what's easiest and least unpleasant—which generally means it's also the least productive thing you can do at that particular time. Too much of your energy will go into small battles with yourself over what to do next and, by losing too many of them, you'll lose your war to achieve the high income you desire. You may even lose your battle to stay in real estate—every year tens of thousands of people leave the business for this exact reason.

One of the solid pillars I built my real estate career on was the standard week. Hot buyers pulled me off it; ready-to-list sellers pulled me off it—but little else could. And, when an interruption was over, I picked up my standard week again. In the beginning, it was two early hours in the office, then out on the street by 9:30 every morning; lunch, then return calls, research houses, and make afternoon calls; dinner, then evening appointments. Every night, I ended my regular workday plus work evening with a short planning session for the next day.

As my skills and knowledge grew, my standard week evolved steadily toward higher and higher production. Everything learned about the area and its inventory of houses helped me reduce the amount of time that adequate research took. And, as my referral business grew, I had less time or need for prospecting.

In my fourth year, I hired a full time secretary and encouraged her to get a real estate license so she could work with my clients on anything I wanted her to handle. She was a tremendous help and only cost me a listing a month. After hiring and training her, I was able to spend most of my time working with clients—when not showing

properties and closing buyers, I'd be running through my techniques
with sellers and listing them. What happened to my income then? It
really took off.

First get efficient, then go for the big volume. After you've done
the first, the second is easy. That's right. Real estate is an easy
business to make big money in—after you've worked hard for two or
three years at developing your professional expertise and building your
clientele.

Keeping to a standard work week is one of the basic methods that
helped me achieve what I achieved as a real estate salesperson. After
taking some training, I worked out a pattern for my weeks. Sure, it
was a demanding pattern—I wouldn't ask anyone to work as hard now
as I did then—but a large part of my results came from always
knowing what I wanted to do at any given moment, and then just
doing that thing. I had goals for every day: every weekday morning I
did certain things; every Sunday afternoon I did certain things. For all
the basic activities that spell success in real estate, there are some
hours of the week that are best to do them in; for every hour of the
day from seven in the morning until nine at night, there are some best
things that you can do to make more money. The limits on how much
you'll do and on how high you'll fly are set by you and nobody else.
Most people do that by never thinking about it. You're different.
You're going to set goals, plan your days around a standard work
week, and achieve great things, aren't you?

Keep at each new standard work week until you grow enough in
professional stature to move up to a higher level. This is exactly what
I did. If you make yourself decide everything every day, you'll make
a lot of bad decisions about how to spend your time. Instead of
wondering what to do next, what a relief it is to operate smoothly and
confidently along previously decided lines, knowing all the time that
you're on target for achieving the success you want. Commit yourself
to a standard work week that's a high production schedule; then stick
to that plan until you're ready for a better schedule that will create
even greater production. You'll be astonished at the heights you'll
reach when you work systematically.

Be sure to make your weekly schedule decisions realistic—don't
attempt too much in the beginning. It's much better to make your first
schedule a little bit too easy—and be able to take on more work
soon—than it is to start at such an impossibly high level that you'll

feel discouraged, guilty, and defeated.

Do your scheduling on paper. Unless you commit it to black and white reality, your plans won't have enough impact to make an impression on your present habits. Review your progress daily—this is crucial, especially in the beginning. Keep working at it—you'll find that developing and getting in the habit of following a powerhouse schedule takes time and effort. What you're looking for is a standard work week that pushes you without beating you, and makes the most effective use of your time that's possible with the degree of expertise you've attained so far.

FINDING MORE HOURS THROUGH TIME PLANNING

If you think about how much a few individuals get done and then compare their output to how little so many people accomplish, it seems like the effective few must have ways of manufacturing minutes.

In a sense, we do. What's amazing is how simple these minute-manufacturing methods are. Let me tell you how to use the plan-your-work, work-your plan method:

1. Tonight, list all the things you have to do tomorrow.

Set priorities on those things by red-flagging or numbering the most important items. Now you're ready for the most crucial thing in this step, which is to commit yourself to completing your top priority items at the earliest possible hour tomorrow.

2. Tonight, review your daily activity goals.

These are all the things that your plan calls for you to do each day—prospect with fifteen people, for example—in order to make your money and other goals come about. Compare your list of things to do with your daily activity goals; then work up an hour by hour plan for tomorrow that'll make the best possible use of your time.

3. Tomorrow, follow the plans you develop tonight.

It's really that simple—but let me warn you, in the beginning you'll often be shocked at how firmly you can commit to the next day's plans, only to have the things you didn't do last week, last month—even last year—come crashing down and blow your plans sky high. Or your old work habits, your old personal commitments, your lack of familiarity with all these new techniques, prevents you from carrying out your plan as well as you want to.

Don't worry about it—just keep planning your tomorrows and working your plans to the best of your ability until these new habits become you. Then you'll find that it's happening with much less stress and effort on your part. Remember, a new habit only takes root in your personality when you follow it for twenty-one days. This means doing it, not just wanting to, not just trying to. And you can't mark those three weeks off in bits and pieces—to make your new standard work week stick, you've got to put together a string of twenty-one days in which you plan your work and work your plan every day.

It will take some practice and some learning by trial and error. You may have to become more assertive with a few people who have been wasting your time. You may have to get very tough with the worst offender in this regard—that person might possibly be yourself.

Build plenty of flexibility into your plans. Avoid locking onto a rigid schedule so tightly that, if anything prevents you from carrying it out in every detail, you'll lose your friendly attitude. One of the main purposes of time planning is to reduce frustration, not expand it.

Follow the plan-your-work, work-your-plan concept and you'll find a lot more productive minutes in every day than you ever knew were there. These manufactured minutes add up quickly into extra productive hours that will add important money to your income. Foresight cuts waste motion and lost time to the absolute minimum.

Every highly productive person I've talked to about this subject has told me that they plan tomorrow tonight, and they consider this small, basic idea one of the most important elements in their success. What an upsurge of productivity there'd be if all the people who control their working time suddenly adopted this system. Slowly, very slowly, that's happening; but most people never plan their days; they simply crash into whatever comes their way. And, just to make sure the confusion is complete, they put off everything they can, which turns everything that happens into a crisis. The future is always filled with nasty surprises for those of us who never look at it a day early.

If you've been playing that tune all your life, please invest the time and effort it'll take to learn how to create an effective workplan each night, and then put it into effect the next day. Do this, make this habit your constant companion, and it will revolutionize your productivity. The time to start is this evening. That's right, tonight. No matter how busy, tired, or discouraged you are, you can make a start on this vital new habit tonight. You can list at least five things you need to do tomorrow.

In the beginning, you'll need about fifteen minutes a night to plan each tomorrow, but as you gain experience with this technique, the time required for it will drop drastically. What'll happen is that you'll be thinking—and maybe making notes—all through the day of what you'll need to do tomorrow. When you sit down in the evening for a few quiet minutes to complete your plan, you'll be able to make all the necessary decisions, and then commit yourself to them, with quick confidence.

What a relief it is to have all your work decisions made, and simply go out and do the job. Believe me, all it takes is commitment to success—which means commitment to accepting the pain of change, commitment to accepting lots of trivial rejection, commitment to doing the most productive thing at every given moment.

Be sure to include your life's most important people and things in your time planning—otherwise you'll create forces that'll tear you down faster than your hard work can build you up. Schedule time for:

1. Family.

Please, treat your family better than you treat your clients—they're more important to you in the long run, aren't they? Yet so many of us forget that truism in the day-to-day hustle to make a buck—and this attitude is so counterproductive, so unnecessary, so harmful to your life. Schedule time for the family. Keep track of the days and things that have special significance to each person you love—anniversaries and birthdays, the school activities your children want you to attend, the events you've promised your spouse you'll attend together.

You can find a new client anytime by knocking on ten doors, but your family is unique and irreplaceable. So if you have to be late for a date with them—call. And, when something is especially important to your spouse or child, don't let the possibility of losing a fee override the certainty of disappointing them. A missed anniversary will be remembered in sorrow twenty years after—a fee you might possibly miss will be forgotten in as many days. One of the main reasons you plan your time and push yourself along all day every work day is to have time for your family.

2. Appointments.

If you have one appointment a week, you won't miss it—but when you get busy, you'll miss scheduled listing and sales appointments unless you keep track of them on paper. Maybe you don't think you're busy enough to need an appointment book. Don't worry—if you follow the suggestions in this book, you soon will be. When the surge of business that's coming at you hits, don't add to your burdens by having to learn how to schedule your time too.

3. Religion.

If you have one, as I do, don't lose it getting rich. That's stupid. I mean it. If you're supposed to go to church, go to church. I know I was supposed to go, and I wanted to go, but sometimes my best buyer would call. Finally, I went to the pastor and said, "Father, make me an usher. That way I have to be here." It worked. Other things are important besides making money—commit yourself to doing those things outside of business that are of the greatest importance to you. They are the things that make life worth living; they give you the strength to keep on going instead of burning out about the time you start to make some real money.

4. Research.

Our business is based on keeping up with the market and with the latest developments in financing and owning real property. All these things are constantly changing; the only way you can gain—and then keep—professional status is to constantly be updating your knowledge. Every day you're not fully occupied with clients, schedule time for viewing property. When should you do that? During the least productive hours for prospecting.

5. Play.

If you work hard, you're entitled to play hard. If you'd rather not do that, go off for some high-quality loafing when you've earned it. I'm fortunate in knowing many of the top real estate people on this continent, and I can tell you that most of them play as hard as they work—and they don't feel guilty about it either because they know they've earned it. If you haven't done enough yet to feel good about taking time off, don't. Wait until you've convinced yourself that you've earned it. Otherwise, guilt feelings will wipe out the benefits you would've received had that vacation, in your own mind, been well-deserved. We can't fool ourselves as much as we think we can.

6. Prospecting.

Until you've built up a referral business, the limit on your income is how much you prospect. Commit to prospecting, schedule it, and don't fight a battle with yourself every day—just get out there and do it. Now you know the phraseology; you know how to build the right attitude; you know how to make it all easier for yourself—so you know that you can do it all.

7. Health.

The tensions and pressures that are built into this business will get to you fast if you don't heal yourself every day with some physical exertion. Why? Because tensions and pressures throw more adrenaline into our blood than is good for us—and the only way to get rid of that excess adrenaline is through physical exertion. This is very basic. Your body has only one way to react to pressure and tension, and that is the same way it reacts to fear—by running or fighting.

Any physical exercise can take the place of the fighting, but for most people, competitive sports create as much tension and pressure as their work does. Keep that in mind when you select your exercises for healing tension and pressure, and give yourself every possible break. Your highest priorities for exercise and recreational activities, as you battle to establish your real estate practice, should be to heal yourself, to protect and improve your health, and to avoid creating new problems for yourself. Jogging may be a better choice than tennis, and walking may be better than jogging. For many people, doctors now recommend a brisk half-hour walk instead of jogging. Whatever exercise you choose, commit yourself to it—you'll feel better, make more money, and enjoy life more and longer.

8. Specialty.

By now, you should have a good idea of what your first listing specialty is going to be. Will you devote your primary efforts to your listing bank? Possibly you've decided to specialize on by-owners, or to work open houses most heavily. Whatever listing specialty you select, be careful to provide enough of the right hours for it in your daily time planner.

9. Friends.

Something has to give if you're on a strong drive for success, and what's likely to snap is your relationships with old friends. For many people, this is too rough—they cave in when the peer pressure to stay average hits them, and they remain as they are. But if you're strong enough to resist this pressure—and you'll have to be if you're going to succeed in becoming a new and remarkably more successful person, there'll come a time, perhaps much sooner than you expect, when it comes down to choosing between success and your old friends. Before long, you'll be growing emotionally, professionally, and financially in noticeable ways—but most of your present friends will be staying on the same levels they occupy now.

Before long, the old relaxed feelings and the community of interests that pulled you together in the first place will be gone, never to return. Very few friendships can survive a considerable change in the status of one friend that's not approximately matched by a similar development in the other person. When you turn into an eagle, you can't eat sunflower seeds with a pigeon anymore.

Accept that—life is set up this way. Don't worry about it because there's nothing you can do, short of giving up your drive for success, to hold onto the past. If that parting of ways is going to happen it will, naturally, and in due time. You're sitting there playing cards with old friends and suddenly your beeper goes off. You toss in the hand, stand up, and say, "I'm sorry but I have to go present an offer now."

If your friends don't understand, if they resent it, that's their privilege. If (I really should say *when*) you become uncomfortable with your old friends, find new friends among the many who, like you, are moving up—or find them among the people who already are at the level you want to reach.

WHAT I MUST DO

In *How to Master the Art of Selling®*, I related the way in which I came into possession of the shortest and most powerful piece of wisdom about time planning that I've ever heard. These words have been framed on the walls of every home and office I've had since I first acquired them some fifteen years ago. They're as compelling today as they were then because these twelve words are timeless. And, to everyone with the spark of genuine ambition, they are priceless. Here they are:

I must do the most productive thing possible at every given moment.

Put that where you can see it at your desk and at your home workplace. If you really commit yourself to that motto, it'll drive you all day long. At times you'll swear it's driving you crazy too—you'll hate it, but you'll also know it's making money for you like nothing else can. I sincerely hope you'll take this short sentence to heart—I'm trying hard to teach it to you because it's the key precept that I've lived by since the real beginning of my real estate career after six months of failure.

I must do the most productive thing possible at every given moment. Keep looking at this marvelous epigram. If you really get it into your bones, you'll stop procrastinating; you'll stop letting the minutes of your life slip away without benefit; you'll stop finding excuses and start finding clients. Is lying on the beach in Tahiti productive? If you're satisfied that you've earned it, absolutely! Live by the fabulous twelve words and you'll become the person you should be—the person of your dreams—because greatness is latent in all of us.

14

FORMS AND CORRESPONDENCE—USING YOUR TOOLS EFFECTIVELY

I'm kind of a nut about putting the facts and figures that relate to what I'm doing on graphs. I discovered early that it isn't enough to simply gather the numbers. Unless they're organized to show the forest instead of the trees, you can't see where you're going. In other words, putting your numbers on graphs tells you what your destination is. If you're headed for trouble, it's really nice to know about it before you get there so you can make sure you don't.

Let me give you an example. In 1968, I quit using the comparable market analysis. Guess what popped up on one of my graphs next? My listing-sold percentage had dropped twelve points. In other words, I lost 12 percent of my listing income because I got a bit too smart. Here's the thought that turned me toward trouble: "I know the values—why do I have to go through all that bother with the CMA? I don't need it." So I had to find out the hard way that sellers don't believe the spoken word like they believe the neatly written figures on a carefully researched CMA. The practical result of skipping the CMA step was that I stopped taking listings at the right values.

COMPARATIVE MARKET ANALYSIS

PROPERTY ADDRESS_____12345 Success Circle_____ DATE _____

FOR SALE NOW	BED RMS	BATH	DEN	SQ. FT.	!ST LOAN	LIST PRICE	DAYS ON MARKET	TERMS
12460 Happy Lane	3	2		same	25,000	58,300	141	VA
13601 Million Dol	3	2		same	25,000	57,090	42	VA
16104 Success Cir	3	2		same	25,000	57,750	80	FHA

SOLD PAST 12 MOS.	BED RMS	BATH	DEN	SQ. FT.	1ST LOAN	LIST PRICE	DAYS ON MARKET	DATE SOLD	SALE PRICE	TERMS
12412 $ Drive	4	2		more	26,000	57,090	52		57,090	VA
16104 Success	3	2		same	25,000	56,650	48		56,100	VA
12105 Happy Ln	3	2			25,000	57,750	71			VA

EXPIRED PAST 12 MOS.	BED RMS	BATH	DEN	SQ. FT.	1ST LOAN	LIST PRICE	DAYS ON MARKET	TERMS
14106 $ Drive	3	2				56,090	120+	Cash to Loan
12104 Happy Lane	3	2				58,300	120+	10% + 2nd

F.H.A. — V.A. APPRAISALS

ADDRESS	APPRAISAL	ADDRESS	APPRAISAL
16401 Success Circle	56,650		
16201 Success Circle	57,200		
16201 Success Drive	57,090		

BUYER APPEAL   MARKETING POSITION

(GRADE EACH ITEM 0 TO 20% ON THE BASIS OF DESIRABILITY OR URGENCY)

1. FINE LOCATION _____ %   1. WHY ARE THEY SELLING _____ %
2. EXCITING EXTRAS _____ %   2. HOW SOON MUST THEY SELL_____ %
3. EXTRA SPECIAL FINANCING_____ %   3. WILL THEY HELP FINANCE .... YES___NO ___ %
4. EXCEPTIONAL APPEAL_____ %   4. WILL THEY LIST AT COMPETITIVE MARKET VALUE . YES___NO ___ %
5. UNDER MARKET PRICE _____ YES____NO____ %   5. WILL THEY PAY FOR APPRAISAL .... YES___NO ___ %

RATING TOTAL_____ %   RATING TOTAL_____ %

ASSETS_____
DRAWBACKS _____
AREA MARKET CONDITIONS _____

RECOMMENDED TERMS _____

TOP COMPARATIVE MARKET VALUE .... $_____
PROBABLE FINAL SALES PRICE .... $_____

If you're new in the business and are thinking of avoiding the work that well-prepared CMA's require, please remember that this happened to me in my fourth year. I'd set some records by then. I had knowledge, skill, and confidence—but it still hurt me in the wallet when I tried to shortcut the CMA-writing step when I presented my research. You new people, please don't go out on a listing appointment without a carefully prepared CMA. I don't have to tell the professionals that—they know it.

One final tip on this form: *have the sellers put their initials on it,* and leave a copy with them. Why does a pro have his sellers initial the comparable market analysis? So that in effect they say in writing, "Yes, I have been informed as to what the actual value is." It makes them think.

ESTIMATED SELLERS PROCEEDS

If this form is called the Sellers' *Cost* Sheet in your office, I suggest that you go to a copy shop and have them run off a supply of these forms with the word *Proceeds* substituted for *Cost.* Why? Would you rather hear about how much you're going to pay, or how much you're going to get?

I'd love for you to join me and the other Champions in a goal: let's make sure the sellers net as much as we've told them they will. I used to make sure they netted more. To dramatize this, I'd have two checks drawn: one for the amount I'd told them they'd get, another for the amount of the overage. Then I'd hand deliver both checks. Why go to all that trouble for people who are moving away? Referrals, my friend, referrals. In real estate, they are what makes the honey sweet. Here's what I'd say:

"Max and Corinne, I wanted to come by and personally bring your check because I promised that it would be for $16,800, but I made a mistake."

They'd brace themselves for bad news, take a quick look at the check, and stare at me in surprise when they saw it was for the exact amount they expected, $16,800. Then I'd hand them the second check and say,

"I goofed in my figuring—I got $275 more for you than we thought we would."

ESTIMATED SELLER'S PROCEEDS

SELLER'S NAME _____ DATE _____

PROPERTY ADDRESS _____

BROKER _____

SALES REPRESENTATIVE _____ SELLING PRICE $ _____

ENCUMBRANCES:

First **Mortgage** ....Source: Seller [ ] Lender [ ] Document[ ] ....$

Second **Mortgage** .....Source: Seller [ ] Lender [ ] Document[ ] ....

Other Encumbrances .....Source: Seller [ ] Lender [ ] Document[ ] ....

TOTAL ENCUMBRANCES .... $

GROSS EQUITY $

ESTIMATED SELLING COSTS

Policy of Title Insurance .... $

Estimated Escrow Fees ....

Termite Inspection and Report ....

    (Possible repairs not included) ....

Prepayment privilege, if any

    GI.......None ....

    Conventional...Varies, but safe to figure 6 months' interest ....

        on unpaid balance

Reconveyance fee (only if existing loan is being paid off)...............

Lender's Demand or Beneficiary Statement ....

Proration of interest on existing loan ....

    (Interest is always 1 month in arrears. Allow 1 month's interest maximum)

FHA or VA loan discount fee of new loan ....

Brokerage ....

Other ....

Other ....

      APPROXIMATE TOTAL COSTS $

      APPROXIMATE SELLER'S PROCEEDS
      (Gross Equity Less Total Costs) $

POSSIBLE CREDITS OR DEBITS $
    Proration of property tax
    Return of balance in Impound Account

This estimate has been prepared to assist the seller in computing his costs. Whenever possible we have used the MAXIMUM charges that can be expected. Lenders and escrow companies will vary in their charges; therefore, these figures cannot be guaranteed by the broker or his representatives.

I have read the above figures and acknowledge receipt of   Presented by: _____
a copy of this form.

_____   Address: _____
Seller

_____   Phone No.: _____
Seller

When they finished oh'ing and ah'ing, I'd say, "You didn't expect this check—so it's fun money. After you get moved, have some fun with it. Now I'd like to ask you, Max and Corinne, if you know of anyone that might also need my services."

For $275, people came up with lots of names. Try this technique—you'll love it.

SALESPERSON'S COMMENTS

Whenever you have a new listing on tour or caravan, have five or ten salespeople fill out this form as they come through. If your listing

---

SALESPERSON'S COMMENTS

WHAT WILL MAKE THIS LISTING SELL?

SELLER'S NAME: LEWIS JONES
ADDRESS: 4621 Euclid St., Anytown, Arizona
SECTION #: 8
LISTED BY: SAM SMITH
LISTED PRICE: $58,950
DOWN PAYMENT: 10% - VA-FHA
                        (Circle One)
INSPECTED PROP.: YES   NO
SHOWN PROPERTY: YES   NO

YOUR APPRAISAL OF PROP.: $58,500

YOUR OPINION OF DOWN PMT. OK

COMMENTS: Nice enough — should sell at these terms — messy neighbor hurts.

SALESPERSON: John Salesman

is priced above market, the salespeople's comments will give you a substantial reason for going to your seller for a price reduction. Use the summary form. The information has more impact when presented this way; also, summarizing the salespeople's comments gives you a chance to omit any that might offend your clients.

SALESPERSON'S COMMENTS

WHAT WILL HELP THIS LISTING SELL?

DATE _____

SECTION # _____

LISTING # _____

SELLER'S NAME: _____

ADDRESS: _____ D.P. _____ PRESENT LIST PRICE _____

SALESMAN	COMMENTS & SUGGESTIONS	SHOULD SELL AT $_____	DOWN $_____

LISTING SALESMAN: _____ DATE _____

PROSPECT CARD

It's a temptation to scribble information about our prospects on whatever piece of paper is handy. But when it's time to call the people back, either we can't find that scrap of paper, or we can't decipher our scribblings on it. Have a standard way of recording routine information—it's the fast, reliable, professional method of doing this essential

PROSPECT CARD

P.R.   L.B.
                                              SALESPERSON Sizzling

SOURCE: (SEE SOURCE LISTS) Doorknocking, FSBO   DATE _____

NAME____ John & Mary Jeffries ____ OCC. ___ Welder _____

ADDRESS____ 12345 Success Circle ____ PHONE(S) 956-3050 _____

NEEDS:	HAS:
BEDROOMS: 3 PRICE RANGE _____	FAMILY SIZE ____ 2-John Jr., Christy
DEN/F.R.:_____ DOWN ___ G.I.	OWNS____ x ____RENTS _____
STYLE:___ Ranch ____ MO. PMTS. 200.00	SELL TO BUY x EQUITY 3,000
POSSESSION:___ anytime ___ INCOME 880.00	LIST ___ x ____ TRADE _____

REMARKS/ADDITIONAL NEEDS _____ H __ F __ C __

FRONT

RECORD OF PROPERTIES SHOWN OR SUBMITTED TO THIS PROSPECT

DATE	ADDRESS	REACTION — GOOD	BAD	MAYBE
		☐	☐	☐
		☐	☐	☐
		☐	☐	☐
		☐	☐	☐
		☐	☐	☐
		☐	☐	☐
		☐	☐	☐
		☐	☐	☐

DISPOSITION ☐ SOLD ☐ BOUGHT ELSEWHERE ☐ GOT AWAY ☐ LISTER ☐

BACK

work. Forms that are designed for the specific job allow you to put more data in less space; when you want to find and use the data, they let you do it faster. These considerations prompted us to develop this prospect card; please feel free to reproduce it for your own use.

PERSONAL HOT SHEET

Many realty boards circulate daily updates for their weekly multiple listing books. These updates, often called hot sheets, are for the exclusive use of the members of the Board of Realtors® that issues them.

HOT SHEET

ADDRESS	NAME	PRICE & TERMS	DATE LISTED	DATE EXPIRED	PHONE

You also need your own personal hot sheet, or listing control form. This is the single piece of paper on which you show the important selling facts for all of your own listings. Keep one copy on your desk and another in your car. When you're carrying more than ten listings, as you soon will be after putting this book's material to work, the personal hot sheet is a necessity. This form helps wonderfully to keep your mind focused on selling your own listings. I don't know about you, but I always wanted to get my buyers happily involved in a listing of mine that suited their requirements. Unless you maintain an up-to-date personal hot sheet, you'll often fail to take full advantage of every opportunity that comes along to bring one of your listings to the attention of buyers or other agents—that is, you'll miss chances to sell your listings. When you only have three or four, you may find that hard to believe, but it's a different game when you're a heavy hitter.

NOTES AND LETTERS THAT BUILD YOUR FUTURE

You're interested in working toward a 100% referral business, right? Start with an idea that's as important to developing a referral business as *I love you* is to developing a lasting relationship: show appreciation to the people who help you. The average salesperson feels that he's done all that needs to be done when he says, "Thanks." Champions write their thanks because appreciation that comes in the mail on a piece of paper is an event that's long remembered. Instead of avoiding this as a task, they go out of their way to take advantage of this tremendous opportunity. Every day, they send tokens of respect and recognition—thank-you notes such as those given below—to people who can, and very often do, become clients and boosters of theirs. If you're serious about earning a Champion's ample income, you'll make this your daily habit—beginning today.

MOST BEAUTIFUL HOME THANK-YOU NOTE

Dear Mrs. Coolier:
    I enjoyed our brief chat this morning, and I'd like to thank you again for the effort that you and Mr. Coolier have lavished on your home. Your skill has made our community a finer place to live in, and your pride of ownership is an inspiration to everyone who passes by your home.

As a professional serving the real estate needs of this area, I treasure people such as you and your husband. Thank you both for your contribution to the quality of life here in Middleford. .

Sincerely,

THANK YOU FOR THE LISTING CARD

When done with professional skill, a listing presentation covers a wide variety of questions. But the listing decision is so highly emotional, and often it's so crucial to the homeowners' plans and finances, that they often regret approving the agreement after the salesperson leaves. Then they may become somewhat dubious of the agent they listed with. This card is designed to rekindle the spark of confidence that inspired them to list with you, and to further establish the rapport that's so vital to a mutually successful agency relationship.

THE THANK YOU FOR THE LISTING CARD

Now we'll go to work...

CHAMPIONS UNLIMITED

Inside: ...in serving you to get happily moved. You can be assured that my company and I will do everything possible to consummate a successful sale for you. Cordially,

Always send this card immediately after taking a listing; it will greatly increase your ability to communicate with your sellers.

FOR SALE BY OWNER THANK YOU NOTE

By-owners are challenging and exciting. Beyond a doubt, they provide the most fulfilling form of prospecting that's available in the resale home field. This card is designed to show the service and sincerity that you have to offer in wishing to help a by-owner. For best results, mail one of these cards the same day you see the people. Better yet, handwrite the words—but get them in the mail fast.

THE "FOR SALE BY OWNER", THANK YOU NOTE

May I take a moment...

CHAMPIONS UNLIMITED

Inside: ...to thank you for showing me your lovely home. I sincerely wish you the best of luck in selling it. If you should find need to employ a professional real estate firm, I would appreciate the opportunity to show you all the excellent benefits we have to offer. Best of luck,

THE ANYBODY WHO DOES ME RIGHT CARD

All of us are surrounded by people we rely on for our everyday existence. Because these people work at such ordinary jobs, they rarely get much praise for the services they render. Nothing that costs so little is appreciated more than recognition for a job well done. Why not send a note of thanks to those who toil for us? Not only is it a fine, upstanding gesture, but the results in the form of referrals will amaze you.

FOR EFFORTS ABOVE AND BEYOND THE CALL OF DUTY CARD

For efforts above and beyond the call of duty.

Inside: It's with great pleasure that we wish you a happy anniversary. About a year ago, you let us serve you in finding your new home. We are proud to have you as one of our clientele and hope you will enjoy many happy years in our home. Sincerely,

♆ CHAMPIONS UNLIMITED

THE THANKS FOR REFERRAL CARD

The dream of every dedicated real estate salesperson should be to build a business that's solidly based on referrals. The easiest people to work with are the buyers and sellers sent to you by former clients of yours. The difference between the referral and the prospect behind a door, or the buyer off the street, is huge. With the referred person, you don't have to prove your honesty and expertise—someone they respect has vouched for you.

Sincere thanks . . .
For referring the Smiths to me. You can
be assured that I will do my best to help
them and justify your confidence in me.
Cordially,

Cherish your referrals. To everyone in real estate, and especially to the new agent, they are pearls beyond price; every referral means that former clients had so much confidence in your professional ability that they took the emotional risk of recommending you to a friend. Along with a considerable opportunity for financial gain, a referral puts a heavy responsibility on you to live up to the confidence your former clients have shown in you.

LETTER OF INTRODUCTION

When you're starting to work a new listing bank, send this message to the residents there. If possible, address them by name. And use the tip given for the next mailing piece to make sure that your letter gets read promptly.

Dear Homeowner:
May I take this means of introducing
myself to you? My name is _____, and
I'm with (name of your company). I'll be
representing homeowners in your
neighborhood, and will stop by in the next
few days to meet you personally.
Sincerely yours,

NEW ON THE MARKET CARD

Send one of these to the ten homes across the street and the five on each side of all your new listings. Here's a tip that'll put a lot more power in notes like these that you send out. Use blank envelopes and have them hand addressed. Check with your broker; unless local ordinances or your board's rules require you to, don't use your company name on the return address. Don't even use the office address if it sounds commercial—give your home address instead. A pro uses hand addressed blank envelopes because they look like personal mail, and they get opened first. Do you know that lots of people never even open mail that looks commercial? So don't use the same envelope all the time. Once they've opened your blank envelope, they'll read this message because the *Guess what* catches their interest.

THE NEW "ON THE MARKET" CARD

OPEN HOUSE INVITATION

Here's the form mentioned in Chapter 7; it'll help you cash in on open house opportunities. Remember: an open house that isn't done right isn't worth doing at all.

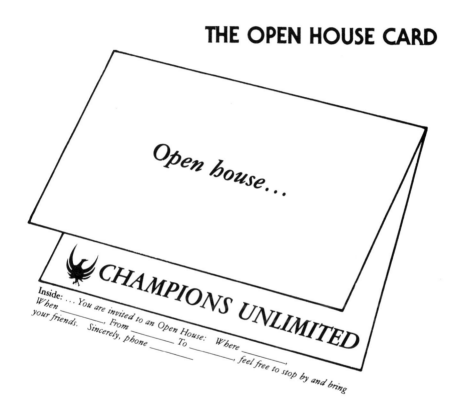

THE OPEN HOUSE CARD

MORE LISTING TOOLS

Here are three more forms that'll put punch in your prospecting time. You're authorized to make copies of all of them for your own use.

MARKET SURVEY

This powerful tool for your listing bank is discussed thoroughly in Chapter 9.

Name _____

MARKET SURVEY

	Yes	No
1. Do you feel the area is improving?	☐	☐
2. How long have you lived in the area?	☐	☐
3. Do you feel the shopping facilities are adequate for the area?	☐	☐
4. Do you folks drive to work in a car pool or commute alone?	☐	☐
5. Where are you employed?	☐	☐
6. Do you have a full time real estate professional serving your family's needs?	☐	☐

When you have finished asking the questions, say, *"Thank you so much for your time. I will let you know of any interesting developments in your area."*

THE MOST BEAUTIFUL HOME ON THE BLOCK
AWARD

Chapter 8 tells you how to use this powerful clientele-builder in connection with the most-beautiful-home thank-you note given above.

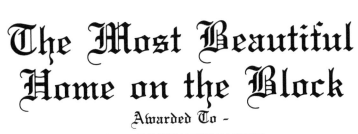

The Most Beautiful
Home on the Block

Awarded To –

Name   THE JOHN JOHNSON FAMILY
2095 S. Marshall Drive
Phoenix, Arizona

Date   January 1, 1983

Thank You,
Your Home Truly Shows Pride In
Ownership, Outstanding Landscaping,
Maintenance, and Attractiveness.

Presented By   CHAMPIONS UNLIMITED

LISTING BANK CONTROL SHEET

Step 2 in Chapter 9 details how to organize your listing bank in a notebook with a supply of this form. You're welcome to reproduce it for your own use.

LISTING BANK ACTIVITY REPORT

- Name _____ Wife _____

Address _____ City _____ Zip _____

Children   Age   (Thank You) Notes

1 _____ _____   A _____   F _____
2 _____ _____   B _____   G _____
3 _____ _____   C _____   H _____
4 _____ _____   D _____   I _____
5 _____ _____   E _____   J _____

Dog _____ Cat _____   Phone _____

Referrals
Name _____   Address _____   LISTER/ BUYER

Hobbies _____   Sports _____

Calls

Use Other Side

15

THE MOOD OF THE MOVE

Many times we do things without really knowing why or how we're doing them. Now that we've come to the final chapter, I'd like to talk to you about how the achievements of my real estate career actually came about. I'm not doing this for self-assertion, but to bring out some clues to the essentials of success that lie deeper than techniques and learned phrases.

Notice that I said *clues* to those essentials. I don't claim to have all the answers in this area—human motives and needs, the world we live in, and our limitations and strengths are far too complex to be covered fully in several books, let alone in one chapter. But if you're new to real estate, I think that in many ways you're probably very much like I was at the same stage of my career—you're probably motivated by similar hopes, limited by similar fears, and headed in similar directions to those I was taking then. So the emotional problems that pounded me as I pursued the goals of my early career have a lot in common with the strains you're feeling now.

It's not enough simply to cope with your own emotions, difficult though this is. To be successful in real estate, you must also have a practical understanding of the emotions churning through your clients.

By now, you know that I believe fervently in the tremendous value of training—until you have some professional tools, you can't put any knowledge to work that you might have about the deep-lying essentials of success. I've spent an enormous amount of time analyzing why I was able to take so many listings and then get so many of them sold. In my last year, I was hitting about a 95% sales ratio on listings taken—out of every twenty of the listings I wrote, eighteen or nineteen of them would sell.

Why was I able to do things like that? Equally important, why had I wanted to pay the heavy price—in hard work and long hours away from my family—for doing them?

When I first started thinking about this, one thing bothered me more than any other: the difficulty of even knowing, let alone fully comprehending, the motives at work inside the core of our personalities. All of us have a clear understanding of our surface motives—we know when we're hungry, hot, or whatever—but I'm convinced that very few human beings understand the roots of their personal motivations and *de*motivations.

If you agree with me on that, you'll also agree that understanding the emotions that drive other people is a vast, intricate, and difficult business. But, puzzling though it is, imprecise though your answers will sometimes be, how much you make in real estate depends to a considerable extent on how well-suited your actions are to the client's emotional situation. Ignoring these problems and opportunities, or depending on luck and a fatuous grin to cope with them, is a fool's business.

Let's look at the makeup of a strong listing presentation for an example. We've analyzed the area, we've seen all the comparables, and we've gathered other data. Now we're in the process of preparing our performance. From here on out, we're getting ready to put the spotlight on ourselves. Our purpose is to perform so well that the sellers will want to trust us with the marketing of their largest and most emotional asset, their home. Shouldn't this be our goal?—to have them feel, "Here's a real estate person who really understands—who really cares!"

Having empathy for your clients and knowing their situation is crucial. We have to become skillful at synchronizing our moves with a wide variety of client emotions. How well we do this has a powerful effect on our incomes as salespeople. In fact, I can't think of anything that will have more to do with how much you make than your ability to feel empathy toward your clients. Without this ability, your knowledge of inventory and technique won't be more than 50% effective.

True, there'll be days when it seems that there's no empathy left in your being. You'll feel that somebody—anybody—has to pour about a ton of empathy on your head before you can give even one more ounce of sympathetic understanding to another client. We're human too; our wells of empathy can run dry just like anyone else's.

But if we're going to be Champion listers, we have to organize our feelings; we have to discipline our emotions; we have to increase our inner strength. We have to do all these things until we have an ample supply of empathy every day for the people we're working with professionally. That's our job. We work with people who are suffering severe pain from the major upheavals that are taking place in their lives. Always keep this firmly in mind: what we do in real estate symbolizes what is happening to our clients' lives; we are the people who pull the levers that move them in and move them out. Selling a cherished home, facing the personal turmoil of moving to a new area, worrying about making far greater financial decisions than they as homeowners are accustomed to make, coping with whatever situation, sometimes a family tragedy, that has forced their home on the market—all these are intense forms of change that are painful to bear.

What does the average salesperson who's struggling to survive in this business have for those people? A vacant smile and a breezy, what's-in-it-for-me manner that pounds home his ignorance of, and indifference to, their emotional pain. Champions know more about techniques and real estate, but that's not the only reason they list more—they care more about more people.

Like everybody else, Champions have serious personal concerns of their own; but you'd never know it from the way they handle themselves when working with clients. You have serious personal concerns too; if you allow them to dominate your feelings and thoughts during working hours, you'll never achieve more than a fraction of your potential income in real estate.

In the office where I had a desk during most of my active real estate career, there were a few other agents who had discipline, knowledge, motivation, and the ability to accept rejection and keep on working. Why didn't they set the same records I did?

At one time, I thought it was primarily because I worked harder and longer than anyone else did. Over the years, I've come to realize that, although I'd never minimize the essential part that hard work and long hours must play in anyone's outstanding success, there was something more going on in mine. I call it *understanding the mood of the move*.

Champions, work at intensifying their natural ability to feel the overall emotions that the sellers have as they get into the pain of moving, of selling their home, of breaking their ties and seeing a part of their lives disappear forever.

Please start asking yourself, "How do I feel about how they feel?" If your attitude is, "I couldn't care less," don't be surprised if they couldn't care less about listing with you. Most people know when you can't stop thinking about yourself long enough to feel for them. There probably aren't two clients in a hundred who'll admit it, but one of the main reasons people pay real estate fees is to get attention and sympathy while a matter that's of great importance to them is being resolved.

Just let your mind fly for a moment. Here's a family, a husband and wife with two small children. He's climbing the ladder of achievement in the corporate structure, and part of the price this family pays for the man's success is that they have to move every eighteen months. He's growing, and in his kind of career, this means going where the next rung on the ladder is. What's happening to the rest of the family when they're moving every year and a half? Do you think that maybe the wife's heart bleeds a little every time she thinks about jerking their kids out of school again? Do you think there's any pain as she thinks about getting in the car for the last time in yet another neighborhood and once more waving a final goodbye to good friends? Do you suppose there's any agony of soul as she realizes that once again she's going to watch her little Terri and her little Davey say goodbye to the playmates they thought they'd have forever? In her children's sorrow and tears, she knows she'll read a real tragedy on moving day, one that's all too familiar to her. When you walk in the door for your afternoon appointment, all these things are going around inside her head. Will she resent it if you're indifferent? Will she hate you for showing that you're thrilled at the chance to make money off her again? You bet she will.

If you're going to list these people, will you agree with me that you'll have to handle her differently than the woman down the street who dislikes her home, despises the neighborhood, and can't wait to move out? They're both in the same basic situation—they have a house to get sold—but there's a vast difference in their emotions. I hope you'll remember what we talked about in the first part of this book—that emotion, not logic, controls the decision. With many people, you'll never hear anything about emotion. No, no, they're too logical for that. But if you could dig deeply into their eventual decision, you'd see some familiar explanations, and realize that their logical decision was dictated by emotion too. You'd discover that people secure enough to let their pain show aren't the only ones who hurt.

What I'm concerned about is that maybe you're only listing the homes of people you relate to easily and without thinking. If that's the case, you have a problem: you'll work at listing all kinds of people, but you've cut yourself off from listing many, and probably most, of them by not being emotionally in tune with their needs. To be a strong lister, you have to relate to many kinds of people. The way you relate to people is to consciously put yourself into their circumstances in your mind. As with all skills, the more often you do this, the better you'll be at it.

If I were talking to the wife and husband in the family that's being transferred again, I'd be more concerned with relating to her than to him. He's excited; he has his promotion; his ego has just received a big boost. And this is happening to a man who's ambitious, successful, and engrossed in his work. It's his life. In this traditional family, the wife is more concerned with the children, and maybe with the thought that they're not getting all the father they need. So, when you talk to this couple, you can't be overly excited about the husband's promotion or you'll turn the wife off by being insensitive to her emotional needs.

Now let's look at another listing situation that a change in the husband's job creates. Here's a man who, instead of getting the promotion he's worked for and thinks he's earned, is making a lateral move. Maybe he's being moved to get him out of the way, or maybe it's because the company needs him somewhere that he doesn't think will further his career. As he sits in their living room waiting for you to come over, he's mad at his company. But he's also mad at himself for failing to get the promotion, and for not having the confidence to quit. So he's going to move again, and there's no joy in it for him.

When you walk in there, you're part of the company he's mad at because you're the vehicle that's going to move him. And he's especially afraid of making a mistake in listing his house because of his insecure position at this point. When people are excited and happy about the move, they'll be more in line with your research on market value than people who are unhappy about the move will be. When your clients are looking forward to a bright future, they're more willing to cut their roots with the past. But if they don't want to leave and it's a fearful move toward an uncertain future, they want more security when they sell the home. What does that mean? They'll want more money. In this situation, you may have to take the property higher than market to begin with.

Today we frequently run into cases where it's a change in the woman's career that puts the couple's house on the market. It won't help your chances of listing them to express astonishment at this fact. When you walk into a home you want to list, quit thinking about yourself. Start asking questions so you can understand why they are doing what they're doing. There's a reason for the move. Until you know that reason, you can't start feeling their feelings.

Let's talk about taking the listing where the reason for moving isn't exciting and up, or even horizontal—it's definitely down and discouraging. Although these situations are touchy to work with, they're more likely to give you the opportunity to render great service to someone who really needs it. The focus of this book is on making money—but do you know something that's very important? You'll make more if you believe very strongly in yourself and in what you're doing. Though you won't get much praise in public for helping people through these troubled situations, in the place that counts—the privacy of your own mind—you'll know. Few things will help you get through the tough spots more than being genuinely and quietly proud of the service you render your fellow human beings.

In very few divorce situations can the listing be taken—and held until the sale of the property closes—unless the agent exercises great tact and understanding. Don't take sides. This is crucial. The husband is quick to resent another woman; the wife is quick to resent another man. You have to play it very professionally with both of them—but be especially courteous and deferential toward the spouse of the opposite sex. Keep it constantly in mind that if either person suspects you of making moral judgments about their marital affairs, you're not going to be their agent. You're working now with very emotional people; the great pain they're feeling makes them turn to anger, resentment, and non-cooperation at the slightest hint of provocation.

Here's a couple who have been married fifteen years. Suddenly the husband, who is now forty, started to grow in new areas of his life. From the beginning of their marriage, he had been the dominant figure and the primary, almost the only, source of the family's income. He put his wife into the homemaker role and she thought that was what he wanted. They both gave the marriage all those good years—but now he's changed and she hasn't. Sound familiar? It probably does, unfortunately.

When you go into that kind of emotionally supercharged situation, you're as much an undertaker as you are a real estate agent. You're working with grief—a marriage has died. You're there to help bury it. As quickly as possible, the husband wants to get rid of this hurt he knows he's putting her through. The wife, on the other hand, is afraid to list the property because she subconsciously knows that the moment the sign goes up, her feelings of insecurity are going off the chart. She's losing her husband, her home, her roots, even her occupation. When the sign goes up, she'll have to face up to making her own way working outside the home after fifteen years away from the job market.

But we're not there as marriage counselors; we can't re-engineer society. All we can do to help is to get them the most money for their home in the shortest possible time. To earn that chance, you must handle both those people so very carefully.

If you're a man, you must also just sit there and think, ''How would I feel if this was happening to me? How would I feel, after fifteen years of helping this man grow, and of having the security of this marriage, if I suddenly learned that I'm going to be on my own? I've never worked. What am I going to do?''

If you're a woman, your problem might be to make sure you don't display so much empathy for the wife that the husband decides you're adding to his already heavy load of guilt. If he comes to that decision, they won't list with you because they both have to approve the listing agreement.

Build a performance that relates to their needs. How would you handle yourself in this listing situation: the family is selling because someone in it has passed away.

Think about these basic situations in advance because you'll be meeting them soon. Prepare the words and the attitudes you'll need to meet these tests with professional assurance and success. The way to do it is to consciously think about how they feel.

Put yourself in this situation for a moment. The husband is a successful entrepreneur who's been in business for himself all his adult life; he's a good family man with a solid image in the community. For years, his favorite recreation has been golf at the country club. He thought he was in fairly good health. Then, in one minute, the doctor tells him it's all over for him in that town. A lung problem. He has to move to a drier climate.

His motivation to move is health, but he's saying to himself, "I've never been knocked down—I won't be now. If we don't get the money I want, I don't care, I'll stay. We sacrificed for twenty years to get my business on a firm footing, and now, after ten years in this house I expected to live out my life in, well, I'm just not giving it away."

Look at his wife. She loves him. And because it might mean three or five more years together, she wants to get the move over with.

If you go in there and run a standard routine off on them without connecting your emotional level to theirs, you're not going to reach them—and you're not going to list them. These people have been turned inward by circumstances. First, you must gain their attention; secondly, you must gain their liking and trust; only then do you have the opportunity to gain their business. You can't get this process started unless you can hook your emotions to their emotions. You must let her feel your heart—you must make him feel you're letting his ego know you understand—Man, I'm with you! If they don't feel that, your techniques won't be more than about 50% effective.

Think about financial crisis. Here's another common reason for moving. This one causes so much pain that the sellers often lock themselves into highly irrational attitudes. Have you ever known people who were about to have their home repossessed?

Let me tell you about a couple who have everything they want. Then he makes one bad move in business—and loses everything. But he has confidence in himself. So he doesn't put the home on the market. Instead, he falls one payment behind, then two.

By making some fast, hard decisions, this couple could have $20,000 in cash after paying off their debts—not much to people who, six months earlier, thought they were worth ten times that. But it's a whole lot to someone who'd otherwise be flat broke while adjusting to a different job and a downgraded lifestyle. However, they don't see it because of pride and the pain they're going through.

Then they fall three payments behind. What do they do? Stick to their price. Some real estate salespeople are putting pressure on these people, not realizing that it's the worst thing they can do because this man doesn't care anymore.

I had many cases of people selling under financial pressure, but one was a vivid example of how stubborn people in this position can get about turning their troubles into complete disaster. I sat across the table from Bob Brown (not his real name, of course) and I couldn't believe what I was hearing. As I went through my usual questions to establish rapport, to get them to like and trust me, I sensed that this was no ordinary situation. When I asked him how much he owed on the home, he said, "It could've been free and clear."

I looked at him. He was about twenty-eight, and he didn't project the image of having done that himself at his age. The usual things flashed through my mind: Daddy had given them the house; a rich uncle left him a small fortune. But I said, "How do you mean that?"

"Well, let me tell you what I did," he said. "I was working in sort of a clerking job, and two years ago I decided I'd had it with what they were paying me. Then a guy came in with an idea about vending machines. I liked the idea. I raised some money with our relatives and went into business with this man. Tom, I made $75,000 last year—here's my checkbook, you can see for yourself."

His wife smiled wistfully and looked down. I felt that she was living that year over again a little. "What's the situation now?" I said.

"It was a partnership. We went to Hawaii on our first vacation ever. We had a fantastic time for three weeks. When we came back, my partner was gone. All the money was gone. He'd been charging for three weeks. The bills you would not believe. There was nothing left to operate with. I quit."

"You can do it again," I said.

He shook his head. "I'm afraid I can't—in fact, I don't even want to."

"What are you going to do?"

"I'm going back to being a clerk," he said.

His wife said, "I couldn't stand it either. He was gone all the time and that's just not for us. It was meant that we should lose everything."

"Well, I hate to say this, Bob, but I don't have, and I never have had, a defeatist bone in my body. Now, you're going to hire me to market your home, and I'm going to get every dime out of it for you that I can."

We went over the comparable market analysis, and suddenly they changed. "Is that all we can get?" he said.

I told Mr. Brown that it was, and he said, "Oh, we'd never do that—we'd never sell for that price."

I said, "This is the quick sale price, which is what you need to go with to beat foreclosure, but it'll still pay off all your bills and give you $20,000 cash to start over with."

"It's not enough," Bob said. "I'd just as soon let the house go back."

"You're kidding," I said. "Am I hearing this right?"

It took me a solid month of negotiating with the lender to keep Mr. and Mrs. Brown out of foreclosure, but I did it. It took me another month to finally get Bob Brown to trust me. Why so long? Because Bob Brown's heart had been cut out. We got it sold, and they had a very, very happy feeling about the transaction. I did too. There's an example where, if an agent who wasn't concerned had gone in there and alienated them, we'd have another human being make a dreadful mistake. There are different forms of suicide, aren't there? Bob Brown and his wife were about to commit the kind where people retreat within themselves and close the world off.

As a real estate professional, you have more than a job—you have an absolute obligation to do everything in your power to feel like your clients feel.

So it's critical, as you get ready to go into their home for the listing appointment, that you be emotionally prepared to understand their feelings. You can't do that if you hit their door with your head full of your own business and personal concerns. Get rid of those thoughts before you get in your car to drive over there. They won't like it if you bring your problems into their time of painful change. Nothing happens in real estate until people like and trust you—and they will if you're professional enough. This means that, first, you share their feelings; second, you know real estate.

INDEX